MW00804376

Publius and Political Imagination

Modernity and Political Thought

Series Editor:
Morton Schoolman
State University of New York at Albany
and
Kennan Ferguson
University of Wisconsin–Milwaukee

The unique collection of original studies of the great figures in the history of political and social thought critically examines their contributions to our understanding of modernity, its constitution, and the promise and problems latent within it. These works are written by some of the finest theorists of our time for scholars and students of the social sciences and humanities.

Titles in the Series

The Augustinian Imperative: A Reflection on the Politics of Morality by William E. Connolly

Emerson and Self-Reliance by George Kateb

Edmund Burke: Modernity, Politics, and Aesthetics by Stephen K. White

Jean-Jacques Rousseau: The Politics of the Ordinary by Tracy B. Strong

Michel Foucault and the Politics of Freedom by Thomas L. Dumm

Reading "Adam Smith": Desire, History, and Value by Michael J. Shapiro

Thomas Hobbes: Skepticism, Individuality, and Chastened Politics by Richard E. Flathman

Thoreau's Nature: Ethics, Politics, and the Wild by Jane Bennett

G. W. F. Hegel: Modernity and Politics by Fred R. Dallmayr

The Reluctant Modernism of Hannah Arendt by Seyla Benhabib

William James: Politics in the Pluriverse by Kennan Ferguson

Merleau-Ponty and Modern Politics after Anti-Humanism by Diana Coole

Aquinas and Modernity: The Lost Promise of Natural Law by Shadia Drury

Carl Schmitt and the Intensification of Politics by Kam Shapiro

Impressions of Hume: Cinematic Thinking and the Politics of Discontinuity by Davide Pangia

Publius and Political Imagination by Jason Frank

Publius and Political Imagination

Jason Frank

ROWMAN & LITTLEFIELD
Lanham • Boulder • New York • London

Published by Rowman & Littlefield
A wholly owned subsidiary of The Rowman & Littlefield Publishing Group, Inc.
4501 Forbes Boulevard, Suite 200, Lanham, Maryland 20706
www.rowman.com

Unit A, Whitacre Mews, 26-34 Stannary Street, London SE11 4AB

Copyright © 2014 by Rowman & Littlefield

First paperback edition 2016

All rights reserved. No part of this book may be reproduced in any form or by any
electronic or mechanical means, including information storage and retrieval systems,
without written permission from the publisher, except by a reviewer who may quote
passages in a review.

British Library Cataloguing in Publication Information Available

The hardback edition of this book was previously cataloged by the Library of Congress as
follows:

Library of Congress Cataloging-in-Publication Data

Frank, Jason A.
Publius and political thought / Jason Frank
pages cm.—(Modernity and political thought)
Includes bibliographical references and index.
1. Federalist. 2. United States—Politics and government—Philosophy. 3. Constitutional history—
    United States. 4. Hamilton, Alexander, 1757–1804—Political and social views. 5. Madison,
    James, 1751–1836—Political and social views. 6. Jay, John, 1745–1829—Political and social
    views. I. Title.
JK155.F73 2014
320.97301—dc23
2013032044

ISBN 978-0-7425-4815-2 (cloth : alk. paper)
ISBN 978-1-4422-7707-6 (pbk. : alk. paper)
ISBN 978-0-7425-4816-9 (electronic)

∞ ™ The paper used in this publication meets the minimum requirements of American
National Standard for Information Sciences Permanence of Paper for Printed Library
Materials, ANSI/NISO Z39.48-1992.

Printed in the United States of America

The imagination of Americans, even in its greatest flights of fancy, is circumspect and cautious. Its impulses are restricted and its achievements unfinished. These habits of restraint are found in political society and to an unusual degree favor the tranquility of the people and the stability of the institutions they have adopted.

—Alexis de Tocqueville, *Democracy in America*

Engagement in politics entails a disciplined imagination.

—Michael Oakeshott, *On Human Conduct*

Contents

List of Abbreviations

DHRC   Merrill Jensen et al., eds., *The Documentary History of the Ratification of the Constitution*, 20 vols. (Madison: Wisconsin Historical Society Press, 1976–).

F   Jacob E. Cooke, ed., *The Federalist* (Middletown, CT: Wesleyan University Press, 1961).

RFC   Max Farrand, ed., *The Records of the Federal Convention of 1787*, 2 vols. (New Haven, CT: Yale University Press, 1966).

Acknowledgments

This book has benefited from the questions and comments of participants in several political theory workshops, colloquia, and conferences. I thank my hosts at the University of Michigan, Yale University, University of Essex, University of Exeter, SUNY Albany, Cornell University Law School, and Humboldt University. Special thanks to Karuna Mantena, Iain Hampsher-Monk, Bernadette Meyler, Aletta Norval, Arlene Saxonhouse, Mort Schoolman, Andrew Schaap, and Liz Wingrove.

Chapter 1 examines how the paradoxes of popular authorization I explored in *Constituent Moments* are navigated by Publius in *The Federalist Papers*. It was originally written for a conference I co-organized with Tracy McNulty at Cornell in 2006 ("Taking Exception to the Exception"). I would like to thank, in addition to Tracy, the other conference participants, in particular Susan Buck-Morss, Bonnie Honig, and Kam Shapiro. An earlier version of this chapter was published in *Diacritics* 37, nos. 2–3 (2007), and I am grateful to the editor Bruno Bosteels and two anonymous reviewers for their helpful suggestions. I would also like to thank the Johns Hopkins University Press for permission to reprint the essay here.

Chapter 2 presents the book's core argument and was originally published in *Political Theory* 37, no. 1 (2009). The essay was greatly improved by the extensive and thoughtful suggestions of the editor Mary Dietz and two anonymous reviewers. Many thanks to them and also to Sage for allowing me to republish.

Chapter 4 engages with prominent Straussian readings of *The Federalist* and was written for a series of conferences on postwar conservative political thought organized by Peter Hohendahl and Gerhard Shütz at Cornell and Humboldt. I am very grateful to Peter and Gerhard for the opportunity to participate in that productive international conversation, and to the other participants in those events. An earlier version of this chapter was published in Peter Uwe Hohendahl and Erhard Schütz, eds., *Konservative politische Kultur nach 1945 in Duetschland und in den USA* (Verlag Peter Lang: Europäischer Verlag der Wissenschaften, 2012), and I thank Verlag Peter Lang for allowing me to republish it here.

Chapter 5 was written for a remarkable joint session of the European Center for Political Research in St. Gallen, Switzerland, organized by Sofia Näsström and Dario Castiglione ("'We, the People': A New Object of Democratic Analysis"). Many thanks to the organizers and participants in that wonderfully productive seminar, in particular Arash Abiza-deh, Cristobal Kaltwasser, Paulina Ochoa Espejo, and Annie Stilz.

Mort Schoolman and Kennan Ferguson have been encouraging sup-porters of this project since its inception, and I am very grateful for their thorough reading of the manuscript and also for their generous editors' introduction. It is an honor to be included in Modernity and Political Thought, and I thank Mort, Kennan, and Jon Sisk for extending the range of the series and agreeing to include a book on an author—Publius—who is not one.

I have received generous financial and intellectual support from friends and colleagues at Cornell University. In addition to those already mentioned, I would like to thank Glenn Altschuler, Robert and Helen Appel, Richard Bensel, Val Bunce, Mathew Evangelista, Mary Katzen-stein, Judith Peraino, Aziz Rana, Hunter Rawlings, Camille Robscis, and Sid Tarrow. I am also grateful to the terrific political theory graduate students at Cornell, who are a constant source of insight and critique. I owe a special debt to Kyong-Min Son and Kevin Duong for their help putting this manuscript together. Finally, for the past nine years Isaac Kramnick has been a remarkable colleague, mentor, and friend, from whom I have learned a great deal not only about *The Federalist Papers*, but also many other things. He will not agree with everything in this book, but Isaac is an inspiration and it is a pleasure to acknowledge my grati-tude to him here.

Series Editors' Introduction

Jason Frank's *Publius and Political Imagination* is volume sixteen of *Modernity and Political Thought* (*MPT*), the Rowman & Littlefield series in contemporary political theory. Frank's study follows recent volumes, also addressing questions of the modern world's political endowments, on David Hume by Davide Panagia, Carl Schmitt by Kam Shapiro, Aquinas by Shadia Drury, Merleau-Ponty by Diana Coole, and William James by Kennan Ferguson.[1] Shortly following the appearance of Frank's work on *Publius*, a volume on John Rawls by Donald Moon will be published, and planned volumes beyond these include works on Karl Marx by Wendy Brown, Aristotle by Mary Dietz, Thomas More by Peter Euben, J. S. Mill by Kirstie McClure, Friedrich Nietzsche by David Owen, and Sheldon Wolin by Nicholas Xenos.

Our recent and planned volumes are all developments that grew out of *MPT*'s well-known inaugural volumes by William Connolly, Richard Flathman, Stephen White, George Kateb, Tracy Strong, Jane Bennett, Michael Shapiro, Thomas Dumm, Fred Dallmayr, and Seyla Benhabib, on Augustine, Hobbes, Burke, Emerson, Rousseau, Thoreau, Smith, Foucault, Hegel, and Arendt, respectively.[2] As those who are familiar with these authors' previous works will expect, their studies adopt a variety of approaches and pose diverse and creative questions about key figures in the history of political theory. Contributors to *Modernity and Political Thought* critically examine ways in which major political theorists can help to shape our understanding of modernity—not only its origins and constitution but also its overt and latent problems, promises, and dangers. In addition to the works themselves, a central goal of the series has been to illustrate how the history of political thought can be brought to bear on modernity's political present to acquire deeper insight into its possible political futures.

Jason Frank's *Publius and Political Imagination* is the first *MPT* volume to take as its focus not a single author but a collaboration between political theorists, in this very special case the collective known by the pseudonym Publius. Alexander Hamilton, John Jay, and James Madison together wrote the public essays later famously collected as *The Federalist Papers*. Publius, of course, became the most influential of the American Founders, particularly as the United States Constitution was being debated among the newly independent states. *Publius and Political Imagination* is a continuation of work Frank earlier began in *Constituent Moments: Enact-*

ing the People in Postrevolutionary America, a remarkable theoretical investigation into the original political event and most fundamental political
principle in the American context from which its modern democratic
society has developed, namely the *question of the people*.[3] Not the people
per se, the historical and political phenomenon on which the birth and
evolution of a modern democratic society may or may not actually depend. Rather, the *question* of the people. While admitting of many variations, in its essentials this question can be formulated in this way: Who,
or where, are the people in whose name the founding of American democratic society is authorized and held to be legitimate, if, at the moment of
its founding, the people neither are present nor can be present but are
presupposed and, in fact, only come into existence after being formally
constituted in such founding declarations as "We the People . . . "? An act
of founding, in other words, appears to paradoxically create the people at
the very moment it invokes the people as justification for the political
order it originates.

   Whereas one might conclude from this that the paradoxical character
of the birth of a democratic society may threaten to invalidate the democratic character of its inception and of its politics thereafter, Frank does
not settle on so readily simplistic a judgment. As evidenced by the
American Constitution and the broadcast events of the revolutionary and
postrevolutionary eras encompassing it, "the people are a political *claim*,"
as Frank puts it, "an act of political subjectification, not a pregiven, unified, or naturally bounded empirical entity" (*CM*, 3). Precisely because
they can only be represented and are never empirically present as a
whole, the people themselves are "enacted" through politics. Drawing on
the thought of Jacques Rancière, in effect, Frank explains, the people are
brought into existence by political claims through founding acts of representation and through all antecedent and subsequent acts of representation. To be enacted, however, is not just to actually come into existence or
to necessarily even exist in fact at all. On the contrary, what is decisive is
that through their enactment the people exist as a *virtual* body.

   To what do the people owe itself as this historical possibility? Repeatedly played out in the events of the revolutionary and postrevolutionary
eras, through this dense history of political contests and protests, demon-
strations and movements, memorials and celebrations of battles as well
as the battles themselves, and authorized by founding documents and
reproduced in the politics to which such birth certificates give birth, enactment is an ongoing process not merely establishing the people as a
represented body. Enactment, Frank proposes, is the constitution of the
people as a body "in *excess* of any particular representation." The power
of the people, as it were, is rooted in the people being "enacted through
representational claims and *forever escaping* the political and legal boundaries inscribed by those claims" (*CM*, 3; our italics). All the ways in
which the people are historically represented enable them to come into

existence as a force that *transcends* their far more politically limited representational forms. Such representational "excess" or "surplus" as Frank also describes it, which leverages the people's escape from the confines of their representational enclosures, releases the people to then *itself* enact a history of political dramas whereby it continually *authorizes itself as a people.* "Constituent moments," as Frank explains, "refer to a mode of subjectification premised on speaking on behalf of a people that is not . . . yet." It is this "speaking on behalf," in a register of presumed plenipotentiality, which produces the people as a self-authorizing historical possibility.

Without a doubt, Frank's theoretical intention is to problematize the acceptance common in academic and non-academic communities that in the American political context the people are no longer, if they ever were, an authentic and viable political entity, but rather a concept that acts to mystify and obscure far less democratic political realities. Though seeking to disturb this cynical reading, he is equally alert to how the image of the people has been co-opted for ideological purposes. Frank concedes that the people are often commandeered as a fiction to instrumentally justify any number of opposing political positions, policy decisions, and outcomes, and perhaps in large part are ironically created by the very constitutive excess accounting for the people as a virtual self-authorizing historical force. Moreover, he affirms that the myth of the people may be as potent a resource with which political demagogues in democratic, no less than undemocratic, societies mesmerize the people to subdue their capacity for judgment and manipulate their political will in the interest of nonpopulist, elite, self-serving ends. And to the extent to which the people do live up to their name, Frank concurs that it is merely their electoral presence that has held the political viability of the people in good stead. Only when such political dissembling is acknowledged can we clearly recognize the impoverishment of a democracy plodding its way through problems and crises with a lethargy secured by representative institutions that have disenfranchised the will of the people.

While he grants the validity of the alleged legitimation deficit plaguing democracy in America, for Frank political realities are more complicated still. The people not only survive but *surmount* their representative institutions. The excess that grounds the people as a real historical possibility, one expressed in a record of distinguished and undistinguished political achievements since the revolutionary era, at the same time reinforces the inherent ambiguity of constitutional representative institutions. On each occasion that such institutions speak in the name of the people, they actualize the people as an unintended outcome, so that the people increasingly take on a body that increasingly comes into view and are thus ever more ready with every representative invocation to take up a position in the public square. Rather than the commonly accepted unilateral thesis, which identifies representative institutions with an illusory popular democracy, Frank proposes a constitutive surplus. He seeks to account for the figure of the people in American political and cultural traditions without which they would be lifeless narratives whose top-heavy forms would collapse for want of substance to animate them. Yet this figure of the people whose real historical life Frank wants to recover is no sanitized force for political good only. Despite the glaring performative contradiction entailed, the people boast of a political record of frequently acting to their own detriment in whole or in part, to which its history of denying rights to minorities testifies.

As his thesis runs against the dominant social scientific and political theoretical discourse maintaining that the people are little more than an obfuscation blinding us to the undemocratic truth of America's democratic politics, Frank's thesis is quite radical. Political efficacy runs deeper than representative democracy knows. Efficacy is the relentless condition of political possibility anchored in a surplus indebted to the ineliminable richness of the language of representation. Excess is that surplus of meaning and voice whose multiple layers and multiple speakers work to construct a real people with real powers even as representation's language functions to contain both. As Frank puts it eloquently, since the Revolution there has been present a real people with a real power springing from their "own unrealized futurity." In this light the people take on an almost messianic quality, a promise regularly renewed as a possibility attached to a surplus of meaning indelibly inscribed beneath a representational surface that unwittingly creates such depth on each occasion it sublimates it in an attenuated praxis. Representative government contradicts itself, and it cannot help but do so by constituting a people who stage a history of dramatic political acts exceeding the limited logic of representation. Representative democracy thus proves to be democratic despite its "best" intentions.

In addition to Rancière, Frank draws on the work of Kenneth Burke, who captures the central dimension of his argument in a speech proposing that in America, rather than the worker or the proletarian, the "people" ought to be adopted by the Communist Party as a symbol of its normative commitments by virtue of its rhetorical power to articulate a universal ideal.[4] What strikes Frank about Burke's proposal—which was met with a poor reception by his Marxist-Leninist colleagues—is its tacit understanding that in the American context the rhetorical power of the idea of the people flows from the way in which a postrevolutionary people may be "doubly inscribed." In the aftermath of revolutionary transformation, that is, the people may become instantiated as "a source of public authority" as well as "a source of resistance to public authority." The American people in the aftermath of the Revolutionary War attest to this. Burke's strategic embrace of the rhetorically constructed power of the American people to accomplish radical ends thus agrees with the role the people have actually played in Frank's reading of American political and cultural history, and played in large part precisely as a result of the constitutive surplus accompanying the rhetorical configurations of the American people since the revolutionary era. For Frank, Burke's theory of the political potential of rhetorically constructed agency perfectly expresses what has already and always been the case historically, though it should be stressed that both Frank and Burke mean to enlist the prescriptive political value of the people once it has been enabled rhetorically.

Our last point regarding the prescriptive political value of a rhetorically constructed people taps directly into themes running from *Constituent Moments* through *Publius and Political Imagination*. In *Constituent Moments*, to be sure, Frank favors the radical side of the "double inscription," specifically the political dramas of the postrevolutionary era that in a variety of forms *resist* public authority. In Frank's words, for example,

> This double inscription of the people enables what I call constituent moments, when the underauthorized . . . seize the mantle of authorization, changing the inherited rules of authorization in the process. . . . [C]onstituent moments enact their claims wholly on the democratic authority of the people themselves: out of these enactments a new democratic subject emerges. (*CM*, 8)

Frank's argument here emphasizes the ways and extent to which the constitutive surplus he has discovered to be the most profound effect of American politics since the revolutionary era, namely how the people have been constructed as a political *possibility*, has created the people as a political *reality—as a new democratic subject*. The historical evidence he marshals on behalf of his theoretical argument then becomes the focus of his attention for the greatest part of his discussion. Once he has laid out the conceptual structure of his argument—constituent moments, constitutive surplus or excess, the people as a not . . . *yet*, double inscription, and so forth—Frank's interest lies with the actual emergence of the people whose construction is assembled from the historical events and processes on which his concepts are based. A discussion too rich and nuanced to adequately summarize, several of its early highlights are sufficient to establish the strength of Frank's thesis.

Taking the revolutionary era as his historical point of departure, Frank does not dispute historians who are right to consider both Thomas Paine and Thomas Jefferson to have authored works—*Common Sense* and the collective "we" of the Declaration of Independence, respectively— that are indifferent to or naively uninformed of the conflicting perspectives among the American people toward the necessity for revolution. What Frank does dispute is whether the historical attention to Paine's and Jefferson's glosses on their contemporaries arrives at the deeper significance of their writings. Far more important in his estimation is how Paine's and Jefferson's manifestos do not describe a people, they enact one, and thus imagine the people as their own *future* achievement. They create a mandate moving the people to become a self-fulfilling prophecy. Hence Paine and Jefferson assisted in the construction of a people who would *retrospectively* validate the call to arms that at the time of their proclamations was only incipient.

One major implication of Frank's interpretation of Paine's and Jefferson's contributions to the Revolution is that while it has been claimed, and with good reason, that the representatives of the people at the Constitutional Convention in 1787 acted less *on behalf of* than *in place of* the people, thus introducing into the Founding a deficit in democratic legitimation, this would only be part of the historical narrative. Even if it were the explicit intention of the Founders to create a constitution that weakened the voice and the power of the people, its effect was not to subdue but to enable the people. Regardless of how conservative with regard to the question of the people the Founding may have been, it robustly constructed the very politicized people about whom the Founders were skeptical, critical, and fearful. Whatever else the American political tradition may be, it traces the creation of the people who, as a virtual power, were in their potentialities embryonic and mature, fragmented and concentrated, unreliable, formidable, transcendent, and even sublime, all at the same time.

For the American Revolution to have broken out, of course, the enactment of the people, its constitution as a surplus, had to have been prepared in advance of Jefferson and Paine. The people necessarily preexisted the Revolution itself. Thus Frank takes the American Founding as only one constituent moment in a continuous chain of political claims bringing the people into existence. As part of the reconstruction of the early history of the emergence of the people as an incipient political force, Frank begins his examination of the revolutionary era against the backdrop of the 1688 Glorious Revolution. What he means to bring to the surface is the predominant role of language in the constitution of the people as an incipient political power.

While the American colonists' prerevolutionary resistance to British practices of taxation during the 1760s and 1770s is well known in its outlines, Frank studies more closely the debates surrounding the legal-constitutional interpretations of political representation these acts of resistance precipitated as an early though unsuccessful means of resolving the conflict. For a time, he explains, the legitimacy of the British impositions turned on fundamental questions of representation, in the first instance, and in the end on the question of whether the British or perhaps the colonies themselves had the sovereign power to determine such matters as taxation. Frank's point here is that these interpretive disputes over the legality of representation and the location of sovereignty all worked to *discursively* produce the unintended and—for the British—quite unwelcome consequence of constructing the people who became set on winning their sovereignty. The people as a sovereign people were created as a possibility through a process inaugurated as an interpretive disagreement and subsequently complicated, in the American context, by the question of who really are the people now supposedly in possession of the sovereign power to determine who legitimately represents them. Frank underscores the elusiveness of an emerging sovereign people and how this question of the people stirring in the revolutionary era was carried over into the postrevolutionary period in a far more intense form as an expanding plurality of claims to represent the people arose. Thus the question of *who are the people* becomes inextricably tied to the question of *who can represent the people*. As he puts it succinctly, this conflation provokes a "perpetual crisis in representation" as these claims amount to a "dilemma of constituency." What Frank wants us to understand from his more intimate exegesis of a familiar history lesson is that the debates leading to the twofold question of who the people and their representatives are offers

> a case study in how a contest around what is supposedly supplemental—in this instance the nature of political representation—comes to construct the object it purportedly supplements: the people represented. . . . In these postrevolutionary debates over political representation, the people became simultaneously more ambiguous and more powerful. . . . This transformation established important conditions for postrevolutionary constituent moments. (*CM*, 15)

An essential element in the construction of the people as a political agent, these debates were not the only factor whose causal significance Frank thematizes. As he reminds us, the revolutionary era was also punctuated by a succession of state and local constitutions with their multiple "declarations of independence" all associated with what he describes as "a dizzying array of self-created revolutionary institutions [that] spoke for the people." Frank does an especially sensitive job of conveying the swarm of more or less legal, more or less organized, more or less collective though always improvisational revolutionary and postrevolutionary political dramas that contributed to the "expansive articulation of the people," to the people as the "excess" defining the constituent moment.

With the concepts of "excess" and the "dilemma of constituency" it spawns, Frank makes comprehensible a variety of postrevolutionary developments often taken to present a spontaneous and confusing array of historical contingencies difficult to relate to a coherent set of antecedent causes. Rather than leaving them as such accidental events, he distils these developments into two general reactions to the problem of representing an equivocal people—the forces for constitutionalism most closely associated with the Federalists and their parallel nemeses struggling to preserve the myriad governmental and often extra-governmental democratic forms heir to the revolution and regularly conscripted to the Anti-Federalist camps.

Whereas historians and political theorists have painted these reactions in mutually exclusive terms, Frank focuses instead on the ways the conflicts between the Federalist and Anti-Federalists functioned to create the people as a power superior to any legislative claim to represent them. In one of the early and great ironies of American history, he suggests, by contradicting the provisions of the Articles of Confederation the extra-legal standing of the national and state constitutional ratifying conventions the Federalists endorsed tacitly constructed the people as such a self-authorizing power against the Federalists more or less explicit intentions to the contrary, while the Anti-Federalists' open opposition to the process of ratification implicitly appears to favor only representative bodies acting on behalf of the people through the legal confederation of state and local institutions prevailing at the time.[5] As a consequence of the overflowing synergy of their struggle, however, Federalist efforts to *contain* the power of the people and the Anti-Federalist drive to *empower* the people both in their own ways constituted the people as an excess far beyond the struggle itself and into present times.

It would be mistaken, then, to simplify Frank's argument by parsing the interests of the Federalists and Anti-Federalists on one side or the other of a democratic divide, as though a debate about the Constitution could be simply limited to whether or not it was democratic. Considering the work of H. L. A. Hart, Stephen Holmes, and Sheldon Wolin, Frank points out that political theorists are either eager to embrace the Constitution's apparatus of popular representation as an unvarnished democratic achievement (Hart and Holmes), or just as one-sidedly eager to defend the position that the people are a democratic power only insofar as they exist outside of and escape the limitations of legal-constitutional provisions regulating that power (Wolin). And political theorists who stress the democratic character of the people's constitutionalization wholly credit the Constitution with defining the people's political identity, while political theorists who reject constitutional representative democracy locate the people's political identity wholly outside the Constitution. Yet, as we have seen, Frank's approach to the question of the people avoids such interpretations and their antinomies. Rather, the Constitution paradoxically *constitutes* the people's political identity and its power as *both contained by and in excess of* the written and spoken words that speak in the people's name. As a constituent power the people are a paradoxical inside and outside, a democratic power *outside* their prescribed limits precisely because the outside originated *within* as a democratic act of constitution itself. Frank's argument—that "the Constitutional 'We the People' is not wholly subsumed in the text that represents it"—is a perfect refinement of this paradox (*CM*, 31).

With the theoretical infrastructure of his argument elaborated, Frank then turns to the postrevolutionary history it is meant to illuminate and to be further illuminated by. *Constituent Moments* now focuses on the forms taken by the enactment of the people, on the episodic eruptions of dilemmas of popular self-authorization and how they are received, engaged, accommodated, and managed in the politics and political culture after the American Revolution and beyond. *Constituent Moments'* cases of popular enactment range compellingly from the fascinations of the culture of popular constitutionalism attached to the ambiguity of the people following their constitutionalization; the representative status of the political enactments of crowds along with the anxieties about the mercurial nature of crowds and large public assemblies in such political enactments; the dilemmas of political self-authorization *re*-enacted in Democratic-Republican Societies of the 1790s in part for the benefit of teaching lessons in civic virtue; to how the dilemmas of popular authorization are brilliantly addressed by the prominent American thinkers Whitman and Douglas.

Throughout its entirety Frank's work places him among the minority of political theorists who have come to appreciate that, while actions are always praised for speaking louder than words, actions are invariably and robustly prefigured in the virtual agent constructed by the word. In every discursive construction of the people and in every political drama of popular self-authorization, the question of the people is reopened and the people themselves redefined and reanimated. So among the many ideas that keep the reader company throughout Frank's work, perhaps there is one that is most vital and that more than any other constitutes the transition to *Publius and Political Imagination.* Wherever the people are incipient and their self-authorization an irrepressible political possibility, the question of the people remains forever unanswered and their democracy an unfinished project they may one day imagine.

We are grateful to Jon Sisk, vice president and senior executive editor for American government, American history, public policy, and political theory of Rowman & Littlefield, for his thoughtfulness and professionalism that make it possible for authors and editors alike to produce their best work. His support of a series dedicated to examining authors through the lens of modern thought has led to a compilation of volumes that, as a whole, refigure the relationship between critical thinkers and the contemporary world. Under his stewardship, Rowman & Littlefield's *Modernity and Political Thought* continues to define a seminal approach to the study of classical, medieval, modern, and contemporary political theory today.

Morton Schoolman, State University of New York at Albany
Kennan Ferguson, University of Wisconsin at Milwaukee

NOTES

1. Davide Panagia, *Impressions of Hume* (Lanham, MD: Rowman & Littlefield, 2013); Kam Shapiro, *Carl Schmitt and the Intensification of Politics* (Lanham, MD: Rowman & Littlefield, 2009); Shadia Drury, *Aquinas and Modernity: The Lost Promise of Natural Law* (Lanham, MD: Rowman & Littlefield, 2008); Diana Coole, *Merleau-Ponty and Modern Politics After Anti-Humanism* (Lanham, MD: Rowman & Littlefield, 2007); Kennan Ferguson, *William James: Politics in the Pluriverse* (Lanham, MD: Rowman & Littlefield, 2007).

2. See William E. Connolly, *The Augustinian Imperative: A Reflection on the Politics of Morality* (Lanham, MD: Rowman & Littlefield, 2002); Richard E. Flathman, *Thomas Hobbes: Skepticism, Individuality, and Chastened Politics* (Lanham, MD: Rowman & Littlefield, 2002); Stephen K. White, *Edmund Burke: Modernity, Politics, and Aesthetics* (Lanham, MD: Rowman & Littlefield, 2002); George Kateb, *Emerson and Self-Reliance* (Lanham, MD: Rowman & Littlefield, 2002); Tracy B. Strong, *Jean-Jacques Rousseau: The Politics of the Ordinary* (Lanham, MD: Rowman & Littlefield, 2002); Jane Bennett, *Thoreau's Nature: Ethics, Politics, and the Wild* (Lanham, MD: Rowman & Littlefield, 2002); Michael J. Shapiro, *Reading "Adam Smith": Desire, History, and Value* (Lanham, MD: Rowman & Littlefield, 2002); Thomas L. Dumm, *Michel Foucault and the Politics of Freedom* (Lanham, MD.: Rowman & Littlefield, 2002); Fred Dallmayr, *G. W. F. Hegel: Modernity and Politics* (Lanham, MD: Rowman & Littlefield, 2002); Seyla Benhabib, *The Reluctant Modernism of Hannah Arendt* (Lanham, MD: Rowman & Littlefield, 2003).

3. Jason Frank, *Constituent Moments: Enacting the People in Postrevolutionary America* (Durham, NC: Duke University Press, 2010). Hereafter *CM*, with paginations in parentheses in the text.

4. Frank takes up Burke's 1935 speech, "Revolutionary Symbolism in America," to the American Writers' Congress convened by the American Communist Party. See *Constituent Moments*, 6–9.

5. Frank further develops this argument in the first chapter of *Publius and Political Imagination*. Refusing to unambiguously align the Federalists with the side of state power, despite their intentions, and the Anti-Federalists with the side of extra-governmental popular politics, is in general a point developed in *Publius*, and that he argues explicitly in his conclusion.

Introduction: The Imaginary Republic

The American Founders have rarely enjoyed the authority they do in contemporary political discourse and constitutional jurisprudence, and not only among so-called constitutional conservatives or advocates of original intent. "When in doubt," Jill Lepore writes, contemporary Americans "left, right, or center, deploy the Founding Fathers."[1] It has not always been this way. Historians have demonstrated the varied fortunes of the Founding Fathers over the course of American history, including the recent past.[2] We need only think of Thurgood Marshall's famous Bicentennial address in 1987 in which Marshall worried that ceremonial commemorations of the Founders invite "a complacent belief that the vision of those who debated and compromised in Philadelphia yielded the 'more perfect Union' it is said we now enjoy." Marshall went on to admit that he did "not find the wisdom, foresight, and sense of justice exhibited by the Framers particularly profound."[3] It is hard to imagine a prominent figure in our public life making such an admission today.

It is fitting to begin a study of *The Federalist Papers* with some reflection on the outsize authority of the Founders in our politics and in our jurisprudence, especially since this study will focus on the importance of the political imagination in *The Federalist*'s political theory: The authority of the Founders over the politics of the American republic is first and foremost a question of political imagination. As the following chapters will show, *The Federalist* did not only offer familiar arguments defending the institutional architecture of the Constitution, or defending the norms that underwrite that document; Publius also offered an alternative vision of the American republic and of American citizenship (and also of American *empire*—see No. 11). *The Federalist Papers* is at once an exercise in the political imagination and a reflective account of the importance of political imagination to republican politics. Publius did not only conceive of the imagination in terms of dangerous and delusionary enthusiasm or the bewildering "labyrinths of an enchanted castle,"[4] but attended to how the political imagination becomes ensconced in institutions, inscribed in belief, and embodied in political practice.[5] This book's focus on political imagination will illuminate aspects of Publius's argument that have been obscured by most familiar accounts, and, in doing so, will offer a different orientation to this initial question: How and why do we subordinate our contemporary politics to the authority of the Founders?

Some of the issues posed by the Founders' authority over our politics are at least as old as the republic itself. I am thinking of such familiar questions as these: Why should the decisions and policies endorsed by a relatively small group of white, propertied men at the end of the eighteenth century have binding authority on the political life of their posterity, particularly in a democratic polity committed to government of the people, by the people, and for the people? Can our commitment to constitutionalism be made compatible with our commitment to popular sovereignty and democratic legitimacy? Why inflate this brief period in the nation's history with a significance and meaning that trumps all others?

The democratic skepticism suggested by these questions is not new and was expressed by some of the most prominent Founders themselves. "Some men look at constitutions with sanctimonious reverence," Thomas Jefferson famously warned, "and deem them like the ark of the covenant, too sacred to be touched. They ascribe to the men of the preceding age a wisdom more than human."[6] Jefferson's radical theory of generational sovereignty, and his related suspicion of the "magic" that lent unquestioned authority to the word "constitutional," has been reiterated by subsequent generations of American citizens who have wrestled with different aspects of what is often called the "counter-majoritarian difficulty" of American constitutionalism.

Democratic theorists in our own time have offered rigorous and historically sensitive efforts to resolve this difficulty—and dispel the "magic"—through theories of "pre-commitment" (Jon Elster and Stephen Holmes), "co-originality" (Jürgen Habermas), "duelist democracy" (Bruce Ackerman), and "redemptive constitutionalism" (Jack Balkin).[7] However, one important approach to the puzzle of the Founders' authority over our politics does not dispel the magic but rather attends to how it is engendered and sustained across time through the concept of Founding itself.[8] We might better understand our reliance on the Founders' authority by turning first to how the Founders, or at least some of them, came to understand that reliance and project it on to their posterity.

Many of his late eighteenth-century contemporaries would have agreed with John Adams that they lived in a time in which "the greatest lawgivers of antiquity would have wished to live." "How few of the human race," Adams pondered, "have ever enjoyed an opportunity of making election of government . . . for themselves or their children?"[9] "The case and circumstances of America present themselves as in the beginning of a world," Thomas Paine similarly wrote in *The Rights of Man*: "We are brought at once to the point of seeing government begin, as if we had lived in the beginning of time."[10] While suspicious of the violence—the "accident and force," as Publius described it in *Federalist* No. 1—associated with the Great Lawgiver paradigm, many American

Founders nonetheless understood the formative political actions undertaken between 1776 and 1789 as modified, modern variations on the ancient example. But how should we assess this self-understanding and its
impact on their political theory? Was it anything more than a case of
mystification? Were the Founders deluded and enthralled by the shining
example of ancient Rome?

In "The Eighteenth Brumaire of Louis Bonaparte," Karl Marx described modern revolutionaries' reliance on the "ghosts of Rome"—their
"imitations of Brutus, Grachus, Publicola, the tribunes, the senators, and
Caesar himself"—as a "process of world-historical necromancy."[11] "Just
when [the living] appear to be engaged in revolutionary transformation
of themselves . . . in the creation of something which does not yet exist,"
Marx explained, "precisely in such epochs of revolutionary crisis they
timidly conjure up the spirit of the past to help them; they borrow their
names, slogans, and costumes so as to stage the new world-historical
scene in this venerable disguise and borrowed language."[12] For Marx, the
inspiring examples of the ancient world were so many "ideals, art forms,
and self-deceptions" that modern revolutionaries invoked to "exalt the
new struggles" and "exaggerate their given task in the imagination."
These imaginary ghosts of Rome "deadened the awareness" of the revolutionaries and prevented them from grasping the true meaning of their
(class) struggles, but their "dramatic effects" also had real historical efficacy and served the action contexts of their time.[13] It did so because these
ancient examples motivated and sustained the heroic and self-sacrificing
action required by such struggles, which Marx believed could never have
been successfully fought on the basis of disenchanted material interests
alone.

Marx, of course, was primarily concerned with the French Revolution
and its legacy, but the most influential scholarly attempt to understand
the significance of the Great Lawgiver paradigm on late eighteenth-century American political thought—in the work of the conservative historian Douglass Adair—surprisingly parallels Marx's analysis in important
respects. In *Fame and the Founding Fathers*, Adair set out to combat the
deflationary emphasis Progressive historians like Charles Beard had
placed on the material self-interest of the Founders, and, in doing so,
demonstrate the formative power of ideas and imagination on their actions and motivations. More specifically, Adair's influential essay sought
a new and more persuasive answer to a frequently recurring question in
American history: "How can we account for this amazing concentration
of political ability in a single generation born into a tiny nation on the
fringe of the Atlantic?"[14] Adair's answer was their "almost obsessive
desire for fame," or, more precisely, their prevailing tendency to be "fan-
tastically concerned with posterity's judgment of their behavior." "The
love of fame," Adair explained, "is a noble passion because it can transform ambition and self-interest into dedicated effort for the community,

because it can spur individuals to spend themselves to provide for the common defense, or promote the general welfare, and even on occasion to establish justice in a world where justice is extremely rare."[15] The love of fame, in other words, can generate the enthusiasm and self-sacrifice necessary to fight a revolution and found a republic, and according to Adair, the Founders took their template from "the very specific and concrete type of fame" offered by Plutarch and other ancient writers: "the GREAT LAWGIVER AND FOUNDER OF A COMMONWEALTH."[16] For both Marx and Adair, then, the appeal to classical antiquity, and especially to the inspiring exemplars of Lycurgus and Solon, Numa and Publius, allowed leading figures of these eighteenth-century revolutions to hitch their passionate self-interest to higher and more noble ambitions—to inaugurate an unfinished revolutionary tradition in the one instance and to found a durable constitutional republic in the other.

Marx's and Adair's accounts have plausibility and offer preliminary orientation to the problem of political imagination, but neither speaks directly to the basic questions of legitimacy raised above. For Marx—as for Jefferson, for whom "the dead have no rights"—this "necromancy" signals a delusional and illegitimate dependence of the living on the dead: "The tradition of all dead generations weighs like a nightmare on the brains of the living." For Adair, the question of legitimacy, insofar as it is raised at all, resides in the superior wisdom and farsightedness of the founding generation. Hannah Arendt moves beyond both accounts and takes the imagined relationship to the Founding to be central to the subsequent authority of the republic. In *On Revolution*, Arendt offers a provocative, if also enigmatic, discussion of how important it was that the Founders conceived of themselves *as* Founders to the project they set out to achieve. Arendt's point is not simply that their self-understanding as Great Lawgivers led to the virtuous and disinterested action required to overcome the considerable political obstacles of the Crisis Period and successfully establish a new constitutional government. Arendt writes that the spirit in which the Founders conceived of themselves *as* Founders was not out of an ambitious love of fame but "sprang from the simple recognition that either they were Founders and consequently would become ancestors, or they had failed. What counted was neither their wisdom nor their virtue, but solely the act itself."[17] This is the basis of what Arendt considers a productive ambiguity in American "constitution worship," because the object of that worship is at "least as much the act of constituting as it was the written document itself." It is the imagined attachment to the *act* of Founding, Arendt insists, that is most important for the political latecomer:

> the remembrance of the event itself—a people deliberately founding a new body politic—has continued to shroud the actual outcome of this act, the constitutional text, in an atmosphere of reverent awe and has

shielded both event and document against the onslaught of time and changed circumstances . . . the authority of the republic will be safe and intact as long as the act itself, the beginning as such, is remembered whenever constitutional questions come into play.[18]

For Arendt, a particular mode of political imagination and remembrance is internal to the authority of American constitutionalism. But what precisely does remembrance have to do with democratic legitimacy? It obviously plays no necessary role in Jefferson's account of generational sovereignty, for example, but neither does it play an important role in less radically democratic traditions of political liberalism, whether developed in its social contract/deontological or utilitarian/consequentialist strains. The thought experiment of the social contract, and the "devices of representation" that preoccupy so many contemporary democratic theorists, are very different from Arendt's imperative to remember a specific inaugurating political act.[19]

Arendt's understanding of the internal relationship between legitimacy and remembrance in the American republic is based in her broader account of the classical republican concept of Founding. The concept comes initially from Biblical, Greek, and Roman antiquity, and is associated with such figures as Moses, Solon and Lycurgus, Romulus, and Brutus, as well as Publius Valerius, the figure Hamilton chose for the pseudonymous authorship of *The Federalist*. In its basic outline, Founding is associated with the deliberate act of instituting a new polity and basing that foundation in law. It is important that it is an act of deliberate will, that it marks a break with existing institutions (it is not simply a transition), and that it culminates in a legal code of some kind (that it is, in Frank Michelman's words, "jurisgenerative").[20]

We already see implied in this basic definition how the concept of Founding intermingles violence and validity. On the one hand, Foundings are often achieved by acts of fratricidal violence—Cain slays Abel, Romulus kills Remus—and they mark a rupture in the existing fabric of law. However, they are also the product of deliberation and will, and establish a rule based in law rather than tyranny. Many of the dilemmas that preoccupy contemporary democratic theorists concerning legality and legitimacy, the norm and the exception, constituted and constituent power, are powerfully dramatized in such ancient texts as the *Book of Exodus* or Livy's *History of Rome*. Such narratives insist on the political importance of the injunction to remember the Founding, and the centrality of rituals of remembrance to both the authority of law and to the ethos of the people who live under the law. Publius and other American Founders argued that the magic of such injunctions and rituals of veneration could only be dispelled in a "nation of philosophers," which Publius believed was "as little to be expected as the philosophical race of kings wished for by Plato" (*F*, 340).

It was Machiavelli's modern recovery and revision of the Great Law-giver that bears the most relevance to Arendt's account, because it was through Machiavelli's work that the distinctly modern question of how to institute a new political authority without appeal to tradition or inherited law, on the one hand, or some kind of transcendental claim to absolute validity, on the other, is most clearly posed and examined. "It ought to be remembered," Machiavelli wrote in *The Prince*, "that there is nothing more difficult to take in hand, more perilous to conduct, or more uncertain in its success, then to take the lead in the introduction of a new order of things."[21]

Machiavelli was nearly obsessed with the possibilities of human agency and with the question of how to engender stable public authority out of crisis and conflict—how public authority might emerge from the secular realm of human action alone. Machiavelli turned to ancient texts, and especially Livy's *History*, to examine how authority is created and sustained over time when confronted with the corruption, contingency, and fortuna that define human affairs. John Pocock argues that this complex understanding of the dynamics of founding and refounding was the "archaism" that Machiavelli placed in the heart of political modernity.[22] For Machiavelli, the *virtù* of the Great Lawgiver and the glorious example of his action, were able to engender the authority necessary to establish a subsequent order of law, so long as *virtù* and glorious action were remembered by citizens when they faced destabilizing forms of corruption in their own time. Machiavelli argued that through restorative acts of refounding, oriented by narratives of remembrance, the political realm might generate its own norms and principles, rather than importing them from the external realms of morality or religion.

Machiavelli's republicanism has been revived by contemporary democratic theorists seeking a normative alternative to political liberalism and communitarianism, and negative and positive liberty, but the neo-republican revival and its efforts to formalize this tradition has focused little attention on Machiavelli's modern reworking of the Great Lawgiver. When the concept of Founding has entered the conversation, as in recent discussions of constitutional moments and constituent power, it has typically neglected the aspects of Founding that both Machiavelli and the ancients found most important: the glorious exemplarity of the Founder's actions that captivated the political imagination of those who came after and were called upon to remember. This emphasis on the extraordinary *act*, on glory and assertive *virtù*, seems dangerously aesthetic, charismatic, and martial to most democratic theorists. Such "silly creation myths" resonate all-too clearly with ugly nationalism, chauvinistic and exclusionary patriotism, or the irrational sacralization of politics.[23] Judith Shklar once expressed this objection in an essay examining the unfortunate role of myth in American politics. Shklar specifically lamented the hold that "the great legislator had on our political imagination," and the "thoroughly mischievous" effect this myth has had on clear-headed political inquiry and analysis.[24] As Shklar knew well, many of the American Founders were aware of these mythologizing tendencies even as they cautiously embraced their political importance, and none more so than Publius.

Although Hamilton, Madison, and Jay wrote *The Federalist Papers* under the pseudonym of Publius, they also carefully distinguished America's postrevolutionary experiments in constitution making from the ancient model. Already in *Federalist* No. 1 Publius writes "it seems to be reserved to the people of this country to decide the important question whether societies of men are really capable of establishing good government from reflection and choice or if they are destined to depend for their political constitutions on accident and force" (*F*, 3). In later essays, Publius explicitly associates the illegitimacy of Founding based on "accident and force" with the Great Lawgiver. "It is not a little remarkable," he writes in No. 38, "that in every case reported by ancient history, in which government has been established with deliberation and consent, the task of framing it has not been committed to an assembly of men; but has been performed by some individual citizen of pre-eminent wisdom and approved integrity" (*F*, 239–40). He goes on to note that the degree to which the acts of these extraordinary citizens are "clothed with the legitimate authority of the people, cannot in every instance be ascertained" (*F*, 240). As I will examine more closely in chapter 1, Publius invokes the Great Lawgiver in a section of *The Federalist* that confronts Anti-Federalist arguments against the illegitimacy of the Philadelphia Convention and the ratification procedure that it established, most notably its unauthorized and illegal rejection of the amendment procedures established under the Articles of Confederation. Following an argument first elaborated by James Wilson during the ratification debates, Publius appeals to the higher lawmaking power of the people themselves as a way of confronting a key Anti-Federalist argument against the Constitution's legality. In *The Federalist*, the people themselves become the Great Lawgiver, but this transformation, as we will see, is not without its own dilemmas and paradoxes, and it certainly does not resolve the intermingling of violence and validity associated with Founding. Publius and many other Founders believed that the American experiment in collective foundation, the people as Great Lawgiver, was one of the most important postrevolutionary American innovations in the long tradition of republicanism, but some of the central theoretical issues had been posed by previous political theorists, most notably Jean-Jacques Rousseau in book 2, chapter 7 of his *Social Contract*.

While Publius warned against recurrent appeals to the people's constituent power in *The Federalist*—especially in No. 49's critique of Jefferson's democratic radicalism—he also argued that the American replacement of the Great Lawgiver with the people not only extended this power to the existing people of his time but to the people unfolding across an extended and unknown future. This argument is appropriately conveyed in the very last *Federalist*, No. 85. Citing David Hume's essay on "The Rise of the Arts and Sciences," Publius writes, "To found and balance a society on general laws is a work of such great difficulty that no human genius, however comprehensive, is able by the mere dint of reason and reflection to effect it. The judgments of many must unite in the work; Experience must guide their labour; Time must bring it to reflection. And the feeling of inconvenience must correct the mistakes they inevitably fall into in their first trials and experiments" (*F*, 594). Far from what now goes by the name constitutional conservatism, Publius in his last essay projects the authorizing authority of the people into an unmarked horizon of future acts, reforms, and constitutional revisions, which brings us back to Hannah Arendt.

The form of remembrance that Arendt proclaims a central component of constitutional authority is focused on the act of founding itself, understood as an act of collective political agency. While Arendt's emphasis is on a single moment of founding, like Publius, her understanding of the agency involved in such acts of political initiation, and beginning anew, uncouples the act from a single temporal anchor, and projects it across a subsequent history of refoundings. Put differently, far from participating in "silly mythmaking" Arendt calls for a form of political remembrance that can actually work to disenthrall citizens from the very idea of a single decisive founding that sets the normative horizon in law and politics for everything that follows from it, and to bring to public attention the exemplary acts and struggles of those agents who have attempted to refound in subsequent American history.

There are other ways of approaching the problem of remembrance, the importance of our imaginary relationship to the Founders, and its role in securing constitutional legitimacy than the one that Arendt develops in *On Revolution*. For example, remembrance can speak to the way that a republican citizenry must see themselves "in the same boat as the founders," as existing in an unbroken and self-correcting tradition of constitutional development.[25] Remembrance can also help shape broader narratives of moral and ethical orientation in which the law is always embedded, as Robert Cover emphasized in his work.[26] Remembrance can also confer the identity-shaping "stories of peoplehood" that Rogers Smith has recently examined. These need not be mutually exclusive approaches, but they emphasize different orientations to how we understand and evaluate our reliance on the authority of the Founders. What all of these inquiries have in common is a critique of forms of democratic and constitutional theory that argues such imaginary considerations can be easily dismissed or bracketed from our public life. The political life of remembrance is poorly grasped if it is only understood in its most hagiographic or fundamentalist forms. With the stage set by these larger questions, it is time to turn directly to Publius and the political imagination he has both reflected upon and helped shape. It will help to first bring a familiar picture into view before elaborating upon what this familiar picture leaves out.

II.

Publius—the pseudonymous voice of Alexander Hamilton, John Jay, and James Madison—is the author of eighty-five essays urging the ratification of the United States Constitution. These essays appeared several times a week in New York City newspapers between October 1787 and August 1788 and were later assembled in book form as *The Federalist*. Although the essays were very hastily written as polemical defenses of the Constitution against its Anti-Federalist opponents, they also aimed to provide a systematic explanation of American constitutionalism and, perhaps, of America itself.

Already in 1788 Thomas Jefferson declared *The Federalist* to be "the best commentary on the principles of government which ever was written," and many subsequent generations of American readers have agreed.[27] Clinton Rossiter hailed *The Federalist* as "the most important work in political science that has ever been written, or is likely ever to be written, in the United States," and "the one product of the American mind that is rightly counted among the classics of political theory."[28] Martin Diamond argued it was the text that most lucidly declared the ends of the "American regime" and set the horizon of its political discourse.[29] Gary Wills described it as a national urtext through which Americans explain themselves to themselves as a people.[30] Even trenchant critics of *The Federalist* like Sheldon Wolin concede that more than any other single text, it initiated the American "public hermeneutic."[31]

Apart from the Declaration of Independence and the Constitution itself, there is arguably no other text in the canon of American political thought that has received more exhaustive commentary from historians, political theorists, political scientists, legal scholars, and others. An important question to ask at the beginning of another examination of *The Federalist*'s political theory is whether its inflated, even mythological, status has rendered important but underarticulated elements of Publius's text obscure or illegible. It is the wager of this study that it has, and that recovering some of these subdued elements and minor tones will not only enrich our understanding of the text itself—illuminating textures and preoccupations we might not otherwise see—but, doing so, bring the text into a productive dialogue with issues and dilemmas contemporary political theorists wrestle with still, but for which *The Federalist* usually has not seemed relevant.

It is well known that in *The Federalist* Publius argued against the decentralization of political authority under the Articles of Confederation, which had created a confederation of thirteen sovereign states rather than a central government capable of acting in the national interest. Publius worried, for example, that national commercial interests suffered from intransigent economic conflicts between states, and that federal weakness undermined American diplomatic efforts abroad. Broadly, Publius argued that the government's impotence under the Articles obstructed America's emergence as a powerful commercial empire. Publius was also critical of the power assumed by state legislatures under the Articles — and of the questionable character of the men serving in those assemblies. The farmers and artisans who rose to power in postrevolutionary America seemed to Publius and other Federalists too beholden to narrow economic and regional interests to serve the broader public good. Of particular concern to Publius were state legislatures passing prodebtor legislation and paper money laws that threatened creditors' property rights. Although revolutionary Americans typically worried about the conspiracies of the elite few against the liberties of the people, Publius's concern was with tyrannical legislative majorities threatening the rights of propertied minorities. According to Publius, the Articles provided no safeguards against the vices of the people themselves. He argued that the Revolution's enthusiasm for liberty had diminished popular appreciation for the need for governance. "Excesses of democracy" threatened to corrupt postrevolutionary republican governments and sink them into popular licentiousness and vice. Publius understood the 1786 insurrection of debtor farmers in Western Massachusetts — Shays' Rebellion — as a terrifying symptom of this broader crisis.

Publius argued for an increase in the "energy" of the federal government to respond to this crisis. However, the national government's increased power would have to be based in republican principles and retain a federal distribution of power; there would be no return to monarchical rule or consolidation of central authority. The task, as Publius stated in *Federalist* No. 10, was to find a "Republican remedy to the diseases most incident to Republican government" (*F*, 65). *The Federalist*'s new science of politics sought to establish republican government on principles that departed from classical republicanism, to prevent the United States from falling into predicted cycles of decline and regeneration that afflicted past republics. The new federal Constitution promised to break these cycles of decline and establish a more durable and powerful *novus ordo seclorum*.

On this issue, there were two essential interrelated components of Publius's arguments, which have been the focus of much of the political theory commentary on *The Federalist*: the American states' vast territory and an innovative theory of political representation. Montesquieu and other influential republican theorists had argued that republican government was only possible over a small territory because free republics depended on a virtuous citizenry that shared interests and values and whose loyalty was engendered through direct participation in public affairs; popular liberties were sustained only by a virtuous citizenry. A large republic's diversity, classical republicans feared, would lead to divisive factional politics that would undermine it. The loyalty of citizens in a large state, moreover, would be achieved by threat of force rather than virtuous commitment to the public good. Publius's Anti-Federalist opponents frequently invoked these theories in their arguments against the Constitution.

Publius rejected this prevailing theory of small republics and argued instead that, far from being a weakness, the American republic's vastness and extent was an advantage. Rather than relying wholly on the citizenry's virtues to prevent factionalism, Publius argued that institutions could be arranged so as to mitigate its harmful effects. Political representation, which Publius called "the great mechanical power in government," was the key (*F*, 84). In a large republic there would be so many different factions, Publius reasoned, that no majority faction could win elections and tyrannize over minorities. Instead, these factions would cancel each other out and typically elect representatives capable of an enlarged, refined view of the public good. While Publius believed that "the people are the only legitimate fountain of power," *The Federalist* emphasizes that institutions' organization should obstruct majorities and protect the people from the tyrannical tendencies of their own democratic will.

Publius's emphasis on how institutional organization might "ameliorate popular systems" exemplifies a broader shift in how he understood the strategy of republican governance, which I explore in chapter 3. In earlier forms of republicanism—including the "Country" republicanism that profoundly influenced American revolutionaries—the power of government was directly opposed to the liberties of the people. Publius, by contrast, argued that the Constitution established an economy of governmental power and popular liberty: government would rule not by directly limiting the liberties of the people, but would indirectly channel them to prevent harmful excesses. This institutional strategy of indirect governance is also exemplified in Publius's famous arguments about checking governmental power. While popular accountability through elections was a crucial "external" check, Publius argued also for the importance of "auxiliary precautions" in the internal organization of the government itself. The separation of powers between the three branches of government would create internal checks and balances within the government to prevent, first, one branch from dominating the others, and second, the general governmental from overreaching constitutional limits on its power. Whereas earlier republican theories of "mixed government" had associated the separate branches with different social classes, Publius's theory derived the authority of all branches from the people themselves. There was no constitutionally sanctioned division of social classes or estates.

Several aspects of this familiar portrait of *The Federalist* will be taken up and examined in the chapters that follow, but in order to illuminate their relationship to aspects of Publius's argument concerning the political imagination that have typically been neglected. A sketch of the ratifying context in which *The Federalist* initially appeared will also direct us to these neglected questions by revealing the crisis of political authority confronted by Publius and the importance of political imagination to navigating the dilemmas produced by this crisis.

III.

On July 26, 1788, the New York State Convention in Poughkeepsie ratified the United States Constitution, making New York the reluctant "eleventh pillar to the Federal Edifice."[32] It had been a long and contentious ratifying season. For almost a year, New York newspapers were filled with essays debating the proposed Constitution and the future of the young American republic. Even before the first *Federalist* appeared in late October of 1787, several prominent Anti-Federalists—writing under such pseudonyms as Centinel, A Federal Farmer, Cato, An Old Whig, and Brutus—had railed against the dangers the Constitution posed to the popular liberties won by the Revolution. Whether the Constitution would save or betray the Revolution was an essential point of contention between Federalists and Anti-Federalists, but all recognized the heightened significance of the "great national discussion" unfolding in the conventions, in the press, and in the streets—not only for America, but for the entire world.

New York's Convention lasted longer and was more bitterly divided than any other ratifying state's. New York Federalists won a very narrow procedural victory of thirty votes to twenty-seven—hardly the longed-for authority of unanimous consent. Moreover, the convention passed twenty-three "explanatory" and "recommendatory" amendments detailing the rights reserved to the people and noting multiple "deficiencies" marring the very Constitution they had ratified. "It was," one historian writes, "an equivocal victory for the Constitution's supporters, but it was enough to bring the state into the Union."[33] In the convention's final days, participants on both sides openly worried that "the body of the people" would "not be satisfied" with the convention's final decision. Governor George Clinton, New York's most prominent Anti-Federalist, assured delegates that he would use all his power and influence to persuade the public to accept the convention's final vote.[34] Indeed, Americans throughout the states worried that formal ratification of the

Constitution would not stand unless the people felt attached to it. To a degree now difficult to realize, the dominant public sentiment in the face of the newly ratified Constitution was "massive uncertainty."[35] John Adams succinctly captured the problem that the New York delegates and broader citizenry faced: "A Constitution is a Standard, a Pillar, and a Bond when it is understood approved and beloved. But without this intelligence and attachment it might as well be a Kite or Balloon, flying in the air."[36] The United States Constitution had been formally ratified, but whether it had achieved binding authority over the citizens of New York and the rest of the Union remained an open and deeply troubling political question.

Three days before the New York Convention's final vote, more than 5,000 people marched in New York City's "grand federal procession" celebrating the successful ratification in ten state conventions—a sufficient number to make the Constitution operative—and urging ratification in New York. An estimated 20,000 spectators watched what one Federalist called "our Procession-Politico,"[37] a spectacle of flags and "showy" floats winding through the streets of lower Manhattan. At the procession's end, 6,000 citizens were invited to an extravagant public feast organized by Revolutionary War hero Pierre L'Enfant. Led by horsemen with trumpets, the marchers formed ten divisions, each including various trades that had united with the merchants in favor of the new federal Constitution: foresters, farmers, gardeners, tailors, bakers, brewers, butchers, carpenters, hatters, blacksmiths, boat builders, potters, clergymen, physicians, and more. Room was made for "strangers" and the president and students of King's College (now Columbia).

Each order carried "the principal instruments or symbols of their estates," with "flags and colors" ornamenting these emblems;[38] the procession was "splendid with a variety of Carts, Banners, and other emblematic contrivances, all very appropriate to the subject of the day."[39] A "Federal Printing Press," for example, accompanied the "Printers, Bookbinders, and Stationers" of the seventh division. Printers distributed broadside odes "among the multitude," praising the Constitution:

> Crown'd with auspicious Light,
> Columbia Eagle rise;
> Thine emblems bless our sight,
> Thine Honors greet our Eyes!
> Nations admire thy rising Dawn, and shall salute thy Day,
> While Generations yet unborn, receive the genial ray.[40]

One newspaper reported that a small flag flew above the Federal Printing Press, "on which was inscribed the word 'Publius's in gold letters."[41]

While singularly extravagant, New York's federal procession followed many others that ratifying season, including processions in Baltimore, Boston, Charleston, and Philadelphia.[42] Together these parades comprised the "largest and most elaborate processions" America had ever seen.[43] The processions' centerpieces were small but seaworthy frigates pulled through city streets by teams of thirteen horses, firing thirteen-gun salutes at intervals. These ships were the symbolic focus of nationwide proratification Federalist pageantry in the spring and summer of 1788. Playing on the metaphor of the ship of state, these frigates were also meant to presage a glorious future of commercial and military empire. Federalists christened these ships with different names: "The Constitution" in Boston, "The Federalist" in Baltimore, "Union" in Philadelphia, and "the Hamilton" in New York City. (See figure I.1.)

Newspaper reports emphasized the majesty of these events and elaborated in great detail on their flags' symbolism and the extravagance of their pageantry. Observe, one writer gushed, "the magnificent display of Standards, Insignias, Mechanical Arts, the Federal Ship, &c, &c."[44] Several reports claimed these pageants defied description, and that "mere description must [therefore] fall short of the appearance of it."[45] One observer described the New York procession as "the most brilliant ever seen in America," and noted "probably few of the oldest cities in Europe ever excelled in a procession of the kind."[46] It was, in short, "the most natural, tasty, august, and sublime Scene ever before exhibited in America."[47]

While celebrating the federal processions' majesty, several observers also contrasted them with two more familiar forms of eighteenth-century political spectacle: the revolutionary rituals of the "people out of doors" and the pomp of monarchical ceremony. Like the Constitution they celebrated, these federal processions were said to navigate between the political extremes of "democratic excess" and monarchical tyranny. They

Figure I.1. *The Federal Ship Hamilton.* Engraving in Martha J. Lamb, *History of the City of New York, Vol. 2.* New York: A. S. Barnes, 1880.

drew on both the popular authenticity of the one and the solemn authority of the other. The federal processions were festival and ceremony,
celebrations and consecrations, rituals of liberty and rituals of order. Contemporaries marveled repeatedly at the "remarkable regularity & decorum that prevailed"[48]:

> No wild intemp'rance here is found
> No riots in the street resound.[49]

Indeed, what most "excited surprise," according to one account, was "to
see a numberless multitude, in view of a tempting collation, not only
adhering to every rule of decorum . . . but tho' under the influence of
public passions, verging on enthusiasm, peaceably . . . retiring without a
single instance of rudeness or intemperance."[50] The sober decorum of
this "numberless multitude" provided an edifying spectacle for emphati-
cally *post*revolutionary citizens.

The processions provided a cohering spectacle of calm and deliberate
citizens divided into artisanal orders and characterized by the industri-
ousness of a commercial society. "Instead of trophies of war . . . which
graced the triumphs of antiquity," the famous lexicographer Noah Webster wrote, "we here beheld the plough, the ship and all the implements
of useful arts."[51] James Wilson argued that these spectacles, far from
useless extravagance, worked in perfect conjunction with liberty and the
laws of nature. While "public exhibitions have been the favorite amuse-
ment of some of the wisest and most accomplished nations," he wrote,
too often these spectacles had been orchestrated to captivate the people
rather than to enlighten them. Republican spectacle, on the other hand,
would become an essential part of the edifying authority of the new
regime. Wilson and other commentators thus drew attention to popular
constitutionalism's aesthetic dimensions. Speaking at Philadelphia's July
4 federal procession, Wilson concluded,

> Public processions may be so planned and executed as to join both the
> properties of Nature's rule [utility and ornament]. They may instruct
> and improve while they entertain and please. . . . They may preserve
> the memory, and engrave the importance of great political events. They
> may represent with peculiar felicity and force, the operation and effects
> of great political truths. The picturesque and splendid decorations
> around me furnish the most beautiful and brilliant proofs, that these
> remarks are FAR FROM BEING IMAGINARY.[52]

In the spring and summer of 1788, Federalists enlisted the "peculiar
felicity and force" of these spectacles to achieve several interrelated goals:
to stage a spectacle of popular unification obviously missing in the contentious debates over ratification, to inflate the authority and seeming
inevitability of the Constitution, and to bind Federalists to a compelling
image of national destiny.[53] *The Federalist Papers* can be read as a part of

this larger effort. Time and again Federalists and Anti-Federalists both referred to the "great national discussion as itself an edifying or educative spectacle." "A greater Drama is now acting on this Theatre than has heretofore been brought on the American Stage," Washington wrote in 1788, "or any other in the World. We exhibit at present the Novel and astonishing Spectacle of a whole People deliberating calmly on what form of government will be most conducive to their happiness."[54]

The figurative spectacle of the "great national discussion" was thus supported by carefully orchestrated spectacles of a more literal sort. Like the more famous festivals that would sweep revolutionary France in the following years, federal processions were rituals of assent that enacted a political unity they claimed to merely represent, to establish an aura of authority over the formal institutions of a fledgling government: they aspired to ensure that the Constitution became "a Standard, a Pillar, and a Bond" rather than a mere "Kite or Balloon."

As might be expected, not all observers reveled in the theatrics of the federal processions. Anti-Federalists worried that Federalists were "stealing the show" by means of pageantry and parade.[55] Thomas Greenleaf, publisher of the Anti-Federalist *New York Journal*, was one of these. Greenleaf had been demonized by New York Federalists for publishing essays critical of the Constitution (his was the only New York City newspaper to do so). The day of the procession, the *Journal* predicted it would resemble the exaggerated theatricality of royal coronation—playing on standard Anti-Federalist fears of consolidated government and the "energy" of the executive branch under the proposed Constitution. Greenleaf also suggested that the participation of elected representatives from the state legislature was in fact unrepresentative of their constituencies and therefore unauthorized: "We are informed, that some of the *representatives* this day will appear royally splendid; others in fancy dresses which credit taste: among the most striking of these, which are not common, is the *grotesque*."[56] In predicting the procession would be a "grotesque," Greenleaf associated it not with somber order and natural correspondence but with caricature, comic distortion, and flamboyant exaggeration: he deflated the Federalist organizers' pious pretense by emphasizing the procession's trumped-up artificiality.

Greenleaf worked the same vein the next day in a longer article. Although his account of the procession was largely admiring—he noted that "it was conducted in a regular and decent manner," for example, and that the ship Hamilton "added greatly to the beauty of the parade"[57]— Greenleaf ridiculed the shoddy stage effects that undermined the authority that Federalists had hoped the procession would possess:

> The stages were of various sizes, and mostly very slight, insomuch that the poor potters were separated from their clay, and no longer had power over it; the stage fell! and, alas! the clay became exposed to the

power of every passer-by. It was really laughable to see the variety of phizzes on that occasion. The poor antis generally minded their own business at home; others who were spectators at an awful distance, looked as sour as the Devil. As for the feds, they rejoiced in different degrees—there was the ha, ha, ha! and the he, he, he![58]

Greenleaf's was the first account of the New York procession to be published, and after it appeared Federalists vociferously attacked his efforts to "ridicule" the procession and "burlesque" the citizenry.[59] Greenleaf objected that the "innocent humor" of his account did not aim at "giving offense or injuring the feelings of any one," but Federalists nonetheless assailed his "misrepresentations" as efforts to diminish their event's respectability. What New York Federalists hoped to sell as authenticity of unanimous popular expression, Greenleaf exposed as shoddy stage effect.

When news arrived on July 26 that the State Convention in Poughkeepsie had finally ratified the Constitution, New York's Federalists were jubilant—and eager to avenge themselves on prominent Anti-Federalists. Greenleaf was a convenient target. Following a night of joyous celebration at a local tavern, a Federalist "gentleman mob" attacked Greenleaf's printing shop. According to one newspaper report, "A large number of the Citizens assembled at Mr. Gerenleaf's, broke into the house, and turned his types and other printing materials out into the street."[60] Reports indicate that the mob was primarily motivated by Greenleaf's published mockery of the Federalist procession. This, too, followed a pattern of similar events unfolding over the previous months. Beginning with riots in Carlisle, Pennsylvania, on December 26, 1787, there were multiple instances of mobbing and rioting during the ratifying season, triggered by contests over processions, parades, and celebrations of constitutional ratification. In fact, the majority of reported riots during this period "originated in controversies over celebrations."[61] The hallowed spectacle of the "great national discussion" also involved conflicts over the enactment of political spectacle.

This brief anecdote offers a different perspective on the contentious politics of constitutional ratification than usually provided by political theory scholarship on the American Founding, and it raises some of the issues to be examined in this study. Much of this scholarship has focused on important issues surrounding the formal and juridical organization of political life: the institutional coordination of federal powers, the checks and balances of different branches of government, the role of contending interests and political factions within a republican government, the principles and mechanisms of electoral representation, the role of the judiciary and constitutional jurisprudence, and the procedures of legislative reform and constitutional amendment. In other words, such studies have typically focused on the official procedures exemplified by the events of July 26, while neglecting the popular politics of July 23.

This book, by contrast, will examine the interdependence of formal political institutions and the broader political culture of late eighteenth-century America—and, more specifically, how Publius and his Anti-Federalist opponents engaged this interdependence—through the lens of political imagination. Political imagination refers not only to the festivals, processions, and parades of postrevolutionary America, but to other inescapably aesthetic dimensions of political life and popular constitutionalism: the narrative organization of political reality in the period's political discourses, the appeal to popular imagination to secure the authority of the state and to envision the constituent capacities of the people, the role of sensation and passion in political deliberation, and the disciplining of imagination into a governing sense of individual and collective interest. Publius, as the following chapters show, engaged with all of these themes in *The Federalist*, but it was perhaps John Adams who captured the problem most succinctly. For Adams and his contemporaries, public life was importantly about the orchestration of appearances; their theatrical conception of public life famously and consistently conceived the political world through the central metaphor of the stage. In a remarkable letter to his friend Benjamin Rush, Adams captured the causal power of political aesthetics on public life, its ability not only to "exaggerate," "conceal," "inflate," and "moralize," but to "actuate."[62] "The Scenery of the Business," Adams wrote,

> has often if not commonly in all the business of human life, at least of public life, more effect than the characters of the dramatis personae or the ingenuity of the plot. Recollect within your own times. What but the scenery did this? Or that? Or the other? Was there ever a *coup de théâtre* that had so great an effect as Jefferson's penmanship of the Declaration of Independence? . . . I have a great mind to write a book on "The Scenery of the Business."[63]

Too bad for us that Adams never wrote such a book, which might have been an interesting companion to his institutionally detailed *Defense of the Constitutions of the United States of America*. Adams, however, was not alone among the Founders in his appreciation of the powerful effects of such *coups de théâtre* on public life in postrevolutionary America, nor was he the only one to theoretically reflect on the importance of their political operations. These concerns with political imagination were already at stake in the pseudonymous authorship of *The Federalist*.

IV.

There are good reasons for referring to Publius as the pseudonymous author of *The Federalist Papers*, as I will throughout this study, rather than the authorial parsing of Hamilton, Madison, and Jay. "During the American Revolution and the early years of the Republic," Douglass Adair writes, "the pseudonym is the norm."[64] While pseudonymous writing goes back to biblical times, and was usually motivated by the desire to avoid political and religious censure, the formative influence on late eighteenth-century Americans came from the English Whigs. The use of pseudonyms in such influential texts as John Trenchard and Thomas Gordon's *Cato's Letters* (1720–1723) treated pseudonymous authorship as a positive good, rather than an unfortunate necessity occasioned by censorship. The widespread eighteenth-century American use of classical pseudonyms became especially pronounced in the newspaper debates over constitutional ratification as Federalist and Anti-Federalists assumed the names of classical figures before entering into the public contentions over constitutional ratification: Publius engaged with Brutus, Cato took on Caesar. Writers employed carefully chosen historical analogies to make sense of the political crises of their own time and of their own roles as Great Lawgivers.[65] These pseudonyms could serve different kinds of authorizing functions. They could serve as marks of distinction and social status, as a sign of the author's education, virtue, wisdom, and taste. The use of pseudonyms also formally enabled the impersonalization of political argument so important to ideologies of republican publicity, as Michael Warner has influentially argued. In the ratification debates, Warner writes, "the mutual recognition promised . . . was not an interaction between particularized persons, but among persons constituted by the negating abstraction of themselves."[66] Publius was a fictive persona rhetorically constructed to elicit and represent a national American public; his "very identity dramatizes the [imagined] conditions of authority in a representational polity."[67]

Approaches to *The Federalist* that neglect this imaginary authorship, and attempt to instead identify the different and competing personal ideologies or "voices" of Hamilton, Madison, and Jay, may illuminate competing emphases and even logical inconsistencies of the text,[68] but they also risk reifying what the text says at the expense of what it aimed to do. *The Federalist* was not written to provide a definitive articulation of the political thought of its three authors—there are many traps set in approaching it as a canonical work of political philosophy—but instead to rhetorically achieve a single public goal: the ratification of the proposed federal constitution. Moreover, Publius himself (and also, independently, Hamilton and Madison)[69] urged his public to bracket questions of personal authorship and motivation when considering the weighty issues of constitutional ratification. Already in the first *Federalist*, Publius attempted to frame the manner of debate by urging readers to resist inquiring into the personal motives of both Federalists and Anti-Federalists, and instead judge the work on the cogency of their arguments alone (even if Publius did not consistently uphold this high principle).[70] Publius feared that an emphasis on the motivations and identities of pseudonymous writers would debase public discussion by directing attention to always inconclusive speculations of motivation and intent. "My motives must remain in the depository of my own breast," Publius writes: "My arguments will be open to all, and may be judged by all" (*F*, 6). Scholars who seek the original intent of Publius in the personal authorship of Hamilton, Madison, and Jay—whether by debunking their economic motivations with Charles Beard, or celebrating their noble impartiality as "thinking revolutionaries"—violate Publius's own guidelines for establishing the meaning of his text. The very question of *The Federalist*'s authorship already inaugurates the problem of the imagination, because Publius asks his audience, as a precondition for properly receiving his argument, to imagine being addressed not by a contemporary person but by a classical impersonation.[71] This splits the form of address into two simultaneous registers of meaning: the newspaper communication of a living contemporary and a "metatextual set of associations" with an imagined republican past.[72] The republican present is overlaid, mediated, and framed through reference to these ancient examples.

Hamilton's adoption of Publius Valerius as the composite voice of *The Federalist* raises a larger question about the role of the imagination in the debates over constitutional ratification, and in particular how the imaginary republic and empire of Rome shaped this most authoritative attempt to envision the modern American republic. *The Federalist* does not only "explain America," as Gary Wills would have it, or defend the constitutional edifice constructed in the Philadelphia Convention, but imagines the future "fate of an empire in many respects the most interesting in the world." Publius's rhetorical enlistment of his public's imagination is not merely ornamental, but an essential part of the architecture of his argument, and that argument is not only about explanations and justifications, but involves a world-making act of calling a new polity into being. The glorious example of Rome was important to this effort. Scholars have debated whether classical republicanism was "illustrative" or "determinative" of the political thought of late eighteenth-century America, and the extent to which "the classics exerted a formative influence on the founders." Bernard Bailyn, to take a prominent example, argues that the classics "contributed to a vivid vocabulary but not the logic or grammar of thought, a universally respected personification but not the source of political and social beliefs."[73] Perhaps the key issue at play in these debates is not how the political thought of ancient writers like Cicero, Plutarch, and Polybius, was taken up and transformed in *The Federalist*'s modern republicanism—although that is an important question—but how the stories, exemplars, and figures of ancient Rome helped shape Publius's understanding of the "critical period" of the 1780s and of the tasks of republican foundation discussed above.

Republicanism is as much a rich assemblage of narratives and symbols as it is a coherent political ideology, despite the best efforts of contemporary political theorists to turn it into such. This is why Gordon Wood calls republicanism a "counterculture to monarchy," and Franco Venturi describes it simply as a "form of life."[74] This imaginary republic, as argued above, continues to profoundly shape our own understandings of political foundation and of our relationship to the authority of the Founders.

Publius did not construe the imagination as simply a dangerous threat or superfluous ornament to the serious political issues of authority, law, and sovereignty, but as importantly constitutive of them. Publius recognized that critical periods of revolution and founding required heightened investments of popular imagination to "initiate a new order of things" and secure the authority of the new regime. He helps us see the extent to which the "reality of the modern state arose in part from a construction in imagination," and that "the activated imagination is not a mere historical epiphenomenon, but instead becomes a significant constituent of a political reality formed this way."[75] Rather than treating Publius as espousing a hard-headed realism, on the one hand, or deliberative democratic idealism, on the other, in the chapters that follow I will engage Publius as a political visionary with an acute understanding of the formative role of the imagination in republican politics, past and present.

NOTES

1. Jill Lepore, *The Whites of Their Eyes: The Tea Party's Revolution and the Battle over American History* (Princeton, NJ: Princeton University Press, 2010), 14.
2. See especially Michael Kammen, *A Machine That Would Go of Itself: The Constitution in American Culture* (New York: Alfred A. Knopf, 1986).
3. Marshall Bicentennial Address at www.thurgoodmarshall.com/speeches/constitutional_speech.htm.
4. Jacob E. Cooke, ed., *The Federalist* (Middletown, CT: Wesleyan University Press, 1961), 31. All subsequent citations to *The Federalist* will be to this edition, titled *F* with paginations in parentheses in the text.
5. My use of imagination in this text is indebted to the discussion in Susan Buck-Morss's *Dreamworld and Catastrophe: The Passing of Mass Utopia in East and West* (Cambridge, MA: MIT Press, 2002).
6. Thomas Jefferson, *Thomas Jefferson: Writings* (New York: Library of America, 1984), 1401.
7. Stephen Holmes, *Passions and Constraint: On the Theory of Liberal Democracy* (Chicago: University of Chicago Press, 1995); Jon Elster, *Ulysses Unbound: Studies in Rationality, Precommitment, and Constraints* (Cambridge: Cambridge University Press, 2000); Bruce Ackerman, *We the People, Vol. 1: Foundations* (Cambridge, MA: Belknap Press of Harvard University Press, 1993); Jürgen Habermas, "Constitutional Democracy: A Paradoxical Union of Contradictory Principles?" *Political Theory* 29, no. 6 (2001): 766–81; Jack Balkin, *Constitutional Redemption: Political Faith in an Unjust World* (Cambridge, MA: Harvard University Press, 2011).

8. Angelika Bernal offers a rich exploration of the concept of founding in "Beyond Origins: Rethinking Founding in a Post-Foundational Age" (unpublished manuscript).

9. John Adams, *The Political Writings of John Adams*, ed. George Carey (Washington, DC: Regnery Publishing, 2000), 490.

10. Thomas Paine, *Political Writings* (Cambridge: Cambridge University Press, 2000), 184.

11. Karl Marx, "The Eighteenth Brumaire of Louis Bonaparte" in *Surveys from Exile: Political Writings, Vol. 2*, ed. David Fernbach (New York: Penguin Books, 1973), 147.

12. Marx, "The Eighteenth Brumaire of Louis Bonaparte," 146.

13. Marx, "The Eighteenth Brumaire of Louis Bonaparte," 148–49.

14. Douglass Adair, *Fame and the Founding Fathers*, ed. Trevor Colbourn (New York: W. W. Norton, 1974), 7.

15. Adair, *Fame and the Founding Fathers*, 12.

16. Adair, *Fame and the Founding Fathers*, 13; Adair's emphasis.

17. Hannah Arendt, *On Revolution* (New York: Penguin, 1990 [1963]), 203.

18. Arendt, *On Revolution*, 204.

19. See John Rawls, *Political Liberalism: Expanded Edition* (New York: Columbia University Press, 2005).

20. Frank Michelman, "Law's Republic," *The Yale Law Journal* 97, no. 8 (1988): 1493–1537.

21. Niccolo Machiavelli, *The Prince*, in *Machiavelli: The Chief Works, Vol. 3*, trans. Albert Gilbert (Durham, NC: Duke University Press, 1989), 5–96, 25.

22. J. G. A. Pocock, *The Machiavellian Moment: Florentine Political Thought and the Atlantic Republican Tradition* (Princeton, NJ: Princeton University Press, 1975).

23. On the sacralization of politics, see Emilio Gentile's *Politics as Religion*, trans. George Staunton (Princeton, NJ: Princeton University Press, 2006).

24. See Judith Shklar's "*The Federalist* as Myth," *Yale Law Journal* 90, no. 4 (1981): 942–53.

25. Habermas, "Constitutional Democracy"; Balkin, *Constitutional Redemption*; Michelman, "Law's Republic."

26. Robert Cover, "Foreword: Nomos and Narrative," *Harvard Law Review* 97, no. 4 (1983): 4–68.

27. Thomas Jefferson, *The Papers of Thomas Jefferson, Vol. 14*, ed. Julian Boyd (Princeton, NJ: Princeton University Press, 1958), 188.

28. Alexander Hamilton, James Madison, and John Jay, *The Federalist Papers*, ed. Clinton Rossiter (New York: Signet Classics, 2003), ix.

29. Martin Diamond, "Democracy and *The Federalist*: A Reconsideration of the Framers' Intent," *American Political Science Review* 53, no. 1 (1959): 52–68.

30. Gary Wills, *Explaining America: The Federalist* (New York: Penguin Books, 1982).

31. Sheldon S. Wolin, *The Presence of the Past: Essays on the State and the Constitution* (Baltimore, MD: Johns Hopkins University Press, 1989).

32. *DHRC Vol. XXI*, 1591.

33. Linda Grant De Pauw, *The Eleventh Pillar: New York State and the Federal Constitution* (Ithaca, NY: Cornell University Press, 1966), 261.

34. Grant De Pauw, *The Eleventh Pillar*, 246.

35. On this general point see David J. Siemers, *Ratifying the Republic: Anti-Federalists and Federalists in Constitutional Time* (Stanford, CA: Stanford University Press, 2002), xi–xvii.

36. Cited in Zoltán Haraszti, *John Adams and the Prophets of Progress* (Cambridge, MA: Harvard University Press, 1952), 221.

37. See the documents collected in "Appendix I: The New York City Federal Procession, 23 July 1788," *DHRC Vol. XXI*, 1584–1666, 1584. See also Sarah H. J. Simpson, "The Federal Procession in the City of New York," *New-York Historical Society Bulletin* 7 (1925): 39–57.

38. *DHRC Vol. XXI*, 1602.

39. *DHRC Vol. XXI*, 1610.

40. *DHRC Vol. XXI*, 1605.

41. *DHRC Vol. XXI*, 1647.

42. See Whitfield J. Bell Jr., "The Federal Processions of 1788," *New York Historical Society Quarterly* 46 (1962): 5–39.

43. *DHRC Vol. XXI*, 1627.

44. *DHRC Vol. XXI*, 1621.

45. *DHRC Vol. XXI*, 1655.

46. *DHRC Vol. XXI*, 1619.

47. *DHRC Vol. XXI*, 1666.

48. *DHRC Vol. XXI*, 1603.

49. *DHRC Vol. XXI*, 1622.

50. *DHRC Vol. XXI*, 1658.

51. *DHRC Vol. XXI*, 1658.

52. James Wilson, "Oration delivered on the Fourth of July, 1788," in the appendix of Francis Hopkinson, *An Account of the Grand Federal Procession* (Philadelphia, 1788). Emphasis added.

53. David Waldstreicher, *In the Midst of Perpetual Fetes: The Making of American Nationalism, 1776–1820* (Chapel Hill: University of North Carolina Press, 1997), 93.

54. George Washington, *Writings* (New York: Library of America, 1997), 92.

55. Washington, *Writings*, 93.

56. *DHRC Vol. XXI*, 1605.

57. *DHRC Vol. XXI*, 1615.

58. *DHRC Vol. XXI*, 1616.

59. *DHRC Vol. XXI*, 1617.

60. *DHRC Vol. XXI*, 1619.

61. Waldstreicher, *In the Midst of Perpetual Fetes*, 93.

62. Clifford Geertz, *Negara: The Theatre State in Nineteenth-Century Bali* (Princeton, NJ: Princeton University Press, 1980).

63. John Adams, "Letter to Benjamin Rush, September 30, 1805," in *The Spur of Fame: Dialogues of John Adams and Benjamin Rush, 1805–1813*, ed. John A. Schutz and Douglass Adair (Indianapolis: Liberty Fund, 1966), 39–44, 44.

64. Douglass Adair, "A Note on Certain of Hamilton's Pseudonyms," in Trevor Colbourn, ed., *Fame and the Founding Fathers: Essays by Douglass Adair* (New York: W. W. Norton, 1974), 272–85, 272.

65. Eran Shalev, "Ancient Masks, American Fathers: Classical Pseudonyms during the American Revolution and Early Republic," *Journal of the Early Republic* 23, no. 2 (2003): 151–72; Gaspare J. Saladino, "Pseudonyms used in the newspaper debate over the ratification of the United State Constitution in the State of New York, September 1787–July 1788," in *New York and the Union*, ed. Stephen L. Schecter and Richard B. Bernstein (Albany: New York State Commission on the Bicentennial, 1990).

66. As many scholars have noted, the ideology of "republican print rationality" was not as hegemonic as Warner suggests. Alongside cultural commitments to the authority of impersonal and reasoned argument in the period were conflicting commitments to the authority of sincerity, character, and voice. The authority of tradition also played an important role in the debates over constitutional ratification. Gary Remer argues that these conflicting approaches to authority were enacted in the very use of pseudonyms, which enabled not only the impersonalization of argument, but also the oratorical invocation of classical authority. I follow lines of argument Remer suggests in his essay here: Gary Remer, "Two Models of Deliberation: Oratory and Conversation in Ratifying the Constitution," *Journal of Political Philosophy* 8, no. 1 (2000): 68–90; Michael Warner, *The Letters of the Republic: Publication and the Public Sphere in Eighteenth-Century America* (Cambridge, MA: Harvard University Press, 1990), 42–43. For contrasting accounts that emphasize the authority of sincerity, character, and voice, see Jay Fliegelman, *Declaring Independence: Jefferson, Natural Language, and the Culture of Performance* (Stanford, CA: Stanford University Press, 1993); Christopher Looby, *Voic-

ing America: Language, Literary Form, and the Origins of the United States (Chicago: University of Chicago Press, 1996).

67. Warner, *Letters of the Republic*, 113.

68. See, for example, James Jasinksi, "Heteroglossia, Polyphony, and *The Federalist Papers*," *Rhetoric Society Quarterly* 27, no. 1 (1997): 23–46; Isaac Kramnick, "The 'Great National Discussion': The Discourse of Politics in 1788," *William and Mary Quarterly* 45, no. 1 (1988): 3–33; Alpheus T. Mason, "*The Federalist*—a Split Personality," *American Historical Review* 57, no. 3 (1952): 625–43.

69. The private letters of Hamilton and Madison clearly indicate that their personal views differ from those espoused by Publius. Furtwangler discusses this issue in *The Authority of Publius: A Reading of the Federalist Papers* (Ithaca, NY: Cornell University Press, 1984), 23–32.

70. Publius violated this principled position by frequently characterizing the Constitution's opponents as ambitious local demagogues who feared losing power under the new constitutional order. The legitimacy of pseudonymous writing itself became an object of debate in the period. In one revealing episode, several newspapers in Boston refused to publish essays by pseudonymous Anti-Federalists. Defenders of the ban argued that the public had a right to know the personal "character" of those Anti-Federalist writers when evaluating their arguments, while Anti-Federalists understood it as an act of blatant intimidation and censorship. See, for example, "Old Whig V," in *DHRC Vol. I*, 538–43.

71. See Grantland S. Rice, *The Transformation of Authorship in America* (Chicago: University of Chicago Press, 1997).

72. Jasinski, "Heteroglossia, Polyphony, and *The Federalist Papers*," 23–46.

73. Bernard Bailyn, *The Ideological Origins of the American Revolution* (Cambridge, MA: Harvard University Press, 1992 [1967]), 26.

74. Gordon Wood, *The Radicalism of the American Revolution* (New York: Vintage Books, 1993), 96; and Franco Venturi, *Utopia and Reform in the Enlightenment* (Cambridge: Cambridge University Press, 1971).

75. Raymond Geuss, *Politics and the Imagination* (Princeton, NJ: Princeton University Press, 2010), 69.

ONE

Unauthorized Propositions

The PEOPLE, who are the sovereigns of the State, possess a power to alter it *when* and in what *way* they please. To say otherwise is to make the thing created, greater than the power that created it.

—Anonymous, *Federal Gazette*, 18 March 1789[1]

The we of the Constitution's "We the People" was as much of an artificial construct as the constitution itself. It was its creature, not its creator.

—Sheldon Wolin, *The Presence of the Past*[2]

In *Federalist* No. 40, Publius directly confronted the troubling question of whether or not the Philadelphia Convention of 1787 had been properly authorized "to frame and propose" the new Constitution of the United States (*F*, 258). Publius explored there nothing less than "the ground on which the Convention stood" (*F*, 264), which he identified as the purportedly solid foundation of the people themselves.[3] *Federalist* No. 40 therefore offers a theoretically probing yet avowedly practical reflection on the availability of foundations, and on dilemmas of popular authorization in times of constitutional crisis; it may be productively read as an exemplary eighteenth-century American reflection on what contemporary political theorists often engage as "a state of exception." *The Federalist*, I will argue in this first chapter, provides helpful orientation to how the popular constitutionalism of the revolutionary and postrevolutionary years confronted and navigated—if never fully resolved—some of the most insistent paradoxes of modern democratic theory.

In No. 40, Publius was preoccupied with the theoretical and historical dilemmas surrounding the eighteenth-century American conception of the people's constituent power—that is, the ultimate power of the people to alter fundamental law "*when* and in what *way* they please."[4] However, in contrast to most contemporary theoretical approaches to constituent power—whether influenced by the political theology of Carl Schmitt or the immanentist optimism of Michael Hardt and Antonio Negri—Publius's navigation of the attending dilemmas of popular authorization resisted the turn to metaphysical abstraction and the appeal to a transcendent or immanent absolute. In his approach to the problem of constituent power, Publius insisted on the productive irreducibility of institutional mediation, and the performative elicitation of a retrospective authorization by the people. While accepting the *absence* of a firm ground of legal authorization (the unbroken authority of law), Publius also rejected a wholly extralegal or unmediated appeal to the people themselves (the transcendental appeal to spirit *beyond* the letter of the law). Instead, he endorsed a political navigation of these dilemmas *in medias res*. Confronting the dilemma of constituency—how does the people give birth to itself as a self-authorizing subject?—Publius shifted the register of discourse away from the formal and juridical and toward the informally ethicopolitical. Doing so, he was able to affirm a rupture in law while simultaneously enlisting another register of normative and republican continuity. This chapter outlines Publius's productive encounter with these dilemmas in *The Federalist*, and suggests the relevance of his example for recent debates in democratic theory, too often captivated by the formal rubrics of "norm" and "exception."

I.

The government which [the Federalists] are so enthusiastically fond of is as yet an ideal phantom, a chimera, a mere theory detested and execrated by every true friend to government.
— "One of the People," *Carlisle Gazette*, January 9, 1788[5]

Publius wrote *Federalist* No. 40 as a response to widespread and persuasive Anti-Federalist claims that the Philadelphia Convention had exceeded the mandate granted to it by the Annapolis Convention of 1786 and the Congressional Act of 1787, both of which authorized the meeting of the Philadelphia Convention "for the sole and express purpose of revising the Articles of Confederation" (F, 259). While the Philadelphia Convention was, in Bruce Ackerman's words, "expressly subordinated to existing institutions and procedures," it had nonetheless produced an entirely new constitutional text, and—theoretically more problematic for Publius—an entirely new procedure for its popular ratification.[6] Under Article 13 of the Articles of Confederation, constitutional reform could come about only through the unanimous assent of the thirteen state legislatures.[7] Under the Philadelphia Convention's plan, the ratification of the proposed Constitution would bypass the constituted power of the state legislatures and appeal instead to the constituent power of the people themselves as organized and represented in state ratifying conventions convened expressly for this purpose. The elections of these ratifying conventions, however, were to be organized by the individual state legislatures, thereby signaling the recognized continuity—albeit in diminished form—of their constituted authority. Ackerman describes this combined rejection of and reliance on existing constituted authorities as the "bootstrapping process" of "our unconventional founding."[8]

In the most dramatic break from the legal authority of the Articles, the Philadelphia Convention required the assent of only nine state conventions for successful ratification. It was, and is, widely accepted that the ratification of the Constitution of the United States would have been impossible without this change. The small state of Rhode Island alone had been a notorious spoiler under the Confederation, and had refused even to send delegates to the Philadelphia Convention. New York lost two of its three delegates—John Lansing and Robert Yates—once it became clear that the convention aimed at nothing short of a thoroughgoing revision of the Articles of Confederation and what they considered the abrogation of the constituted authority of the state legislatures. Getting to the heart of the legal matter, and invoking the uncertain vacillation between constituent and constituted power that characterized the debates over constitutional ratification, the Anti-Federalist Patrick Henry pointedly asked the delegates to the Virginia Ratifying Convention, "What right had they [in the Philadelphia Convention] to say, *We, the people?* Who *authorized* them to speak the language of, *We, the people,* instead of, *We, the states?*"[9]

In the ensuing "great national discussion" between Federalists and Anti-Federalists, Publius and other Federalists (foremost among them the eminent early American legal theorist and future associate justice of the Supreme Court James Wilson)[10] invoked the constituent power of the American people as a strategy for overcoming the constituted power of the sovereign states. In this way, Federalists declared themselves more deeply committed to revolutionary principles than their Anti-Federalist opponents, who, because of their appeal to the constituted authority of popularly elected state legislatures, were placed in the uncomfortable position of denying the superior authority of the people at large. By appealing to the people's constituent power Federalists presented themselves as "champions of the people's superiority to their government," while framing their Anti-Federalist opposition as narrow, rule-bound proceduralists.[11] As Steven Skowronek has recently put it, "disillusioned conservatives grasped hold of the concept of popular sovereignty—the most radical idea promulgated during the revolutionary era—to justify a Constitution designed to check the power of popularly elected legislatures."[12]

Gordon Wood and other historians have claimed, perhaps with some exaggeration, that the resulting eighteenth-century American idea that sovereignty is permanently located in the people at large marked "one of the most creative moments in the history of political thought," and was "the decisive achievement of the American political imagination."[13] This conceptual innovation, while prefigured in the work of seventeenth-century political theorists such as Thomas Hobbes, George Lawson, John Locke, and, as we will see, Jean-Jacques Rousseau, emerged slowly in postrevolutionary America from two decades of practical experiments and innovations in the "quasi-legal" politics of the "people out of doors," the eighteenth-century phrase used to denote not only literal gatherings of crowds and mobs, but also "indoor" forms of political association that broke from the authority of constituted government (revolutionary conventions, committees, and congresses).[14] "The idea of the people as a constituent power," R. R. Palmer writes, "developed unclearly, gradually, and sporadically during the American Revolution. . . . It emerged from the grassroots."[15] In their political struggles with Parliament and Crown over fundamental questions of constitutional interpretation, the colonists enshrined, first tacitly and then explicitly, the people as the ultimate locus of *interpretive* constitutional authority; this identification was the discursive precondition for the people being ultimately identified as an agency of constitution-making power, as a constituent power as generally understood. As Larry Kramer writes in his important study of eighteenth-century American popular constitutionalism, "eighteenth-century Americans had an expansive image of popular constitutionalism. They took for granted the people's responsibility not only for making, but also for interpreting and enforcing their constitutions—a background norm that was so widely shared and deeply ingrained that specific textual expression in the constitution was unnecessary."[16]

Invoking this higher popular authority in No. 40, Publius argued that the convention's appeal beyond the constituted authority of the states to the constituent power of "the people themselves," as they were *represented* in the state ratifying conventions, would retrospectively authorize the preamble's authoritative claim to speak on the people's behalf: "We the People of the United States, in order to form a more perfect Union . . . ." Without this prospective future assent, Publius wrote, the Constitution is "worth no more than the paper on which it is written"; it must be "stamped with the approbation of those to whom it is addressed" in order to become a living document (*F*, 264). In a stirring example of what Jacques Derrida characterizes as the "fabulous retroactivity" of instituting moments, whose full authorization always comes after the fact, the people, in Publius's account, must come to recognize their own voice speaking through the preamble's "We the People" in order for its claim to have authoritative effect.[17] James Madison later invoked this "nonsimultaneity of the people's self-foundation,"[18] and its politico-theological resonance, in a speech he delivered as a congressman from Virginia before the House of Representatives in April 1796. The Constitution, Madison claimed in that speech, "was nothing more than the draught of a plan, nothing but a dead letter, until life and validity were breathed into it by the voice of the people, speaking through the several state conventions."[19] The principal difficulty, however, with this retrospective authorization, this appeal to the enlivening "voice of the people," was that the procedures and rules for bringing to articulation the people's voice—the convention's changes in ratification procedure—were the invention of the very body whose work was to be given "life and validity" through them. The dead letter here begets the living spirit. To invoke a common eighteenth-century American trope, the convention's bold act of ventriloquism engenders the very voice ventriloquized.[20] The authorizing people are enacted or elicited by the instituting text that claims to speak on their behalf.

This was, Publius concedes in No. 40, the "most plausible" Anti-Federalist objection to the convention's proceedings, but, contrary to Publius's claims there, it was not "the least urged in the publications which have swarmed against the Convention" (*F*, 263). The Anti-Federalist "Portius," for example, wrote that if the question of improper authorization in the ratification procedure "is not obviated, [it] cannot fail of overthrowing the whole structure, and reduce it to the situation of a baseless fabrick of nocturnal reverees."[21] It was an objection that revealed a troubling performative dimension to the process of constitutional authorization, one structurally similar to the paradox of popular authorization that Derrida explores in his well-known essay on the Declaration of Independence and that many democratic theorists have examined since. In that essay, Derrida writes that the "we" of the Declaration speaks "in the name of the people but this people does not yet exist. . . . If [the people] gives birth to itself, as a free and independent subject, as a possible signer, this can hold only in the act of signature. The signature invents the signer."[22] Like Derrida's reading of the Declaration, but in more institutionally or even procedurally specific terms, *Federalist* No. 40 reveals that the Philadelphia Convention's change in the amendment procedure exemplifies how an instituting or constituent action "performatively produces the conditions that guarantee the validity of the performative."[23] This paradoxical task is not only faced by actors in founding moments—by historical exemplifications of the Great Lawgiver—but also persistently reiterated in the moments of democratic claims making that follow, in which actors, in Alan Keenan's words, "make an appeal that sets the conditions for its own proper reception," an appeal that cannot be fully authorized or justified through reference to already existing rules, procedures, and norms (at least not if rules are poorly understood as establishing the terms of their own application).[24] These moments appear as occasions of groundless "decision" only if we are forced into a theoretical straitjacket of strictly opposing formal rule-governed to exceptional non-rule-governed behavior—if we posit an "absolute decision" in the purportedly normative void where rule-governed behavior (again, narrowly understood) gives out.

Confronting this dilemma in the practical context of late eighteenth-century American debates over constitutional reform, *Federalist* No. 40 dwells on how deeply tenuous was the "boundary between authorized and usurped innovations, between that degree of change, which lies within the compass of alterations and further provisions, and that which amounts to a transmutation of the government" (*F*, 261). Publius's paradoxical embrace of the people's constituent power differs in illuminating ways from Carl Schmitt's influential formulation of this concept, partly because of Publius's insistence that popular voice be instituted or mediated through inherited procedures, even if those procedures are not unequivocally legal, are productively open to institutional improvisation, and are only fully authorized after the fact of their instituting (here the relevant historical question is Publius's reliance on the broadly constitutionalist repertoires of the convention form).[25] For Publius, the people's voice, even as a constituent power, still is and must be institutionally mediated. For Schmitt, on the contrary, constituent power "is not bound by legal forms and procedures; it is always 'in the state of nature,' when it appears in this capacity."[26] He continues, "It is a part of the directness of this people's will that it can be expressed independently of every prescribed procedure and every prescribed process."[27]

There is no paradox in Schmitt's conception of constituent power, because Schmitt's constitutional theory relies on the presupposition of a manifest and unitary popular will as its comprehensive foundation. This has led some—most notably Stephen Holmes—to accuse Schmitt of "democratic mysticism." "It is not obvious," Holmes writes, "that the people can have anything like a coherent will prior to and apart from all constitutional procedures." "Can citizens exercise their sovereign power outside all procedural mechanisms for aggregating their separate wills into one?" The people, Holmes summarizes, cannot act as an "amorphous blob."[28] Holmes nicely illuminates a questionable presupposition of Schmitt's theory of constituent power, but he also loads the argument in his favor by presuming there is either a "coherent will" or none at all, and that this coherence must comprise formal procedures of aggregation (e.g., voting), which, of course, require preexisting formal rules. I will return to this question in the final chapter.

Constitutional self-binding mechanisms do not resolve the dilemmas of popular authorization that Publius explored in No. 40. Holmes and Schmitt are actually united in their all-or-nothing formalism, the one insisting on the democratic precondition of a formal proceduralism and the other on its complete suspension in dramatic moments of constituent willing. Neither theorist dwells, as does Publius in No. 40, on the dilemmas of representation and authorization that inhabit these claiming moments, instead positing a unified authorizing subject constituted by either formal rules or their exceptional rupture. Neither theorist engages constituent power as a *claim* that can only ever achieve a retrospective authorization from the authorizing entity on whose behalf it speaks. Publius, however, engages the question in just this way.

"The theory of the people's constituent power presupposes," Schmitt writes, "the conscious willing of political existence, therefore, a nation." It is significant that Schmitt prefers the language of nation to that more paradoxical and ambiguous language of the people. "The nation," Schmitt writes, "is clearer and less prone to misunderstanding. It denotes the people as a unity capable of political action, with consciousness of its political distinctiveness and with the will to political existence."[29] The "nation" substantializes the indeterminate identity of "the people." Schmitt thereby resolves the paradoxes of collective self-unification in a theological affirmation of undivided and homogeneous national will. For Schmitt, this existential unity of will, the existence of "the nation" manifest in "concrete decision," derives either from "unmediated self-identity" or through the idea that such unity is only brought about through representation.[30] In neither instance, however, nor in his attention to their practical combination in different places and times, does Schmitt's constitutional theory allow for productive ambiguity and ongoing political contestation over how this will is claimed through different acts of representation or institutional embodiment. The dilemmas of popular authorization that emerge from the paradox of the people can be resolved in the enactment of constituent power, as Schmitt suggests, but only for a time. Pierre Rosanvallon has clearly identified the dynamics of this *temporary* resolution:

> The *people as event* can seem to resolve, for a time, the constitutive aporia of representation. In action, as indissociably lived and narrated, the people is given tangibility by what it makes happen. . . . [T]he visibility of the people as actor, whether in the tumult of the street or in the good behavior of the patriotic festivals, periodically allowed the possibility of postponing the conceptual and practical difficulties posed by the distance between the representatives and those they represented.[31]

In his theory of constituent power Schmitt seems to have in mind such revolutionary moments of self-evident popular will, and he cites Moscow in 1917, Berlin in 1918, and revolutionary France in just this regard. In the French Revolution, Schmitt writes, "with complete awareness, a people took its destiny into its hands and reached a free decision on the type and form of political existence."[32] Such was not the case, according to his account, in revolutionary and postrevolutionary America, and this purported failure was an important basis of his disregard for the traditions of American constitutionalism.

With a few notable exceptions, like his qualified praise of Alexander Hamilton's account of presidential prerogative in *The Crisis of Parliamentary Democracy*, Schmitt had little admiration for American constitutionalism in general, and for *The Federalist* in particular, believing that early Americans typically avoided the most fundamental questions of constitutional law, in particular the problem of constituent power.[33] Thus, in his *Constitutional Theory*, Schmitt writes:

> The American constitutions of the eighteenth century lacked a genuine constitutional theory. The most important historical source for the theoretical foundations of this constitution, *The Federalist*, offers insight for the most part into practical questions of organization. The people gives itself a constitution, without the covenant, founded by the general community and society, being differentiated from every other act which constitutes a new political unity, or from the act of a free political decision about its own form of existence.[34]

This last sentence, in effect, denies that Americans directly confronted in the moment of constitutional founding the question of constituent power. I have suggested, to the contrary, that there is instead an attractive *alternative theory of constituent power* in *The Federalist*. Schmitt defines constituent power (*die verfassunggebenden Gewalt*) as "the political will, whose power or authority is capable of adopting the concrete comprehensive decision over the type and form of its own political existence."[35] Constituent power is an unstructured "Urgrund," or "das formlos Formende," "an inexhaustible source of all forms without taking a form itself."[36] It is an "absolute beginning, and the beginning . . . springs out of normative nothingness and from concrete disorder."[37]

For Schmitt, eighteenth-century revolutionary theories of constituent power (most notably, for Schmitt, that of the Abbé Sieyès), with their insistence on absolute beginning and willful self-creation, were living rebukes to Enlightenment rationalism. Their political rearticulation of a willful god capable of creating a world *ex nihilo*, capable of creating an order without being subject to it, was the paradigmatic modern instance of the pure "state of exception." Schmitt believed the revolutionary slogan *vox populi vox Dei* therefore powerfully exemplified the willful political theology that underwrote modern revolutions. As Schmitt made clear in many of his critical readings of modern constitutionalism, however, the very constitutional orders these revolutions founded quickly disavowed this originary power. This disavowal was, in fact, a central component of Schmitt's critique of liberal constitutionalism, which he argued could not account for the legitimacy of the political will that brought it into being, and was thereby incapable of recognizing how this extraconstitutional and normatively unjustified will subtends or haunts existing constitutional arrangements. Schmitt affirmed—as do some of his contemporary radical democratic admirers—the persistence of an extraconstitutional people—"above," "beyond," and "beside" the state—which exposes a gap in the legitimacy of liberal constitutionalism.[38] As William Sheuerman has written, for Schmitt "liberalism's failure to take constituent power seriously, to look into its own troubled (normatively unjustified) origins is . . . its Achilles heel."[39]

This Schmittian theological insistence on normatively unbound but indivisibly unified will—the decision "in its absolute purity"—obscures for contemporary democratic theorists how constituent power was conceptualized and practiced in eighteenth-century America. Publius, in contrast to Schmitt, emphasized that the people can act (just as they can speak) only through representation or delegation. The people, while figured by Publius as the "only legitimate fountain of power" (*F*, 339), can neither speak in their own voice nor act of their own accord. "It is impossible," Publius writes, "for the people spontaneously and universally, to move in concert toward their object, it is therefore essential, that such changes [in fundamental law] be instituted by some *informal and unauthorized propositions*, made by some patriotic and respectable citizen or number of citizens" (*F*, 265; emphasis in the original). In this important passage, Publius relies first on a recognizably Hobbesian argument that, until unified through representation, the people can only ever be a disorganized multitude incapable of moving "spontaneously" or "universally" in concert toward their object (in this case, the creation of a new constitutional order). Without representation, the people remains forever latent; it is representation that gives the people concrete historical existence and a capacity for action, even if the people also always exceed representational capture.[40]

But who is to say whether this representative claim is legitimate, if it is not secured by a pre-established and fully authorized procedure for determining the rules of representation in the first place (an electoral process, for example)? Wouldn't those rules also have to be popularly authorized? Here we glimpse the specter of a familiar infinite regress. As I put the point in *Constituent Moments*, "Determining who constitutes the authorizing people is an inescapable yet democratically unanswerable dilemma; it is not a question the people can democratically decide because the very question subverts the premises of its resolution."[41] Noting, as Publius does, that these propositions and claims undertaken in the people's name must be "*informal and unauthorized*" highlights their ungrounded and performative dimension, their break from the existing procedural norms of constituted authority. Just as quickly as Publius invokes the ungrounded and performative dimension of these "*informal and unauthorized*" claims, however, he attempts to contain this dimension through the invocation of another informal register of normativity—that is, by insisting on the "patriotic and respectable" character of their self-authorized citizen participants. This does not *resolve* the resulting dilemma of popular authorization, but neither does it plunge into the normative void of an absolute decision.

Publius emphasized the importance of informal rules of normative continuity, not to command a predetermined course of action, but to offer a guideline through which the resulting controversy and disagreement could be politically debated and judged. The "great national discussion" between Federalists and Anti-Federalists was powerfully shaped by competing claims of "patriots" over the meaning and scope of their revolutionary inheritance.

II.

> They [the representatives] are the sign—the people are the thing signified.
>
> —"Brutus," No. 3, *New York Journal*, November 15, 1787[42]

In revolutionary and postrevolutionary America there was an acute cultural awareness of the political contestability that necessarily underwrites representational claims. The Imperial Crisis was, after all, characterized by disputes between the colonists and Parliament over what constituted legitimate political representation in the first place (would political representation be "virtual," encompassing the good of the entire realm, or "actual," accountable to the interests of different local constituencies?), and it was prefaced by accusations of misrepresentation leveled against colonial governors. As Wood writes, American politics in the Revolutionary era had made "glaringly evident, that representation could never be virtual, never fully inclusive; it was acutely actual, and always tentative and partial."[43] This evident partiality was made even more glaring in the wake of Independence. While "the revolution professedly made the collective people sovereign, . . . it did not settle how the public will should be institutionalized nor which representations of that will carried greatest weight."[44] As I examined in *Constituent Moments*, postrevolutionary American politics were therefore frequently characterized by competing claims to speak in the people's name. The revolutionary and postrevolutionary American context was charged with a heightened political awareness and suspicion of representational claims, but it was also a period marked by the proliferation of institutions making such claims. John Adams remarked on the early appearance of this dynamic in his "Dissertation on the Canon and Feudal Law" (1765). "This dread of representation," Adams wrote, "has had for a long time, in this province, effects very similar to what the physicians call hydrophobia, or dread of water. It has made us delirious; and we have rushed headlong into the water, till we are almost drowned, out of simple or phrensical fear of it."[45] Constituent power, as it came to be understood and practiced in postrevolutionary America, intensified these dilemmas attending political representation because it is the power that establishes the very rules and procedures through which legitimate political representation is to be construed in the first place. Like other repertoires of popular representation in the revolutionary and postrevolutionary years—the crowd, the committee, the congress—the representative status of the convention, its claim to speak in the people's name, is not wholly secured by formal rules or fully authorized procedures (but, again, neither is it without inherited repertoires). It therefore brings the improvisational dynamics of political representation into public view. In the absence of fixed legal rules and procedures to navigate the dilemmas of authorization posed by the Philadelphia Convention, Publius appealed to another register of informal normativity in *Federalist* No. 40 to assess the legitimacy of those citizens claiming to speak in the people's name—that is, those "respectable and patriotic" citizens who advance a series of needed *"informal and unauthorized"* propositions.

Without formal or procedural rules in place, how were the people to judge the "irregular and assumed" privilege of their self-proclaimed representatives? How will the eventual approbation by the people themselves come to, in Publius's words, "blot out all antecedent errors and irregularities" (*F*, 266)? Publius concludes No. 40 with these questions as he counsels his public against "little ill-timed scruples" and a "zeal for adhering to ordinary forms," in favor of a bold political experimentalism (*F*, 265). It is a bold experimentalism made necessary, Publius argues, by what he and other Federalists argued were the emergency conditions of the postrevolutionary years, the series of domestic and international political and economic crises suffered under the Articles of Confederation.

Simply to abide by established legal procedures (and duly constituted authorities) in times of crisis, Publius writes, would be to sacrifice the "dearest interests of the country" to mere legal formalities. Confronting this sense of crisis and emergency required a change of government like that affected by the Revolution itself. "In all great changes of established governments," Publius wrote, "forms ought to give way to substance" (*F*, 265). A rigid adherence to legal form and constituted authorities would "render nominal and nugatory the transcendent and precious right of the people [now quoting directly from the Declaration of Independence] 'to abolish or alter their governments as to them shall seem most likely to effect their safety and happiness'" (*F*, 265). In this passage Publius established a clear continuity between the extralegality of the Philadelphia Convention's action, and the people's "transcendent and precious" right to revolution. He compares the convention itself to the extralegal "committees and congresses" of the Revolution, thereby acknowledging that "in its origin and in its essential character, the convention was a revolutionary assembly"[46]; "illegality," Bruce Ackerman writes, "was the leitmotif of the Convention from first to last."[47]

Publius ultimately concedes that participants to "the Convention were neither authorized by their commission, nor fully justified by circumstances" (*F*, 267), but that they might be nonetheless retrospectively vindicated (if not justified) by a collective act of political judgment based on the quality of their proposals.[48] Overriding all ambivalence over full and uncontroversial legal authorization, Publius argues, should be "a manly confidence in their country" (*F*, 266). Time and again, Publius situates the trace of arbitrariness he invokes in his appeal to necessity—and that seems to resonate with Schmitt's "state of exception"—within a broader field of normative continuity. "A manly confidence," "considerations of duty," and "patriotism" bridge the formal or legal legitimation deficit Publius confronts in No. 40 (which is thereby not to be equated with legitimacy *tout court*). This tactic does not resolve the dispute but shifts it to another register—from legality more narrowly conceived, we might say, to politics. For example, as suggested above, we can productively understand the debates between Federalists and Anti-Federalists as a patriotic competition over who could authoritatively claim to embody the "spirit of '76" and the legacy of the Revolution. The appeal to the "respectable and patriotic" character of the participants in the Philadelphia Convention simply, but also significantly, shifts the locus of this contest and the terms under which it will be carried out, making it still controversial but no longer focused on questions of formal legality.

Throughout No. 40, Publius insists on both the continuity and the innovation of the convention's plan, basing his argument on a complex tapestry of their rule-following and rule-making activity, their attention to both formal and informal rules of popular representation. He invokes "considerations of duty," for example, as a way of "supplying any defect of regular authority" (*F*, 266). Although the form of the Articles of Confederation are to be abandoned, he argues in another passage, their animating principles will be partly retained.[49] The Philadelphia Convention obviously did not conceive of itself as existing in a kind of normative vacuum, or creating the Federal Constitution *ex nihilo*. "The truth is, that the great principles of the Constitution proposed by the Convention may be considered less as absolutely new," Publius writes, "than as the expansion of principles which are found in the Articles of Confederation" (*F*, 262).

This important aspect of Publius's argument is dismissed by some constitutional scholars and neglected by others who translate the paradoxes of authorization explored in Publius's text into narrowly formal or legal paradoxes alone.[50] In No. 40 Publius is concerned with dilemmas of authorization that are larger and more encompassing than formal legal authorization. Even Ackerman, whose influential work has done the most to recover the democratic and political resources of Publius's argument on popular sovereignty for constitutional moments of "higher lawmaking," treats Publius's arguments in No. 40 preeminently as questions of legality and illegality. Schmitt, for his part, dismisses such arguments as evasions of the fundamental question of constituent power's anormativity. In contrast to these accounts, I believe Publius's arguments productively invoke broader political considerations that highlight the limitations of their animating legal formalism. In his invocation of the "patriotic and respectable" character of the convention's participants, Publius evinced a common eighteenth-century appeal to the ethical orientation of character, on the one hand, and patriotic duty on the other, a different set of principled concerns or guidelines to orient political debate and contest where legal rules give out, to navigate the ineliminable risks and underauthorization of democratic claims making in this instance of constitutional crisis. In No. 40 Publius therefore offers an exemplary enactment and navigation of a dilemma that has become a familiar touchstone in contemporary democratic theory, and that has its canonical expression in book 2, chapter 7 of Rousseau's *Social Contract*.[51]

III.

> We ought to scrutinize the act by which a people becomes a people, for that act being necessarily antecedent to any other, is the real foundation of society.
>
> —Jean Jacques Rousseau, *The Social Contract*[52]

The relevance of Rousseau's account of the Great Lawgiver to this chapter's focus on *The Federalist*'s treatment of constituent power is not based in any discernable influence that *The Social Contract* had on American debates surrounding constitutional ratification, or on Publius in particular. While some of Rousseau's major works, most notably *Emile*, were widely read in postrevolutionary America, *The Social Contract* was little known, and even less approved.[53] Rousseau's discussion of the lawgiver from *The Social Contract* models the dilemma of popular authorization examined above, and thereby helps clarify American debates over constituent power and constitutional ratification. A different understanding of Rousseau's famous chapter from what is usually offered by contemporary democratic theorists will also emerge from this discussion.

Rousseau's lawgiver is a productive and regularly returned to figure in contemporary democratic theory. Some, like Geoffrey Bennington, William Connolly, Bonnie Honig, and Alan Keenan, see the lawgiver as modeling, in different ways, how democratic autonomy invariably reaches for an outside heteronomic support to establish itself.[54] Others, such as Seyla Benhabib, invoke the lawgiver as an instance of an idealized rationality that reconciles legality and legitimacy, rationality and democratic will.[55] While I largely agree with those who see the lawgiver as a figure of heteronomic support—as, in Keenan's words, "a figure for those moments in democratic politics that prove necessary to the people's autonomy without being reducible to its logic"[56]—what is most important about this figure in relation to the argument of *Federalist* No. 40 is not the groundlessness of the lawgiver's actions: the lawgiver, Rousseau openly reminds his readers, has no authority to do what he sets out to achieve. Instead, I am interested in how Rousseau figures the *navigation* of these dilemmas, or how the lawgiver's formative appeals to a people-that-is-not-yet taps into informal and even inarticulate registers of normativity that precede formal codification in law, but without which, in Rousseau's account, no law can survive. Rousseau characterizes this other kind of law as "the most important [law] of all . . . which sustains a nation in the spirit of its institution and imperceptibly substitutes the force of habit for the force of authority."[57] While this law is "unknown to our political theorists," Rousseau writes, it "is the one on which the success of all the other laws depends; it is the feature on which the great lawgiver bestows his secret care."[58] It is the register of law that shapes a people into the kind of people enabled to be at once the sovereign and the subject of law.

Rousseau's lawgiver, in other words, is important not only for theoretically modeling recurrent dilemmas in democratic authorization, but also in revealing how attempts to navigate these dilemmas appeal to the "aesthetic-affective" and imaginary registers of ethico-political life.[59] Like Publius, Rousseau does not posit a groundless moment of decision in his discussion of founding moments, but instead directs attention to the normative resources for navigating these dilemmas of popular authorization *in medias res*.

Rousseau famously invokes the lawgiver as a way of resolving the paradoxical origin through which a people becomes a people—an originary question of the political imagination—a way of resolving what Bonnie Honig (following Paul Ricoeur) has recently called "the paradox of politics," or that we might simply call the paradox of the people.[60] How does a people give birth to itself as a collective subject? How do we inaugurate the imagined relations that give birth to a people as a people? If a people is to itself be an artifact of human autonomy and consent, instead of an accident of history and force, how does it call itself into being?

According to Rousseau, when previous political theorists (Grotius is his intended target) explored how a people gives itself a ruler and how they consent to being ruled by a sovereign authority, they invariably presumed that "a people is *a people*."[61] They presuppose a "civil act" and "public deliberation" that cannot in fact be presumed. "We ought to scrutinize," Rousseau writes, "the act by which a people becomes a people, for that act being necessarily antecedent to any other, is the real foundation of society."[62]

Rousseau's understanding of the people unfolds gradually in *The Social Contract*. The people, for example, cannot promise to simply obey and still be a people. Once there is a master there can be no sovereign. A people simply *is* not, properly understood, if it does not rule itself. It might be an "ordered multitude" enslaved by a common master, or a "blind multitude" anarchically subject to no rule at all, but it cannot be a sovereign people. Since the people, properly understood, is subject to laws, the people ought to give birth to them. And this origin must be unanimous, since even majority rule relies on a prior rule or convention, and therefore only begs the question of its own formal authority (and, once again, the specter of infinite regress). Rousseau's formulation of this problem resonates with Publius's claim that the people cannot move "spontaneously and universally . . . in concert toward their object" (*F*, 265), but need to rely instead on a set of "*informal and unauthorized propositions*":

> The right of laying down the rules of society belongs only to those who form the society; but how can they exercise it? Is it to be by common agreement, by a sudden inspiration? Has the body politic an organ to declare its will? Who is to give the foresight necessary to formulate enactments and proclaim them in advance, and how is it to announce them in the hour of need? How can a blind multitude, which often does not know what it wants, because it seldom knows what is good for it, undertake by itself an enterprise as vast and difficult as a system of legislation?[63]

How does a blind multitude transform itself into a self-legislating people? A familiar paradox appears here that the lawgiver is invoked to resolve:

> For a newly formed people to understand wise principles of politics and to follow the basic rules of statecraft, the effect would have to become the cause; the social spirit which must be the product of social institutions would have to preside over the setting up of those institutions; men would have to have already become before the advent of law that which they become as a result of law.[64]

Just as Sieyès later appealed to the constituent power of the nation to break the vicious circle of preconstitutional legitimacy in the months leading up to the French Revolution, so does Rousseau's lawgiver reflect, in Hannah Arendt's terms, the problem of the absolute.[65] Rousseau himself invoked the theological dimensions of this appeal toward the opening of the lawgiver chapter when he writes that "Gods would be needed to give men laws."[66]

For this reason, Rousseau's lawgiver has sometimes been interpreted as a metaphysical or theological gesture to an absolute beginning, or point of origin. Schmitt's insistence on political theology looms here as well. Indeed, in *Legality and Legitimacy* Schmitt invokes Rousseau's "extraordinary lawgiver" as the very model for the "pure will" of constituent power.[67] More recently, Geoffrey Bennington has given this reading a Derridean turn by insisting on the lawgiver's "absolute exteriority" and "violent illegality." [68] However, Rousseau explicitly distinguishes the act of the lawgiver, however heteronomous, from a simple act of formative and foundational violence. While Rousseau affirms that the lawgiver has "a task that is beyond human powers and a nonexistent authority for its execution," he goes on to remark that the lawgiver "can employ neither force nor argument, *he must have recourse to an authority of another order, one which can compel without violence and persuade without convincing.*" [69]

This invocation of "an authority of another order," while indicating a divine appeal, also opens up a gray area of normativity between force/will/violence, on the one hand, and deliberation/reason/conviction, on the other, or between decision and deliberation. [70] This gray area is an explicitly aesthetic terrain, marked by Rousseau's appeal to the lawgiver's "sublime reasoning, which soars above the heads of the common people." [71] Clearly this "authority of another order" does not provide hard and fast criteria for the people-that-is-not-yet to judge by, but it also does not leave the audience of its address wholly without orientation; it does not present them with, in Bennington's words, a moment of "radical undecidability." The locus of the decision, if we still want to call it that, is in the gathered people (that is not one yet) that are the object of the lawgiver's address. Rousseau emphasizes the careful consideration of what remains latent or "virtual" in the audience of the address; the people is here little more than a prophecy, but that is not nothing. The lawgiver, Rousseau writes, must pay close attention to "conventions," so that "natural relations and laws come to be in a harmony on all points, so that the law, shall we say, seems to only ensure, accompany, and correct what is natural." [72] The lawgiver's productive unconcealing of latent popular dispositions—Kam Shapiro describes it as the virtuosic revelation of the virtual—is itself an artistic and transformative act, even if it "*seems* to only ensure, accompany, and correct what is natural": it does not simply represent what is passively given—the lawgiver is no mere "copyist" [73]—but elicits or enacts the people through mediation. As with Publius, the living voice of the people is called into being through this act of mediation itself. This aspect of Rousseau's political thought sits in productive tension with his familiar tendencies to reject the alienating mediation of representation, to privilege presence, immanence, and transparency. The chapters in *The Social Contract* that follow Rousseau's discussion of the lawgiver—three separate chapters on "the people"—elaborate on the conditions of receptivity and "ripeness" for a people that has not yet become "the people" properly understood, that has not yet responded to, or transformatively recognized itself in, the lawgiver's address.

Publius's dilemma differs in at least one important respect from the dilemmas made familiar to democratic theorists by Rousseau's lawgiver. Where the lawgiver claims to anchor his extralegal authority in a transcendental appeal to a higher power (thereby posing the problem of whether he is a "prophet" or a "charlatan"), Publius's extralegal appeal is to the very people to whom his discourse is addressed. How does the problem change when the "higher power" appealed to is not a deity, not a transcendental anchor, but the immanent voice of the *anticipated* people themselves? Alan Keenan has stated the dilemma succinctly:

> To lay the conditions for the people to become a people, one must appeal to a sense of the people *as* a people; yet the success of that appeal depends on those conditions already being in place, *or at the very least being imaginable.* The paradoxical task of the legislator . . . is to make an appeal that sets the conditions for its own proper reception; one must appeal to the political community in such a way that its members will accept the regulations that will make them into the kind of (general) people able to "hear" such an appeal.[74]

The ensuing political problem revolves around how the people come to recognize the lawgiver's voice as their own when there is no fixed rule or criteria to distinguish between its legitimate and illegitimate articulation or representation. (How could there be? The people in whose higher name the lawgiver speaks is not . . . yet.) I have characterized this as a constituent moment. Constituent moments enact felicitous claims to speak in the people's name, even though those claims explicitly break from the authorized procedures or rules for representing the popular voice. The dilemmas of authorization that spring from these moments appear in both the formal political settings of constitutional conventions and political associations as well as in the relatively informal political contexts of crowd actions, political oratory, and literature. These moments are not only enacted in dramatic moments of revolution and founding, but continually reiterated over a history of democratic claims making. *Federalist* No. 40 offers one of the most compelling and condensed examinations of a constituent moment in the traditions of American political thought.

Although Publius and Rousseau illuminate the everyday contours of judgment called upon to navigate the dilemmas of popular authorization associated with constituent moments, both also isolate the dilemmas faced by the lawgiver/founder to the quasi-mythical time of constitutional creation. Not long after writing *Federalist* No. 40, Publius wrote in No. 49 that he feared that the "public passions" elicited through regular appeals to the people's constituent authority "would in great measure deprive the government of that veneration which time bestows on every thing, and without which perhaps the wisest and freest governments would not possess the requisite stability" (*F*, 340). Such "experiments are of too ticklish a nature to be unnecessarily multiplied," he wrote, and should be reserved "for certain great and extraordinary occasions" (*F*, 341, 339). I will examine Publius's enlistment of political imagination to effect such veneration in the next chapter, and how it can work to prevent those in its thrall from recognizing the democratic productivity of the dilemmas of authorization examined here.

Democratic theorists often argue that the dilemmas of authorization associated with constituent moments are limited to exceptional moments that usurp the reigning norm, rule, and authority, but the dilemmas surrounding unauthorized claims to speak in the people's name cannot be so quickly contained in these exceptional moments. They reveal something about democratic claims-making practices more broadly understood. Returning to the Founding, tapping its resources, may not simply reveal a beacon of "higher lawmaking" where, as Ackerman argues, formal illegality, mass energy, public spiritedness, and extraordinary rationality are united.[75] It may also reveal the extent to which democratic politics is always characterized by the risk of claims made without fully authorized grounds, by self-authorized claims to speak in the people's name. The mythology of Founding and the appeal of our own Great Lawgivers may serve in fact to keep us enthralled or captivated by the extraordinary moments of the appearance of the people's constituent power, enthralled by the exception "in its absolute purity."

An alternative reading of such canonical texts as *The Federalist* may help mitigate this captivation, which is in part captivation by the drama of the exception. "The exception," Carl Schmitt wrote in *Political Theology,* "is more interesting than the rule. The rule proves nothing; the exception proves everything. In the exception the power of real life breaks through the crust of a mechanism that has become torpid by repetition."[76] Captivation by the exception obscures how the enactment of popular claims exemplified in founding moments is not reserved for such extraordinary moments and need not prioritize the sovereignty of the exceptional situation; it obscures how these enactments attend democratic claims made in seemingly everyday or ordinary political settings. This enthrallment threatens to blind us, or deaden us, to the extent to which the extraordinary inhabits and sustains the democratic ordinary, to the way these constituent capacities are continually elicited from within the midst of political life. This is a lesson we can learn from the Founders themselves. Democratic theory would do well to attend to the nuances and contours of these small dramas of self-authorization. This may seem deflationary of "the democratic event" fashionably construed in dramatically fugitive or disruptive terms. Just as the "state of exception" is misdescribed as a dramatic "moment of madness" or as "normative nothingness," so too might the normal be misdescribed as the simple "crust of mechanism" or the "torpor of repetition."

NOTES

1. *Federal Gazette* (New York), March 18, 1789.

2. Sheldon S. Wolin, *The Presence of the Past: Essays on the State and the Constitution* (Baltimore, MD: Johns Hopkins University Press, 1989), 83.

3. Edmund Morgan, *Inventing the People: The Rise of Popular Sovereignty in England and America* (New York: W. W. Norton, 1989), 272.

4. On the problem of constituent power in contemporary democratic and constitutional theory, see Andrew Arato, "Carl Schmitt and the Revival of the Doctrine of Constituent Power in the United States," *Cardozo Law Review* 21 (1999–2000): 1739–47; Andreas Kalyvas, "Popular Sovereignty, Democracy, and the Constituent Power," *Constellations* 12, no. 2 (2005): 223–44; Martin Loughlin and Neil Walker, eds., *The Paradox of Constitutionalism: Constituent Power and Constitutional Form* (Oxford: Oxford University Press, 2007); and Ulrich K. Preuss, "Constitutional Powermaking for the New Polity: Some Deliberations on the Relations between Constituent Power and the Constitution," *Cardozo Law Review* 14 (1993): 639–60.

5. "One of the People," *Carlisle Gazette*, 9 January 1788, reprinted in "The Carlisle Riot and Its Aftermath 26 December 1787–20 March 1788," in *DHRC Vol. II*, 670–708, 674–78, 676.

6. Bruce Ackerman, *We the People, Vol. 2: Transformations* (Cambridge, MA: Belknap Press of Harvard University Press, 1998), 43. See also Bruce Ackerman and Neal Katyal, "Our Unconventional Founding," *The University of Chicago Law Review* 62, no. 2 (1995): 475–573.

7. The final provision of the Articles reads, "And the articles of this confederation shall be inviolably observed by every state, and the union shall be perpetual; nor shall any alteration at any time hereafter be made in any of them; unless such alteration be agreed to in a Congress of the United States, and be afterwards confirmed by the legislatures of every state."

8. Ackerman and Katyal, "Our Unconventional Founding," 477.

9. Patrick Henry, "Speech at the Virginia Ratifying Convention, 4 June, 1788," in *DHRC Vol. IX*, 929–31, 930.

10. The most famous statement of Wilson's argument, and one much discussed in the period, was his first address to the Pennsylvania Ratifying Convention. See James Wilson, "Speech at the Pennsylvania Ratifying Convention, 24 November, 1787," in *DHRC Vol. II*, 339–63; See also Gary Wills, "James Wilson's New Meaning for Sovereignty," in *Conceptual Change and the Constitution*, ed. Terence Ball and J. G. A. Pocock (Lawrence: University of Kansas Press, 1988), 99–106.

11. Morgan, *Inventing the People*, 281.

12. Stephen Skowronek, "The Reassociation of Ideas and Purposes: Racism, Liberalism, and the American Political Tradition," *American Political Science Review* 100, no. 3 (2006): 385–401, 387.

13. Gordon S. Wood, *The American Revolution: A History* (New York: Modern Library, 2003), 159; James T. Kloppenberg, *The Virtues of Liberalism* (New York: Oxford University Press, 1998), 30. On the emergence of popular constituent power in revolutionary and postrevolutionary America see Willi Paul Adams, *The First American Constitutions: Republican Ideology and the Making of the State Constitutions in the Revolutionary Era*, trans. Rita Kimber and Robert Kimber (Chapel Hill: University of North Carolina Press, 1980); Horst Dippel, "The Changing Idea of Popular Sovereignty in Early American Constitutionalism: Breaking Away from European Patterns," *Journal of the Early Republic* 16, no. 1 (1996): 21–45; R. R. Palmer, *The Age of the Democratic Revolution: The Challenge* (Princeton, NJ: Princeton University Press, 1959); and Gordon S. Wood, *The Creation of the American Republic, 1776–1787* (Chapel Hill: University of North Carolina Press, 1969), 344–89. For a discussion of the seventeenth-century Anglophone origins of the concept of popular constituent power, see Julian Franklin, *John Locke and the Theory of Sovereignty: Mixed Monarchy and the Right of Resistance in the Thought of the English Revolution* (Cambridge: Cambridge University Press, 1978).

14. For a detailed discussion of the "quasi-legal" politics of the "people out of doors" see Pauline Maier, *From Resistance to Revolution: Colonial Radicals and the Development of American Opposition to Britain, 1765–1776* (New York: W. W. Norton, 1972).

15. Palmer, *The Age of the Democratic Revolution,* 216, 222.

16. Larry Kramer, *The People Themselves: Popular Constitutionalism and Judicial Review* (New York: Oxford University Press, 2004), 53.

17. Jacques Derrida, "Declarations of Independence," *New Political Science* 15 (1986): 7–17.

18. Alan Keenan, *Democracy in Question: Democratic Openness in a Time of Political Closure* (Stanford, CA: Stanford University Press, 2003), 14.

19. James Publius, "Jay's Treaty (April 6, 1796)," in *The Papers of James Publius, Vol. 16,* ed. J. C. A. Stagg, Thomas A. Mason, and Jeanne K. Sisson (Charlottesville: University of Virginia Press, 1989), 290–301.

20. I examine the political valence of the metaphor of ventriloquism in "Hearing Voices: Imagination and Authority in *Wieland*" in *Constituent Moments: Enacting the People in Postrevolutionary America* (Durham, NC: Duke University Press, 2010).

21. "Portius," *American Herald* (Boston), November 12, 1787. Reprinted in *DHRC Vol. IV,* 216–20, 217.

22. Derrida, "Declarations of Independence," 10.

23. Derrida, "Declarations of Independence," 10.

24. Keenan, *Democracy in Question,* 52.

25. On the revolutionary politics of the convention form, see Wood, *Creation of the American Republic,* 306–43.

26. Carl Schmitt, *Constitutional Theory,* ed. and trans. Jeffrey Seitzer (Durham, NC: Duke University Press, 2008), 128.

27. Schmitt, *Constitutional Theory,* 131. Emphasizing this immediacy, he argues that the "the natural form of the direct expression of a people's will is the assembled multitude's declaration of their consent or disapproval" (131). Even an assembled multitude, however, must be said to represent an entity larger than this empirical gathering of individuals: the people.

28. See Stephen Holmes, *Passions and Constraint: On the Theory of Liberal Democracy* (Chicago: University of Chicago Press, 1995), 148, 167.

29. Schmitt, *Constitutional Theory,* 127. The historical relationship between popular sovereignty, with its impossible referent of the people's will, and the emergence of identarian nationalism has been explored by Bernard Yack. According to Yack, nationalism emerges in response to pressures internal to the discourse of popular sovereignty, particularly those engendered by the dilemma of identifying the people's constituent power. "For if the people precede the establishment and survive the dissolution of political authority [constituted power], then they must share something beyond a relationship to that authority. . . . [T]he nation provides precisely what is lacking in the concept of the people: a sense of where to look for the prepolitical basis of the community." Bernard Yack, "Popular Sovereignty and Nationalism," *Political Theory* 29, no. 4 (August 2001): 517–36, 524.

30. Schmitt, *Constitutional Theory,* 239.

31. Pierre Rosanvallon, "Revolutionary Democracy," in *Democracy Past and Future,* ed. Samuel Moyn (New York: Columbia University Press, 2006), 79–97, 92.

32. Schmitt, *Constitutional Theory,* 127.

33. Carl Schmitt, *The Crisis of Parliamentary Democracy,* trans. Ellen Kennedy (Cambridge, MA: MIT Press, 1992), 45.

34. Schmitt, *Constitutional Theory,* 127. I have altered Seitzer's translation of this passage for clarity. See Carl Schmitt, *Verfassungslehre* (Berlin: Duncker & Humblot, 1965), 78.

35. Schmitt, *Constitutional Theory,* 125.

36. Schmitt, *Constitutional Theory,* 128–29.

37. Carl Schmitt, *Über die drei Arten des rechtswissenschaftlichen Denkens* (Berlin: Duncker & Humblot, 1993), 21, 23–24. Andreas Kalyvas directed my attention to this passage.

38. Schmitt, *Constitutional Theory*, 268–85; see also Andreas Kalyvas, "Carl Schmitt and the Three Moments of Democracy," *Cardozo Law Review* 21, no. 5–6 (2000): 1525–66.

39. William E. Scheuerman, "Revolutions and Constitutions: Hannah Arendt's Challenge to Carl Schmitt," in *Law as Politics: Carl Schmitt's Critique of Liberalism*, ed. David Dyzenhaus (Durham, NC: Duke University Press, 1998), 252–80, 254.

40. In the United States the authority to speak in the people's name derives in part from a constitutive surplus inherited from the revolutionary era, from the fact that since the Revolution the people have always been at once enacted through representation and also in excess of any particular representation. This dilemma illuminates the significance and theological resonance of popular *voice*, with its continually reiterated but never fully realized or unmediated reference to the sovereign people beyond the law, the spirit beyond the letter, the Word beyond the words.

41. Jason Frank, *Constituent Moments: Enacting the People in Postrevolutionary America* (Durham, NC: Duke University Press), 2.

42. "Brutus, No. 3," *New York Journal*, November 15, 1787. Reprinted in *DHRC Vol. XIV*, 119–24, 122.

43. Wood, *Creation of the American Republic*, 600.

44. Marc L. Harris, "Civil Society in Post-Revolutionary America," in *Empire and Nation: The American Revolution in the Atlantic World*, ed. Eliga H. Gould and Peter S. Onuf (Baltimore, MD: Johns Hopkins University Press, 2004), 197–216, 203.

45. John Adams, "A Dissertation on the Canon and Feudal Law," in *The Political Writings of John Adams*, ed. George W. Carey (Washington, DC: Regnery Publishing, 2000), 3–21, 14.

46. John Alexander Jameson, *The Constitutional Convention: Its History, Powers, and Modes of Proceeding* (New York: S. C. Griggs, 1867), 130.

47. Bruce Ackerman, *We the People, Vol. 1: Foundations* (Cambridge, MA: Harvard University Press, 1991), 49.

48. For an elaboration of the importance of the difference between vindication and justification, see Bonnie Honig, "Between Decision and Deliberation: Political Paradox in Democratic Theory," *American Political Science Review* 101, no. 1 (2006): 1–17.

49. On this point see Andrew Arato, *Civil Society, Constitution, and Legitimacy* (New York: Rowman & Littlefield, 2000), 333. "Principles," Arato writes, "have the advantage of being able to draw on moral resources that have not been formalized and that are available when appeal to legal resources would inevitably turn circular at moments of foundation."

50. See, for example, Akhil R. Amar, "The Consent of the Governed: Constitutional Amendment Outside Article V," *Columbia Law Review* 94, no. 2 (1994): 457–508, 497.

51. Jean-Jacques Rousseau, *The Social Contract*, trans. M. Cranston (New York: Penguin Books, 1968).

52. Rousseau, *The Social Contract*, 59.

53. Henry F. May, *The Enlightenment in America* (New York: Oxford University Press, 1976), 178. Gary Wills, however, claims that Rousseau's *Social Contract* had a direct influence on James Wilson's conception of popular sovereignty and constituent power. "Wilson," Wills writes, "had Rousseau's *Social Contract* at his elbow during the ratifying period." Wills, "James Wilson's New Meaning for Sovereignty," 100. Aside from some less-than-definitive quote comparison, however, Wills offers no real evidence for this direct influence, and he does not consider that Wilson might have derived his ideas about constituent power and the political sovereignty of "the people at large" from a close and less canonical source: the practices and evolving repertoires of the Revolution itself.

54. Geoffrey Bennington, "Mosaic Fragment: If Derrida Were an Egyptian . . . ," in *Legislations: The Politics of Deconstruction* (London: Verso, 1994), 207–26; William E. Connolly, *The Ethos of Pluralization* (Minneapolis: University of Minnesota Press, 1994), 137–40; Bonnie Honig, *Democracy and the Foreigner* (Princeton, NJ: Princeton University Press, 2001), 18–25; Keenan, *Democracy in Question*, 50–58.

55. Seyla Benhabib, "Deliberative Rationality and Models of Democratic Legitimacy," *Constellations* 1, no. 1 (1994): 26–52.

56. Keenan, *Democracy in Question*, 50.

57. Rousseau, *The Social Contract*, 99.

58. Rousseau, *The Social Contract*, 99.

59. I take these phrases from the work of William Connolly. See, for example, William E. Connolly, *Neuropolitics: Thinking, Culture, Speed* (Minneapolis: University of Minnesota Press, 2002).

60. Honig, "Between Decision and Deliberation"; Paul Ricoeur, "The Political Paradox," in *Legitimacy and the State*, ed. William E. Connolly (New York: New York University Press, 1984), 250–72.

61. Rousseau, *The Social Contract*, 59.

62. Rousseau, *The Social Contract*, 59.

63. Rousseau, *The Social Contract*, 83.

64. Rousseau, *The Social Contract*, 87.

65. For Arendt's account of the revolutionary problem of "the absolute" see Hannah Arendt, *On Revolution* (New York: Penguin, 1990 [1963]), 189–214.

66. Rousseau, *The Social Contract*, 84.

67. Carl Schmitt, *Legality and Legitimacy*, trans. and ed. Jeffrey Seitzer (Durham, NC: Duke University Press, 2004), 37–83.

68. Bennington, "Mosaic Fragment," 219.

69. Rousseau, *The Social Contract*, 87. My emphasis.

70. Honig, "Between Decision and Deliberation."

71. Rousseau, *The Social Contract*, 87.

72. Rousseau, *The Social Contract*, 88.

73. Rousseau, *The Social Contract*, 90.

74. Keenan, *Democracy in Question*, 52. My emphasis.

75. Ackerman, *We the People, Vol. 1: Foundations*, 179.

76. Carl Schmitt, *Political Theology: Four Chapters on the Concept of Sovereignty*, trans. George Schwab (Cambridge, MA: MIT Press, 1988), 21.

TWO

Publius and Political Imagination

A NATION without a NATIONAL GOVERNMENT is, in my view, an awful spectacle.

— *Federalist* No. 85[1]

American political scientists, historians, politicians, Supreme Court justices, and citizens widely recognize *The Federalist*'s decisive influence on the American political imagination. Less often noted is that *The Federalist* is also about the politics *of* the imagination, and that Publius was actively engaged in those politics during the ratification debates of 1787 and 1788. In *The Federalist*, Publius not only critically addressed the unavoidably political implications of the enthusiastic imagination—its conventionally understood tendency to inflame the passions, betray the intellect, and subvert political authority—but also elaborated a constructive role for the imagination in reconstituting public authority, shaken during the revolutionary and postrevolutionary years. Publius relied on a formative theory of the imagination—partly vernacular but also drawn from prominent theorists of the Scottish Enlightenment—to make his case for constitutional ratification.

Although some thought the enthusiastic imagination endangered governmental stability with, in Benjamin Rush's words, "airy and impracticable schemes," late eighteenth-century political thinkers often invoked the disciplined or instructed imagination to secure institutional regularities of political behavior.[2] In this chapter I will turn directly to Publius's engagement with political imagination. I will first outline postrevolutionary American understandings of the imagination's political dimensions—both enthusiastic and formative—and then explore three central aspects of Publius's restorative appeal to the imagination: the appeal to the public veneration required for establishing and sustaining political authority; the strategies for shifting citizen loyalty from the state and

47

local level to the newly energized federal government; and Publius's rhetorical elicitation of the public's imagination in aestheticized portrayals of Providential nationality. Taken together, these aspects of Publius's argument make up the core of *The Federalist's* aesthetics of (self) rule. In each instance, Publius invoked the imagination as a heteronomic support to navigate the dilemmas of democratic self-authorization explored in the last chapter. Such dilemmas are intrinsic to the normative challenge Publius posed in *Federalist* No. 1 and elsewhere described as "the most momentous [subject] which can engage the attention of a free people" (*F*, 90): to establish a free government from popular "reflection and choice" rather than "accident and force" (*F*, 3).

I.

American political thought has been marked by a powerful continuity of anti-imaginistic discourse.[3] This discourse has arguably had a detrimental impact on the historiography of the founding period, obscuring the constructive role of the imagination in the period's political debates. Scholars have tended to see the Founders, in Gordon Wood's words, as "masters of events, realistic pragmatists . . . modern men in step with the movement of history."[4] There is a great deal of truth in these familiar portrayals of the American Founders as empirically minded realists, but they do not tell the whole story.

There are two broadly familiar interpretive approaches to *The Federalist*, conveniently supported by two equally familiar passages from the text, that inhibit a fuller understanding of the role the imagination plays in Publius's arguments. The first focuses on the American drama of deliberation and consent during the "great national discussion" and the challenge from *Federalist* No. 1 to establish a "good government from reflection and choice . . . [rather than] accident and force" (*F*, 3). The second privileges the new science of politics and Publius's rejection of classical republican attempts to give all citizens "the same opinions, the same passions, the same interests" (*F*, 58). This second reading emphasizes Publius's turn away from civic virtue and his attempt to establish political order on what man *is* (interested, passionate, ambitious, avaricious), rather than on what he *ought* to be (virtuous, patriotic, vigilant, public spirited).

The first interpretation—which I call the deliberative reading—understands political imagination primarily as a vestige of premodern mystification, as the cloak of illegitimate power established on "accident and force" rather than reasoned popular consent. The second interpretation—which I call the realist reading, and will explore more fully in chapter 3—rejects the political imagination as utopian or dangerously blind to the plurality of opinions and passions, and neglectful of the organizing bedrock of interest to political life. Both of these basic lines of interpretation find strong support in the debates surrounding constitutional ratification, but their emphasis (sometimes implicit, sometimes explicit) on the imagination primarily as an obstacle to more enlightened republicanism paints a one-dimensional picture of issues animating these debates.

Scholars have noted—but rarely elaborated upon—Publius's *critical* invocation of the imagination. Throughout *The Federalist*, Publius accuses Anti-Federalists, for example, of appealing to the public's revolutionary bias and "distempered imaginations" rather than to their candid, impartial judgments. Anti-Federalists aimed, Publius writes, to "mislead the people by alarming their passions rather than convince them by arguments addressed to their understandings" (*F*, 155). Their "distempered imaginations" and "gloomy doctrines" captivated readers with "deceitful dreams" drawn from the "halcyon scenes of a . . . fabulous age" rather than from sober observations of political or historical experience (*F*, 151, 35, 193). Publius's partisan caricature discounts the opposing but equally formative appeal to the imagination in some Anti-Federalist writing (briefly sketched below), but also illuminates the political dimensions of the faculty of the imagination in postrevolutionary contexts.

The Anti-Federalist fear of expanded, centralized power is almost always the occasion for Publius's accusations regarding the Anti-Federalist propensity for fantasy. In dwelling on the dangers of federal power, Anti-Federalists "open a boundless field for rhetoric"; they "inflame the passions of the unthinking, and may confirm the prejudices of the misthinking" (*F*, 269). Publius singled out the Anti-Federalist fear of energetic government as a fantastic supposition engendered by Revolution's disfiguring passions, unsupported by serious reflection:

> The moment we launch into conjectures about the usurpations of the federal Government, we get into an unfathomable abyss, and fairly put ourselves out of the reach of all reasoning. Imagination may range at pleasure till it gets bewildered amidst the labyrinths of an enchanted castle, and knows not on which side to turn to extricate itself from the perplexities into which it has so rashly adventured. (*F*, 197)

This unfathomable abyss of speculation engenders an imagination trapped in "labyrinths" of its own making, a hallmark of the "inflammatory ravings of chagrined incendiaries" (*F*, 187).

The Federalist regularly pairs jealousy of power with enthusiasm. While acknowledging the defensive role that the citizenry's jealousy might productively play in a republic (a commonplace of civic republican thought), Publius feared its excesses. "Like Bile in the natural" body, Publius writes, when jealousy "abounds too much in the body politic, the eyes of both become very liable to be deceived by the delusive appearances which that malady casts" (*F*, 437). Jealousy of power is a passion that inflames the imagination, obscures judgment, and "discolors and disfigures every object" (*F*, 391). The objections Anti-Federalists offered to energized state power therefore provide only "imaginary difficulties" rather than "solid objections" (*F*, 83). Their groundless apprehensions are to be considered as "a disease, for which there can be found no cure in the resources of argument or reasoning" (*F*, 180).

While Publius disdained Anti-Federalists' suspicious (some have suggested clinically paranoid) fantasies concerning power, he also recognized these depictions' aesthetic pleasures; Publius feared that the Anti-Federalists might be all-too-readable, at times equating their writings with a seductive literary exercise. "To establish the pretended affinity [between the presidency and monarchy]," Publius writes, "they have not scrupled to draw resources even from the regions of fiction" (*F*, 452). Anti-Federalists, in Publius's account, employed seductive, titillating literary tropes to elicit the suspicion of power. They portrayed the president "with the diadem sparkling on his brow, and the imperial purple flowing in his train . . . [and] images of Asiatic despotism and voluptuousness. . . . We have been almost taught to tremble at the terrific visages of murdering janizaries; and to blush at the unveiled mysteries of a future seraglio" (*F*, 453).

In these accusations Publius both invoked widespread eighteenth-century anti-novelistic discourse and contrasted a decadent literary public with a fastidious, seriously deliberative political public. Publius worried that Anti-Federalists were seducing readers through ingenious deployments of well-known plots from the Revolution, plots that cast the Philadelphia Convention's participants as malevolent conspirators against the people's hard-won liberties.[5] In a passage from *Federalist* No. 29, for example, Publius wrote that reading the work of Anti-Federalist opponents to the new Constitution was like "perusing some ill written tale or romance" (*F*, 185). Rather than presenting the public with "natural and agreeable images," like those Publius provides of "Union" and nature (see below), these zealously republican opponents of the Constitution presented "nothing but frightful and distorted shapes—Gorgons, Hydras, and Chimeras dire."[6] Every pressing political topic of the ratification debates was "disfigured" by their fantastic representations; they transformed "every thing . . . into a monster" (*F*, 185–86). The Constitution (in this case the "necessary and proper" clause) was "held up to the People in all the exaggerated colors of misrepresentation . . . as the hideous monster whose devouring jaws would spare neither sex nor age, nor high nor low, nor sacred nor profane" (*F*, 204). (For their part, Anti-Federalists sometimes compared Publius's texts to "dry trash."[7])

As the imagistic repertoire of seraglios, enchanted castles, labyrinths, and monsters indicates, these portrayals were not simply literary, but distinctly gothic.[8] Like Publius's dismissive portrayal of the "unhallowed language" and "fatal charm" of Anti-Federalists, gothic fiction is characterized by pleasures taken in acute apprehension and forebodings of disaster (*F*, 88, 92). In her work on the American gothic, Cathy Davidson writes that the gothic "questioned the rules of rationalism that, for those in power, conveniently ordered their interest and their status."[9] The American gothic's dark foreboding powerfully countered prevailing tropes of exceptionalism, progress, and triumphant enlightenment. It was rhetorically cunning, then, for Publius to portray the suspicious Anti-Federalist opposition, with their "gloomy doctrines," in this way, and to position himself as the candid spokesman for America's bright future, who would "break the fatal charm which has too long seduced us from the paths of felicity and prosperity" (*F*, 92).

In late eighteenth-century America, fiction itself, especially the novel, was sometimes held to be immoral, unserious, and dangerously unmoored from real-world concerns. Moreover, as Davidson has also shown, in the wake of the Revolutionary War, the novel was closely paired with the Revolution's "democratic excess" and challenge to deferential authority. The novel was popularly figured as "the literary equivalent of Daniel Shays," igniting "apprehensions about mobocracy on both the cultural and political level."[10] Publius effectively drew on this widespread antinovelistic discourse in his portrayal of Anti-Federalists as authors of seductive gothic romance.

Underlying these criticisms of the novel, and of the gothic novel in particular, was a more general worry about the imagination as such. This broader early American anti-imaginistic discourse appears in the writing of Jonathan Edwards, Timothy Dwight, Benjamin Rush, Noah Webster, Thomas Jefferson, and John Adams, as well as Publius (and Hamilton, Madison, and Jay). The case against the imagination was motivated primarily by a longing for social and moral stability, with the imagination posited as the human faculty posing a constitutive threat to that stable order. What Terence Martin characterizes as the "American suspicion of the imagination" is as old as New England Puritanism, but was compounded in the eighteenth century by the Spartan simplicity of classical republican critics of decadence and corruption, and enlightenment odes to science, knowledge, and rationality. According to Martin (as well as intellectual historian Henry May), this suspicion of the imagination was influenced especially by Thomas Reid and the Scottish Common Sense school.[11]

Given these overlapping traditions of anti-imaginistic discourse, the faculty of the imagination posed a distinct problem for the revolutionary and postrevolutionary generation. While they increasingly understood themselves as liberated from captivating attachments to Old World tradition, this tradition disciplined or habituated the imagination and provided settled parameters for its attachments. Without these parameters, imagination threatened to unmoor itself from reality and take untempered flights of fancy, leading to the incapacity to distinguish the real from the figments of one's own imagination. According to Martin, late eighteenth-century American critiques of the imagination have to be understood with this important component in mind; otherwise, their purported realism seems defined by its direct opposition to imagination, or by its appeal to unmediated experience, when actually what was more often called for was a disciplined imagination or an "instructed vision."

Benjamin Rush captured this sense of the Revolution's unmooring impact on the imagination in an essay written shortly before the meeting of the Philadelphia Convention:

> The excess of the passion for liberty, inflamed by the successful issue of the war, produced in many people, opinions and conduct which could not be removed by reason nor restrained by government. . . . It un-hinged the judgment, deposed the moral faculty, and filled the imagi-nation, in many people, with airy and impracticable schemes of wealth and grandeur.[12]

The Revolution had expanded commerce, loosened propriety, height-ened the newly politicized citizenry's expectations, and inflamed jeal-ousy of governmental power. For Rush and many of his contemporaries, these developments had a corrupting influence on a balanced imagina-tion. Like Publius, Rush linked institutional fragility to enthusiastic flights of fancy, a commonly drawn connection in the period. Critiques of the subversive enthusiastic imagination inflamed by the Revolution have too often been mistaken for critiques of the imagination *tout court*, or for attempts to free politics entirely from the imagination's influence. It is a mistake to infer from Publius's critique of the purportedly gothic and literary dimensions of the Anti-Federalist opposition that "*The Federalist* leaves almost no room for . . . imaginary projections," or that "Publius distrusts any work of the imagination—what he calls conjectures and ravings."[13] Historians and political theorists often uncritically reiterate Publius's depiction of the Anti-Federalists' passionately disfiguring imagination, as well as the implied counterimage of Publius as an admir-able proponent of candor (Albert Furtwangler), pragmatism (Daniel Boorstin), realism (Richard Hofstadter), and truth (some followers of Leo Strauss).[14] These emphases provide a one-dimensional picture of how the imagination operates in Publius's argument, and also a one-dimensional picture—an enthusiastic picture—of the imagination itself.

II.

In the eighteenth century, particularly among theorists of the Scottish Enlightenment, the imagination occupied a central role in several over-lapping discourses, and helped to cohere a basic worldview. The imagi-nation was essential not only to the conceptualization of self, motivation, and human nature, but also to establishing the sympathetic relationships that formed the basis of society and economic and political orders, all central concerns of *The Federalist*. This was not yet the Romantic imagination, with its emphasis on creativity and "genius," but a universal faculty that acclimated human beings to their natural and social surroundings. Imagination was construed as the very basis of individual and collective identity.

Many eighteenth-century thinkers, including Publius, understood this broader pre-Romantic conception of the imagination as at once necessary and threatening to social cohesion. If the imagination could stitch together a coherent worldview and regulate human interaction, it was also blamed for much of the unhappiness of social life, particularly in its enthusiastic guise. James Engell suggests that nearly every prominent eighteenth-century discussion of the imagination betrays anxiety about the faculty's instability.[15] Because the imagination was most often used to explain dynamic and relational elements of human life—how people develop, how societies interact and progress—this faculty was also considered a destabilizing force, the basis of interrelated physical and mental maladies, and, of course, of political unrest. The imagination was at once the basis and continued threat to the political order, something also recognized by such canonical political theorists as Plato and Hobbes.

This central tension regarding the imagination played out during the ratification debates. Bernard Bailyn argues that "one of the [Federalists'] most revealing themes . . . is the exhortation to rise to the extraordinary occasion before them by thinking freshly and fearlessly about the problems they faced, and above all not to brood on groundless fears, not to . . . imagine catastrophe around every corner."[16] In a more recent work, Bailyn argues further that Americans' very status as "provincials—marginal, borderland people" freed them "from instinctive respect for traditional establishments," and, thereby, "stimulated their imaginations" and "encouraged them to create a new political world."[17] Thomas Pickering reminded his contemporaries, for example, that while they must not "give a loose to [their] imaginations," their situation called for imaginative rethinking.[18] Similarly for Publius, the imagination was a vital but dangerous political resource; it had to be both relied upon and resisted.

Publius, of course, did not articulate anything like a *philosophy* of the imagination in *The Federalist*—Martin Diamond is right that the text "did not deal systematically with philosophical issues"[19]—and Publius was obviously not engaged with the period's detailed philosophical debates over the faculty. However, public discourse reiterated the broad outlines of these technical philosophical debates about the faculty of imagination. A formative theory of the imagination—partly vernacular but also derived from Scottish Enlightenment theorists—plays an important role in Publius's defense of the new federal Constitution. David Hume's work on the imagination, while hotly debated in its particulars, nicely illuminates how theorists of the Scottish Enlightenment broadly characterized the faculty's instability. I turn here briefly to Hume's account of the imagination not to argue its immediate influence on Publius—although such a case can certainly be made[20]—but to bring Publius's reliance on the formative imagination into focus. Although I don't engage with the scholarship demonstrating (or denying) Hume's influence, I agree with Daniel Walker Howe's assessment that "Hume spoke to the needs of the Federalists because he shared their conviction that political institutions decisively shaped the folkways of a people."[21] The indirect government of the public imagination—not direct didacticism, but indirect coaxing and canalizing of the public imagination encouraged through institutional design (a theme I will develop further in the next chapter)—suggests Hume's influence. Publius did not need to endorse Hume's radical skepticism or even be familiar with Hume's *Treatise* to use a widely available understanding of the customary basis of power in habit and the sedimentation of the imagination.

Hume was a preeminent theorist of the ineliminable role of fancy in politics, and for Hume the imagination was the very basis of moral life. That said, Hume's work invokes imagination in different ways, sometimes with seeming inconsistency. Broadly, imagination for Hume was the very ground of memory, sense, and understanding, because the imagination was the means by which the mind actively associated ideas with each other. In Eva Braun's words, for Hume, "imagination spans the whole cognitive spectrum from sense impressions to thinking."[22] For Hume, the mind reacts to and orders experience according to its own desires, uncertainties, and fears. The drama of the mind and of its passions, as it confronts other people and the world, is directed overwhelmingly by imagination. "We save ourselves from . . . total skepticism," Hume writes in the *Treatise*, "only by means of that singular and seemingly trivial property of the fancy."[23] The fancy is "seemingly trivial" because only as imagination structures the stream of perception are regularities established that serve as "the foundation of our thoughts and actions, so that upon their removal human nature must immediately perish."[24] The imagination is the faculty, then, that habituates us into an ordered world. The furthest thing from trivial, imagination is for Hume the means by which human beings bring regularity to the flux of the world (recall Hume's arguments about the imagination's role in establishing relations of cause and effect). Imagination is, therefore, intimately connected to institutions for Hume, and to habituation. In the *Treatise* the imagination is constrained by resemblance, contiguity, and cause and effect, but these are but habitual associations, and not written into the nature of things. The imagination is at once the faculty of transformative malleability *and* of securing an enabling, sedimented stability. "Nothing is more dangerous to reason," Hume writes in the *Treatise*, "than flights of the imagination."[25] But, as Frederick Whelan emphasizes, this faculty is also "necessary for all reasoning."[26] In the philosophical economy of the *Treatise*, the imagination reveals the dependency of the human mind's highest faculties—its reasoning capacities—on a dangerously delusional faculty.

Hume navigates the imagination's internal ambivalence throughout his work, and so too does Publius in *The Federalist*. The next two sections explore how Publius's account of public veneration and political attachment addresses the formative imagination. The focus in both sections is on Publius's arguments concerning the proposed constitution's salutary elicitation of the public imagination for establishing public authority. The chapter's final section, by contrast, turns to *The Federalist*'s own rhetorical elicitation of the public imagination in alluring images of Providential nationality, in the rhetorical elicitation of a national identity. In each instance, Publius invokes the imagination to respond to a familiar dilemma of democratic theory: how a self-governing people becomes a people in the first place. "Before we ascribe sovereignty to the people," Edmund Morgan succinctly writes, "we have to imagine that there is such a thing."[27] Publius posits veneration, attachment, and identification as three important and overlapping modes of this imagining.

III.

Multiple concerns drew delegates to the Philadelphia Convention in the summer of 1787: the federal government's weakness under the Articles of Confederation, the indignities of engaging European powers, widespread economic insecurity, state legislatures passing prodebtor paper money laws, growing domestic unrest as exemplified by Shays' Rebellion, and so on. For many delegates, these concerns were symptoms of a broader postrevolutionary crisis in authority, expressing a decline in received patterns of deferential politics that Gordon Wood has called postrevolutionary America's "democratization of mind."[28] These expressions of crisis were frequently invoked in the debates of the Philadelphia Convention and throughout *The Federalist*.

For Publius, these years' political volatility resembled the "unceasing agitations and frequent revolutions" that were the "continual scourges of petty republics" (*F*, 177). Although the concern with the "perpetual vibration" of republican politics recurs throughout *The Federalist* (*F*, 50), nowhere does Publius give closer theoretical attention to the unsettling dynamics of public passion than in *Federalist* No. 49, and there the faculty of the imagination plays an important role in the analysis. In No. 49 Publius criticized Jefferson's theory of popular constitutional conventions, which Jefferson had proposed in his draft of a state constitution for Virginia in 1783 and later published as a second appendix to his *Notes on the State of Virginia*.[29] The final section of Jefferson's proposed constitution outlined procedures for constitutional revision that allowed for "altering" the constitution through popular constitutional conventions, as Massachusetts had done in 1780. While Publius acknowledged that Jefferson had included "enlightened" provisions that guarded against the "dangerous propensities" of these intermittent constitutional appeals to the people, Publius also criticized the ease with which Jefferson appealed to the people's constituent power as a corrective to constitutional breaches of power (*F*, 339). While it seemed "strictly consonant," Publius wrote, "to the republican theory, to recur to the same original authority [of the people]," and while such appeals must be allowed "for certain great and extraordinary occasions," these provisions invited dangerous elicitations of public passion that threatened to unsettle the American citizenry's sedimented political imagination and diminish constitutional authority (*F*, 339).

This potential for public unrest was a central reason for rejecting "the proposed recurrence to the people." Regular appeal to "the people" would disturb the public tranquility "by interesting too strongly the public passions"; such "experiments are of too ticklish a nature to be unnecessarily multiplied"; they "would in great measure deprive the government of that veneration which time bestows on every thing, and without which perhaps the wisest and freest governments would not possess the requisite stability" (*F*, 340). The broadly Humean dimensions of this argument—with its marked concern for instituting stable regularities of governance (and not only governance: "the veneration which time bestows on every *thing*") that can earn the habitual "veneration" of the public—are further indicated in Publius's invocation of the "opinion" on which all governments are based. In Publius's formulation, the "practical influence" of opinion on conduct is strengthened when it is imagined or "supposed" to be shared by others and multiplied by past examples.

> When the examples, which fortify opinion, are *ancient* as well as *numerous*, they are known to have a double effect. In a nation of philosophers, this consideration ought to be disregarded. A reverence for the laws would be sufficiently inculcated by the voice of an enlightened reason. . . . [I]n every other nation, the most rational government will not find it a superfluous advantage to have the prejudices of the community on its side. (*F*, 340)

By limiting the occasions and institutional spaces through which these "ticklish" invocations of public passions might occur, Publius hoped to temper public sentiments themselves, to make them more amenable to "veneration" and "reverence." Publius similarly argues in No. 25 that the federal authority's very weakness under the Articles of Confederation necessitated the occasional suspension of the rule of law to confront emergency situations, which thereby deflated the settled authority of law: "every breach of the fundamental laws, though dictated by necessity, impairs the sacred reverence, which ought to be maintained in the breast of rulers towards the constitution of a country" (*F*, 163). The authority of law—for both rulers and ruled—would come only through cultivating "veneration" and "sacred reverence" for the institutions that embodied it.

Earlier in his argument, Publius asked whether it was not "the glory of the people of America, that whilst they have paid a decent regard to the opinions of former times and other nations, they have not suffered a blind veneration for antiquity, for custom, or for names" (*F*, 88), and in the previous chapter we have seen Publius's own subtle engagement with the dilemmas of authorization associated with constituent power. In No. 49 and elsewhere, however, Publius suggests that the proper conditions for establishing a more republican and deliberative polity had to be established by *first* circumscribing the occasions for popular deliberation over fundamental law.

Stephen Holmes has emphasized this constitutionalist concern with enabling constraints and the dilemmas of precommitment,[30] but, like many other liberal admirers of *The Federalist*, Holmes largely neglects Publius's concomitant arguments concerning veneration, authority, and habit. Madison delayed the publication of his now-famous accounts of the Philadelphia Convention for a similar reason: he wanted to wait until the veneration of the citizenry had been established before submitting the convention's disagreements and compromises to public view. He feared that publicly revealing the conflicts behind the convention's seemingly "unanimous" assent of the Constitution would rob it of authority.[31] Scholars have sometimes marveled at how quickly the rancor of the ratification debates supposedly resolved into Constitution worship. Hannah Arendt described it as an admirable "blindness" on the part of early Americans, an "extraordinary capacity to look upon yesterday with the eyes of centuries to come."[32]

It is fitting, of course, that Jefferson was the target of Publius's praise of veneration and the habituated imagination. No founding figure was more outspoken in opposing the authority of custom, including the inherited authority of constitutions themselves. In the letter to Samuel Kercheval examined in the introduction above, Jefferson wrote that "some men look at constitutions with sanctimonious reverence and deem them like the arc of the covenant, too sacred to be touched."[33] Although Jefferson wrote these words in 1816, he had long held the sentiment. In a letter sent to Madison in September of 1789, Jefferson wrote that "no society can make a perpetual constitution, or even a perpetual law. The earth belongs always to the living generation. They may manage it, then, and what proceeds from it, as they please during their usufruct." Madison, evincing the same difference elaborated in *Federalist* No. 49, responded, "Would not a Government so often revised become too mutable & novel to retain that share of prejudice in its favor which is a salutary aid to the most rational government?"[34]

Imagination is central to this argument concerning veneration. Veneration occurs over time, as human beings become familiar with existing institutions. In "ticklish" contexts, conventions of constitutional reform would forever upset the passions and political imaginations of the citizenry and prevent it from settling into an established reverence and awe for existing institutions; they would risk provoking a "universal ardor for new and opposite forms" (*F*, 341). Publius does not replace imagination with reliance on reason, a tactic only suitable in a "nation of philosophers," but rather allows the imagination to become more stable in the duration of its object of contemplation, to provide a stable object to which "veneration" can attach. Knud Haakonssen has nicely summarized this central dimension of Hume's political thought: "When there is uncertainty about . . . authority . . . our habitual ways of thinking and behaving are broken. Under such circumstances opinions and actions are much more likely to be influenced by imagined situations than by actual conditions, and passionate flights of fancy tend to take over."[35]

The regularity of behavior does not eschew the imagination but disciplines it so that its field of (in this case, political) expectations is delimited. As Hume writes in his *Essays*, "to render the passion of continuance, we must find some method of affecting the senses and imagination. . . . Popular superstitions and observances are found to be of use in this particular."[36] Later commentators on American constitutionalism, most profoundly and persuasively Tocqueville and Lincoln, would invoke the enabling, but not wholly rationally justified, authority of early America's civic religion.[37]

IV.

A related imaginistic dilemma appears in Publius's arguments about the obstacle that America's vastness posed for generating attachment to the new federal government. How could citizens break their customary and also more "natural" loyalty to local and state authorities, and refocus their attachment to the new federal government? Anti-Federalists like Brutus worried that under the proposed Constitution all the powers reserved to the states "must very soon be annihilated." The states, they feared, would "dwindle away . . . their powers absorbed in that of the general government."[38] Anti-Federalists worried that this "consolidation" of federal power would lead citizens, in the words of Demosthenes Minor, to "forget . . . local habits and attachments" and "be reduced to one faith and one government."[39]

Publius rejected the claim that the Constitution would "usurp the powers" of the state and local governments. Even if the federal government tended to deflate state authority, however, it could not easily overcome the citizenry's natural tendency toward more intimate loyalty to local governments. The "superiority of influence" that the states have over their citizens resides largely in the ease with which the imagination binds the affections to nearer objects:

> It is a known fact in human nature that its affections are commonly weak in proportion to the distance and diffusiveness of the object. Upon the same principle that a man is more attached to his family than to his neighborhood . . . the people of each State would be apt to feel a stronger bias towards their local governments than towards the government of the Union; unless the force of that principle should be destroyed by a much better administration of the latter. (*F*, 107)

From this eighteenth-century commonplace, Publius argues that appeals to the regularity of contact with local and state law, especially in cases of criminal and civil justice, engender "popular obedience and attachment," because the state's control over justice has its "terrors and constant activity before the public eye" (*F*, 107). State governments are immediately before the eyes of the people who enjoy its protection. From the states, justice and "all those acts which familiarize and endear government to a people are dispensed to them" (*F*, 82). In comparison to these local ties, the federal government does not so excite the imaginations of the citizenry. Because the federal government is "less apt to come home to the feelings of the people," it is "less likely to inspire . . . an active sentiment of attachment" (*F*, 108).

There are exceptions to this local attachment of imagination, as the qualification in the passage—"unless the force of that principle should be destroyed by a much better administration of the latter"—indicates. Although Publius insisted on the imagination's "natural" attachment to local particularities, elsewhere in the argument he was at pains to show the possible redirection of the imagination of attachment from the states to the federal government.

Another common Anti-Federalist objection to the proposed constitution was that the distance of the federal government would force it to rely upon coercion to secure obedience to federal laws (influenced by Montesquieu's theory of despotism). Again, Brutus provides a good example of this Anti-Federalist position when he writes that it is impossible for government to sustain the "confidence, respect, and affection of the people . . . in a republic so extensive as the United States."[40] Without this affection, "the government will be nerveless and inefficient, and in no way will be left to render it otherwise, but by establishing an armed force to execute the laws at the point of a bayonet."[41]

While Publius went to great lengths to assure skeptics that local ties would remain dominant under the newly proposed federal power, in response to this different set of criticisms Publius relied on a quite opposite set of arguments. He now insists on the proposed Constitution's ability to redirect the sentiments of the citizens *away* from the local to the federal level, to institutionally inculcate a sense of national belonging, or

what David Waldstreicher has called the "constitution of federal feeling."[42] In this context, better and more efficient administration is taken as
the key to enhancing attachments to federal power. However, this redirection of attachment is not based simply on the perceived interest of the
citizens, and it is misleadingly characterized as an "economic theory of
public affection."[43] Publius recognized the novelty of his arguments on
these points:

> [T]he more the operations of the national authority are intermingled in
> the ordinary exercise of government, the more the citizens are accus-
> tomed to meet with it in the common occurrences of their political life;
> the more it is familiarized to . . . their feelings; the further it enters into
> those objects which touch the most sensible chords, and . . . put in
> motion the most active springs of the human heart; the greater will be
> the probability that it will conciliate the respect and attachment of the
> community. Man is very much a creature of habit. A thing that rarely
> strikes his senses will generally have but little influence on his mind. A
> government continually . . . out of sight, can hardly be expected to
> interest the sensations of the people. (*F*, 173)

The attachment described goes well beyond the reasoned "confidence" one might have in "better administration." The passage, however,
also poses a difficulty to Publius's overall argument against the Anti-
Federalist opposition. In the earlier argument, Publius had insisted on the
natural attachments to locality to allay concerns that the federal government would impinge upon the states' power; here he suggests that an
increase of federal power and federal superiority in administration will
in fact turn the imagination from the local to the federal government,
securing obedience without the use of force and, thereby, further enhancing federal power. As he puts the point elsewhere, "an intimate intercourse under the same government will promote a gradual assimilation,
of temper and sentiment" (*F*, 405). Publius relied here on the logic of a
self-generating cycle of power—increased federal power will elicit the
public's imagination and affections, therefore further enhancing federal
power—as well as the obverse argument that a weak government is an
unloved (and unlovely) government:

> The most deplorable effect of all is that diminution of attachment and
> reverence which steals into the hearts of people, toward a political
> system which betrays so many marks of infirmity. . . . No government
> any more than an individual will long be respected, without being
> truly respectable, not truly respectable without possessing a certain
> portion of order and stability. (*F*, 422)

The government must be given more power in order to attract the
attachments of the citizenry; the attachments of the citizenry are required
in order for the government to consolidate more needed power. "The
more [the authority of Union] circulates through those channels and cur-

rents, in which the passions of mankind naturally flow, the less will it require the aid of the violent and perilous expedients of compulsion" (*F*, 81). Power here is to work through the elicited imagination of the public rather than through direct force; far from subverting authority, the imagination is here enlisted in its support.

The emphasis Publius placed on the reforming power of administration has led some political theorists to accuse *The Federalist* of neglecting the sentimental terrain of politics altogether. Sheldon Wolin, for example, writes, "*The Federalist* had to invent a new and abstract conception of the citizen who would be national in character, an unmediated subject designed for a politics of intendment."[44] Deracinated interest, in this account, became the only "active principle of the human mind," connecting the citizen with government. I will examine Publius's invocation of interest in the next chapter, but it is worth pointing out here that such interpretations overlook the extent to which new federal power not only could "destroy" natural attachments to local government, but could constitute powerful new attachments in their place. Publius elicited not an "abstract conception of citizen" but a newly constituted, intimate national citizenry. The ability of federal power to "touch the citizens directly" rather than going through the mediation of state government not only consolidated national power, but also established direct sentimental connection. Public sentiments and political loyalty, no longer generated through direct citizen participation and ties of locality, would instead be actuated through a more intimate and direct display of federal power in individual citizens' lives. In this sense, the new federal government's institutional design would not merely organize interests, balance the branches of government, or establish constitutional equilibrium (all of which will be examined in the next chapter); it also would transform the sentimental structure of its citizens, reforming their "tempers, sentiments, and manners." In his defense of the proposed constitution Publius articulates a poetics as well as a mechanics of power.[45]

Herbert Storing's influential interpretation of Federalist and Anti-Federalist thought, which I will examine at more length in chapter 4, also speaks to this point. Storing draws a sharp contrast between the Anti-Federalist's nostalgic reliance upon a virtuous citizenry for maintaining liberty and the Federalist's more avowedly modern reliance on self-interest and institutional design. While Anti-Federalists understood "the whole organization of the polity as having an educative function"—they saw the republic, Storing writes, "as a school of citizenship as much as a scheme of government"—*The Federalist* supposedly had no such formative vision. The force of Publius's argument in *Federalist* No. 10, for example, is its shocking disregard of civic virtue, its rejection of the possibility of "removing the causes" of factions by "cultivating a love of liberty among the citizens," and its invocation, instead, of a novel governmental logic of "controlling its effects" (*F*, 58). Rather than conceiving of government as a "molder of character," Storing writes, Publius saw it as a "regulator of conduct."[46] In *Politics and Vision* Wolin similarly claims that Publius's aim "was not to educate men, but to deploy them, not to alter their moral character, but to arrange institutions in such a manner that human drives would cancel each other out."[47] But does the institutional regulation of conduct itself mold character, form interests, and shape attachments? *The Federalist* argues that it does.

The emphasis these influential, if competing, interpretations place on the role of interest and "better administration" obscures the formative dimension of Publius's argument and the important role of the imagination. They neglect Publius's reliance on the habituation of the citizenry — beyond either interested judgments or reasoned deliberations — to federal attachment and loyalty. The habituation of the formative imagination is also not free of normative consideration because it is attended by considerations on "the degree of authority required to direct the passions of so large a society to the public good" (F, 81). Publius makes clear that the redirected attachments to federal authority will have the benefit of working against "that strong predilection in favor of local objects," and toward an "enlarged view" mediated by the representative institutions of the federal government. Noting how under the Articles of Confederation "the great interests of the nation have suffered on an hundred, from an undue attention to the local prejudices, interests and views of the particular states," Publius argued that an energized federal government would not only enthrall it citizens to its power by "touching" their lives more directly, but that this redirection would lead to a consideration of a broader general interest (F, 318). The imagined redirection of attachment would, in other words, work to habituate the citizenry into an enlarged perspective and loosen the "bias of local views and prejudices" (F, 144). It would habituate citizens into an attentiveness to questions of general — *national* — concern.

Publius's concern with redirecting attachment to federal government and so engendering a habituated sense of national belonging is also enacted in *The Federalist*'s attempt to rhetorically elicit the national attachments of its public, addressing the nation not only as an "imagined community," in Benedict Anderson's sense,[48] but also as a captivating object of aesthetic evaluation. To better illuminate this dimension of Publius's text, we must look beyond the stated differences of principle between Federalists and Anti-Federalists, and toward their competing images of collective belonging; we must consider the political positions that both underwrite and arise from what Robert Ferguson has called the "aesthetics of ratification."[49]

V.

In both form and content, *The Federalist* aspires to interpellate readers into a national body politic, to address them as a national citizenry in addition to "the people of the state of New York." The text works to enact the very national public on which achieving its overarching goal—the ratification of the Constitution—depends. These appeals to nationality are, moreover, not limited to arguments concerning the "utility" of Union. While Publius's arguments for Union seem "superfluous" because they are already "deeply engraved on the hearts of the great body of the people in every state" (*F*, 7), he also urges the reader to "reflect that the object upon which he is to decide is not a particular interest of the community, but the very existence of the nation" (*F*, 590). Before a people can have a particular interest, or be served by useful institutions, as we saw in the last chapter, they must first be constituted as a people. The nation in *The Federalist* is at once the precondition and the desired effect of ratification.[50] As such, *The Federalist* may be said to participate in a broader "effort of symbolic construction," wherein, in Carroll Smith-Rosenberg's words, "late eighteenth-century British North Americans imagined a new nation, constituted a new government—and constructed new identities as subjects of that nation and to that Constitution."[51]

Publius began *The Federalist* not by first elaborating the divisive weaknesses of the Articles of Confederation, but by imagining a unified American geography, language, and history. While Publius announced he would first address "*the utility of the Union to your political prosperity*" (presumably in Nos. 2 through 14), he built these arguments upon the prior poetic invocation of the Providential nation as an alluring object of aesthetic evaluation. The key passage is from *Federalist* No. 2:

> It has often given me pleasure to observe, that Independent America was not composed of detached and distant territories, but that one connected, fertile, wide spreading country was the partition of our western sons of liberty. Providence has in particular manner blessed it . . . for the delight and accommodation of its inhabitants. . . .
>
> With equal pleasure I have as often taken notice, that Providence has been pleased to give this one connected country, to one united people, a people descended from the same ancestors, speaking the same language, professing the same religion, attached to the same principles of government, very similar in their manners and customs, and who . . . fighting side by side throughout a long and bloody war, have nobly established their general Liberty and Independence. (*F*, 9)

The pleasure Publius takes in these imagined scenes of national belonging sanctioned by nature and Providence is an important precondition to the federal government's proper operations, outlined in the subsequent arguments concerning the "utility" of union; it is a necessary supplement to these arguments. Publius's invocation of Providential nationality has led some to argue that "the concept of American nationhood underlies the whole case for the Constitution."[52] Hans Morgenthau, for example, cites this passage as evidence that the Constitution was based in a "pre-existing community."[53] Samuel Beer has elaborated a similar argument.[54] But such accounts of Publius's "description" of a nation neglect the aesthetic rendering of the nation, its productive and performative dimension, as well as the willful inaccuracy of Publius's account of "one united people, a people descended from the same ancestors, speaking the same language."[55] "In proportion as the United States assumes a national form and national character," Publius wrote, "so will the good of the whole be more and more an object of attention" (*F*, 437–38). But *The Federalist* indicates that this "form and national character" cannot be assumed, but must be produced. As suggested above, Publius argues that only as the nation becomes a pleasing object of (aesthetic) attachment will an enlarged view of the good of the whole come into view for the citizenry, loosening the ties of locality, and broadening narrow parochial concerns.

Compare Publius's invocation of Providential national unity to the Anti-Federalist Brutus's similarly aestheticized invocation of the complex fabric of locality:

> The United States includes a variety of climates. The productions of the different parts of the union are very variant, and their interests, of consequence, diverse. Their manners and habits differ as much as their climates and productions; and their sentiments are by no means coincident. The laws and the customs of the several states are, in many respects, very diverse, and in some opposite. . . .[56]

While Brutus and other Anti-Federalists invoke the web of difference in explicitly pastoral terms, Publius converts this difference into dissonance as "unsocial, jealous, and alien sovereignties" (*F*, 9). If, as Publius writes, "a NATION without a NATIONAL GOVERNMENT is . . . an awful spectacle," it is also true that pleasing spectacles of nationality in part compose the nation (*F*, 594). According to Publius, an ugly disunity of fractious regional affiliations typifies the history of confederations (a history detailed at length in *The Federalist*), and, by implication, the Anti-Federalist alternative.[57] Publius held that this counter-spectacle of ugly discord would also fix the national attachments of a unified citizenry, and attest to the ordering power of aesthetic display: "This picture of the consequences of disunion cannot be too highly coloured . . . . Every man who loves peace, every man who loves his country, every man who loves liberty ought to have it ever before his eyes, that he may cherish in his heart a due attachment to the Union of America" (*F*, 272).

In contrast to *The Federalist's* "pleasing and agreeable" images of Union are the awful "spectacles" provided by the "petty republics of Greece and Italy," which engender "sensations of horror and disgust" (*F*, 50). "If momentary rays of glory break forth from the gloom, [if] they dazzle us with a transient and fleeting brilliancy," Publius writes, "they at the same time admonish us to lament that the vices of government should pervert the direction and tarnish the luster of those bright lights and exalted endowments" (*F*, 50). Historians also occasionally reiterate the aesthetic dimensions of Publius's portrayal of the Anti-Federalist opposition as characterized by ugliness, asymmetrical discord, jealousy, smallness, and lack of polish.[58] The Anti-Federalists, for their part, were attentive to Publius's reliance on the language of spectacle and occasionally charged that the Federalists were themselves captivated by monarchical regimes' lost grandeur. In Patrick Henry's words, visions of "Stately palaces" and "dazzling ideas of glory, wealth, and power" held them in thrall.[59]

The Federalist's attempt to imaginatively unify the geographic, social, and political landscape of American in alluring spectacles of Providential nationality was a common literary strategy. In *Letters from an American Farmer*, Crèvecoeur writes that the American "spectacle" is "more entertaining, and more philosophical than that which arises from beholding the musty ruins of Rome," because in America the imagination, "instead of submitting to the painful and useless retrospect of revolutions, desolations, and plagues, would . . . wisely spring forward to the anticipated fields of future cultivation and improvement, to the future extent of those generations which are to replenish and embellish this boundless continent."[60] Crèvecoeur's juxtaposition of the competing spectacles of Old and New World is echoed in Publius's juxtaposition of the turbulent spectacles of past republics with pleasing scenes of a newly national, natural *mise-en-scène*. If Publius frequently characterized the Anti-Federalist imagination as disfiguring, he himself also presented "natural and agreeable images" fitted to "nature's nation."[61] As Robert Ferguson writes, "as unity bespoke beauty and pleasant vistas, so ruin and decay promised ugliness, political entrapment, and local chaos or absence of form."[62] The beauty of the scenes of Providential nationality that Publius depicts is reminiscent of Burke's dictum that to make us love our country, our country ought to be lovely.[63] Or as Crèvecoeur writes, one *"involuntarily* loves a country where everything is so lovely."[64] "A NATION without a NATIONAL GOVERNMENT," Publius writes, is "an awful spectacle" (*F*, 594). Ratification would therefore complete a work of beauty, a beauty required to hold the attention and sustain the identity of an emerging nation; imagination would align the external border of the state with the heart of the American citizen.

Of course, this border demarcates not only a geographical territory, but also the imagined boundaries of belonging. The "true state" of African slaves, Publius writes, was in their "mixt character" as "persons" and "property," "irrational animals" and "members of society" (*F*, 367). "The savage tribes on our western frontier," he elsewhere writes, "ought to be regarded as our natural enemies" (*F*, 156). And women are simply not discussed by Publius at all. These originary exclusions, in the words of one recent constitutional theorist, "eat away at America's legitimacy," but they have also been a source of ongoing political contention and democratic revitalization.[65] Because the enabling boundaries defining "the people of this republic" are necessarily imagined, the political movements mobilized around them have also been importantly re-visionary and poetic, not merely interested or deliberative.

Despite the claims of deliberative and realist approaches, *The Federalist* does not offer only a disenchanted politics freed from the imagination—a politics based wholly in public reason or virtue, on the one hand, or calculations of interest, on the other—but also a politics based in a disciplined or instructed imagination. Indeed, the next chapter will show how interest is itself envisioned by Publius as an effect of such formative influence. At key points in his argument Publius invoked the imagination to secure the authority of the proposed constitutional regime; he converted imagination from a subversive or destabilizing force—the enthusiastic imagination—to a support of power. The interconnected aspects of Publius's aesthetics of (self) rule—the habitual veneration of shared constitutional norms, the redirected popular attachment to federal authority, and the aestheticized identification with the Providential nation—enlist the public imagination to navigate (if not resolve) dilemmas attending the normative challenge to "decide the important question" of whether "good government" can be established from popular "reflection and choice" rather than "accident and force" (*F*, 3).

By figuring the people as inheritors of a revered constitutional tradition, united by and attached to an effective federal government, and identified with a Providential nationality, Publius enlisted the imagination as a heteronomic support to navigate the dilemmas of collective self-authorization examined in chapter 1.[66] The imagination sutures what reason cannot; it establishes the attachments and the provisional boundaries around who comprises the self-legislating people, that "pure original fountain of all legitimate authority" (*F*, 146). This is a precondition of democratic politics, whether that politics is understood as the jockeying of interests or a process of reasoned deliberation. "Democratic citizens," as Danielle Allen writes, "cannot take shape until 'the people' is imaginable."[67]

While dilemmas surrounding the self-constitution of the people are no doubt reiterated over a history of democratic claims making, they are dramatically self-evident at founding moments, leading some to simply characterize them as "paradoxes of political founding."[68] As I noted in the introduction, the political parables of biblical and classical antiquity also model these dilemmas and indicate that foundings are invariably attended by fratricidal violence and the creation of a mythology to retrospectively enlist the support of the people so founded, or convert them into such a people. As Publius put the point, in reference to Lycurgus, ancient parables of political foundation typically mix "a portion of violence with the authority of superstition" (*F*, 241). In this way, Hume noted how "time and custom give authority to all forms of government . . . founded only on injustice and violence," as contemporaries "transfer to their predecessors and ancestors that right, which [the mind] naturally ascribes to the posterity, as being related together, and united in the imagination."[69]

The legitimation deficit entailed by this reliance on unjustified violence and recompensatory myth has been largely disavowed by liberal constitutionalism, perhaps most especially in its American guise. While these questions are not generally emphasized in either democratic theory or the historical scholarship of the American founding—being all but absent, for example, in the debates between liberals and civil republicans[70]—they have played a remarkably important role in the history of American political thought. Like Publius, Americans tend to see "a finger of that Almighty hand" guiding the deliberations of the founding generation (*F*, 238).[71]

Leo Strauss's followers are an exception, as I will examine in more detail in chapter 4. They have frequently emphasized the importance of the classical framework of founding for understanding late eighteenth-century American political thought. Straussian interpretations of the American founding, despite the significant differences among them,[72] typically lionize the founders as "an assembly of demi-gods" whose "thought remains the finest American thought on political matters."[73] According to these interpretations the founders "laid down our most basic rules" and established "the primary terms of our moral and civic discourse."[74] They therefore offer a "qualitatively distinct form of political intelligence."[75] Acutely aware of the impossibility (and, as they frequently proclaim, the dangers) of full democratic autonomy, and of the need for supplemental civic religion and myth, Straussian approaches nonetheless insist on the absolute legitimacy of "the American regime." They base this legitimacy in the extraordinary wisdom of the founding generation, in its capacity to found the regime on "a disinterested and true knowledge of political things."[76] The founders were thinking revolutionaries who founded the regime on permanent political truths that we forget at our peril.

Essential to this approach is a fundamental distinction between the exceptionality of the founding generation and the generally low-sighted repetition of what follows; the "rare and the thoughtful" must be distinguished from "the ordinary and the banal."[77] Although the founders understood the importance of "sacred veneration" and "myth" to perpetuating the regime, by these accounts, they were not themselves dependent on such aesthetic devices. The founders established "a durable regime whose perpetuation requires nothing like the wisdom and virtue necessary for its creation."[78] Without this fundamental distinction between the exceptional wisdom of the founders and the cave of posterity, the sacred origin is deprived of its absolute legitimacy; all is reduced to ideology. Elaborating this point in relation to Madison, Gary Rosen argues that the "sacred veneration" and "patriotic reverence" the founders called for does not detract from the legitimacy of the founding (as it would in the modern social contract theories of Hobbes and Locke), because it is based in a happy coincidence of truth and myth, a fortuitous union of ancient and modern, an exemplification of Aristotle's conception of a "true opinion."[79] Thus the heteronomous rule of a wise and virtuous elite is supposedly made compatible with popular self-government.

Things are different, of course, if we take the more historically plausible Hume as our guide to understanding *The Federalist*'s encounter with the problem of founding. This approach is moreover suggested by Publius himself. In the final installment of *The Federalist*, Publius directly cites Hume to defend the Founders' *departure* from the classical paradigms of the extraordinary lawgiver. Publius's closing reliance on Hume's critique of classical paradigms of founding, while here, as elsewhere, emphasizing the Constitution's incremental and customary development, does not fully displace the political into an evolutionary story of social development. It does, however, seem to diminish the extraordinary significance of the founding along with the exceptional wisdom of the founders, allowing us to glimpse the mythic dimensions of their posthumous sanctification; it raises doubts about the unique authority we habitually attribute to the founding generation for orienting contemporary democratic politics, and it does so on the founders' own authority. Democratic and constitutional theorists tend, in Jeremy Elkins's words, "to simultaneously rely on, and to forget, the mythical character of 'the people's' founding of a constitution."[80] The *Federalist* is similarly reliant on, and wary of, the mythology of founding, and democratic theorists might learn from this productive ambivalence.

Publius counseled "a remembrance of the endearing scenes which are past" to orient political action in the present (*F*, 298) because such remembrance draws a boundary around the politically possible. Like Hume, Publius recognized the necessity of imagined connections to a point of political origin, where the "naturally ascribed" legitimacy of the present is transferred to "predecessors and ancestors" and "united in the imagination."[81] Even contemporary constitutional scholars typically not engaged by debates surrounding the political imagination or the aesthetic dimensions of political life occasionally theorize the centrality of imagining that "we are in the same boat" as those we call founders; or how participants in a constitutional politics "must be able to recognize the project as the same through history and judge it from the same perspective."[82] This imperative requires an imaginative investment that these theories cannot typically account for or fully justify on their own terms.

Publius recognized, where much contemporary democratic theory does not, that the inquiries of reason and the deliberations of a democratic polity must call on a prior investment of the imagination.

Emphasizing how *The Federalist* enlists the imagination is not to debunk its normative claims, but to admire how Publius's recognition of the necessity of these supports did not prevent the broader pursuit of reestablishing a republican government on the people's authority. Theoretical attention to the many ways in which aesthetic investments are enlisted in political life—including in the sanctification of the founding generation's thought—may engender a more detailed appreciation of their workings. Rather than casting off the aesthetic as a remnant of political barbarism, democratic theorists might pay closer attention to how imagination is enlisted time and again at the heart of democratic liberalism, thereby making investments in our sustaining fictions more visible and open to critical engagement and contestation. If imagination invests us in the unbroken authority of a constitutional tradition, it is also the faculty that underwrites the capacity to begin the world anew.

NOTES

1. Jacob E. Cooke, ed., *The Federalist* (Middletown, CT: Wesleyan University Press, 1961), 594. All subsequent citations to *The Federalist* will be to this edition, titled *F* with paginations in parentheses in the text.

2. Benjamin Rush, "The Effects of the American Revolution on the Mind and Body of Man," in *Selected Writings of Benjamin Rush*, ed. Dagobert D. Runes (New York: Philosophical Library, 1947), 331; Terence Martin, *The Instructed Vision: Scottish Common Sense Philosophy and the Origins of American Fiction* (Bloomington: Indiana University Press, 1961).

3. Martin, *Instructed Vision*, 157–58.

4. Gordon S. Wood, "Interests and Disinterestedness in the Making of the Constitution," in *Beyond Confederation: The Origins of the Constitution and American National Identity*, ed. Richard Beeman, Stephen Botein, and Edward C. Carter II (Chapel Hill: University of North Carolina Press, 1987), 112, 69.

5. This claim is at the center of Bernard Bailyn's *Ideological Origins of the American Revolution* (Cambridge, MA: Harvard University Press, 1967), xiii.

6. Publius takes the phrase (without attribution) from book two of *Paradise Lost* (v. 628). John Milton, *Paradise Lost*, ed. Gordon Teskey (New York: W. W. Norton, 2004), 450.

7. Cited in Albert Furtwangler, *The Authority of Publius: A Reading of the Federalist Papers* (Ithaca, NY: Cornell University Press, 1984), 21.

8. Jay Grossman suggests the gothic background to Federalist critiques in *Reconstituting the American Renaissance: Emerson, Whitman, and the Politics of Representation* (Durham, NC: Duke University Press, 2003), 74.

9. Cathy Davidson, *Revolution and the Word: The Rise of the Novel in America* (New York: Oxford University Press, 1986), 237.

10. Davidson, *Revolution and the Word*, 41.

11. Martin, *Instructed Vision*, 57–106; Henry May, *The Enlightenment in America* (New York: Oxford University Press, 1976), 337–62.

12. Rush, "The Effects of the American Revolution," 331.

13. Grossman, *Reconstituting the American Renaissance*, 71–74.

14. Furtwangler, *Authority of Publius*, 61–69; Daniel J. Boorstin, *The Genius of American Politics* (Chicago: University of Chicago Press, 1953), 96–98; Richard Hofstadter, "The Founding Fathers: An Age of Realism," in *The American Political Tradition* (New York: Vintage, 1989 [1948]), 3–22; for example, Thomas L. Pangle, *The Spirit of Modern Republicanism: The Moral Vision of the American Founders and the Philosophy of Locke* (Chicago: University of Chicago Press, 1988).

15. James Engell, *The Creative Imagination: Enlightenment to Romanticism* (Cambridge, MA: Harvard University Press, 1981).

16. Bailyn, *Ideological Origins of the American Revolution*, 352.

17. Bernard Bailyn, *To Begin the World Anew: The Genius and Ambiguities of the American Founders* (New York: Knopf, 2003), ix. See especially the chapter "Politics and the Creative Imagination."

18. Cited in Bailyn, *Ideological Origins of the American Revolution*, 352.

19. Martin Diamond, "Democracy and *The Federalist*: A Reconsideration of the Framers' Intent," *American Political Science Review* 53, no. 1 (1959): 52–68, 61. Morton White has nonetheless attempted to identify a systematic philosophy underlying Publius's arguments in *Philosophy, The Federalist, and the Constitution* (New York: Oxford University Press, 1989).

20. The literature detailing the Scottish Enlightenment's influence on eighteenth-century American political thought, and *The Federalist*, is extensive. For a useful overview vis-à-vis imagination, see Daniel Walker Howe, "Why the Scottish Enlightenment Was Useful to the Framers of the American Constitution," *Comparative Studies in Society and History* 31, no. 3 (1989): 572–87, 573; and Samuel Fleischacker, "The impact on America: Scottish philosophy and the American founding," in *The Cambridge Companion to The Scottish Enlightenment*, ed. Alexander Broadie (New York: Cambridge University Press, 2003), 316–37. Lance Banning lists much of the scholarship on Hume's influence in *The Sacred Fire of Liberty: James Madison & the Founding of the Federal Republic* (Ithaca, NY: Cornell University Press, 1995), 467n35.

21. Howe, "Why the Scottish Enlightenment," 584.

22. Eva Braun, *The World of the Imagination: Sum and Substance* (New York: Rowman & Littlefield, 1991), 84.

23. David Hume, *A Treatise of Human Nature*, ed. L. A. Selby-Bigge (New York: Oxford University Press, 1978), 267.

24. Hume, *Treatise*, 225.

25. Hume, *Treatis*, 267.

26. Frederick G. Whelan, *Order and Artifice in Hume's Political Philosophy* (Princeton, NJ: Princeton University Press, 1985), 99.

27. Edmund S. Morgan, *Inventing the People: The Rise of Popular Sovereignty in England and America* (New York: W. W. Norton, 1989), 153.

28. Gordon S. Wood, "The Democratization of Mind in the American Revolution," in *Leadership in the American Revolution, Papers Presented at the Third Symposium, May 9 and 10, 1974* (Washington, DC, 1974), 63–89. Woody Holton provides a wonderful account of this postrevolutionary crisis in authority in *Unruly Americans and the Origins of the Constitution* (New York: Hill and Wang, 2007).

29. Thomas Jefferson, *Notes on the State of Virginia*, ed. William Peden (Chapel Hill: University of North Carolina Press, 1982), 209–22.

30. Stephen Holmes, *Passions and Constraint: On the Theory of Liberal Democracy* (Chicago: University of Chicago Press, 1997), 134–77. I agree with Jeremy Waldron that Procrustes might be a better mythic figure than Ulysses to model these moments, insofar as they resemble not so much "the triumph of preemptive rationality," as an "artificially sustained ascendancy of one view in the polity." Jeremy Waldron, *Law and Disagreement* (New York: Oxford University Press, 1999), 268.

31. See Madison to Thomas Richtig, September 15, 1821, in Max Farrand, *The Records of the Federal Convention of 1787, Vol. 3* (New Haven, CT: Yale University Press, 1987), 447–48.

32. Hannah Arendt, *On Revolution* (New York: Penguin, 1990 [1963]), 198.

33. Thomas Jefferson to Samuel Kercheval, July 12, 1816, in *Political Writings*, ed. Joyce Appleby and Terence Ball (New York: Cambridge University Press, 1999), 210–17, 215.

34. Thomas Jefferson to James Madison, September 6, 1789, in *The Republic of Letters: The Correspondence between Jefferson and Madison, 1776–1826, I,* ed. James Morton Smith (New York: W. W. Norton, 1995), 631–36, 634; James Madison to Thomas Jefferson, February 4, 1790, in *The Republic of Letters, I,* 650–53, 652. Jefferson's belief that "the earth belongs *in usufruct* to the living" goes unnoticed in most discussions of this dimension of his thought. Usufruct is a right derived from civil law that qualifies the ownership of property by mandating its care and cultivation. Its Latin roots—*usus* and *fructus*—signify "use" and "fruit." This qualifier places obvious normative limitations and obligations on the "living generation," although Jefferson does not fully elaborate these limitations.

35. Knud Haakonssen, "The Structure of Hume's Political Theory," in *The Cambridge Companion to Hume,* ed. David Fate Norton (New York: Cambridge University Press, 1993), 182–221, 196.

36. David Hume, "The Skeptic," in *Essays: Moral, Political, and Literary* (New York: Cosimo Classics, 2006), 170.

37. See Abraham Lincoln, "Address to the Young Men's Lyceum of Springfield, Illinois," in *Abraham Lincoln: Speeches and Writing 1832–1858,* ed. Don E. Fehrenbacher (New York: Library of America, 1989), 28–36, 35.

38. "Brutus I," in *DHRC Vol. I. 21,* 411–21, 414.

39. Cited in Herbert J. Storing, *What the Anti-Federalists Were For* (Chicago: University of Chicago Press, 1981), 10.

40. *DHRC Vol. I,* 418.

41. *DHRC Vol. I,* 420.

42. David Waldstreicher, *In the Midst of Perpetual Fetes: The Making of American Nationalism, 1776–1820* (Chapel Hill: University of North Carolina Press, 1997), 53–107.

43. According to Samuel Beer, Publius's appeal to "better administration" as the ground of enhanced national attachments relied exclusively on arguments of "utility in the broadest sense"—the advantages of union listed, for example, in *Federalist* No. 27—and neglected aesthetic components of national belonging. For Publius, according to this account, utility alone "guided the cathexis" of nationalized citizens. Samuel Beer, *To Make a Nation: The Rediscovery of American Federalism* (Cambridge, MA: Harvard University Press, 1993), 364.

44. Sheldon Wolin, "Tending and Intending a Constitution: Bicentennial Misgivings," in *The Presence of the Past: Essays on the State and the Constitution* (Baltimore, MD: Johns Hopkins University Press, 1989), 82–99, 98.

45. The distinction is taken from Clifford Geertz, *Negara: The Theatre State in Nineteenth-Century Bali* (Princeton, NJ: Princeton University Press, 1980), 123.

46. Storing, *What the Anti-Federalists Were For,* 21.

47. Sheldon Wolin, *Politics and Vision: Continuity and Innovation in Western Political Thought* (London: George Allen & Unwin, 1960), 389.

48. Benedict Anderson, *Imagined Communities* (New York: Verso, 1983).

49. Robert A. Ferguson, "The Forgotten Publius," in *Reading the Early Republic* (Cambridge, MA: Harvard University Press, 2004), 151–71, 157.

50. This nationalization of "the people" helped navigate what democratic theorists call the "dilemma of constituency," or the "boundary problem," by substantializing the identity of the constituent people as the nation. As Bernard Yack has written, "the nation provides precisely what is lacking in the concept of the [constituent] people: a sense of where to look for the prepolitical basis of political community." See his "Popular Sovereignty and Nationalism," *Political Theory* 29, no. 4 (2001): 524; see also Rogers M. Smith, *Stories of Peoplehood: The Politics and Morals of Political Membership* (New York: Cambridge University Press, 2003).

51. Carroll Smith-Rosenberg, "Dis-covering the Subject of the 'Great Constitutional Discussion,' 1786–1789," *The Journal of American History* 79, no. 3 (1992): 841–73, 842.

52. Edward Millican, *One United People:* The Federalist Papers *and the National Idea* (Louisville: University Press of Kentucky, 1990), 65.

53. Hans J. Morgenthau, *Politics Among Nations* (New York: Knopf, 1954), 484–85.

54. Beer, *To Make a Nation*, 320–22.

55. Millican, *One United People*, 65.

56. *DHRC Vol. 1*, 420; later states' rights advocates invoked similar spectacles of regional affiliation, suggesting that, in John Calhoun's words, "the very idea of an American People . . . is a mere chimera." Cited in Beer, *To Make a Nation*, 317.

57. Ferguson, "Forgotten Publius," 161.

58. Wood, "Interests and Disinterestedness," 94.

59. Cited in Storing, *What the Anti-Federalists Were For*, 31.

60. Hector St. John de Crèvecoeur, *Letters from an American Farmer*, ed. Susan Manning (New York: Oxford University Press, 1997), 15.

61. Perry Miller, *Nature's Nation* (Cambridge, MA: Harvard University Press, 1967).

62. Ferguson, "Forgotten Publius," 161.

63. Edmund Burke, *Reflections on the Revolution in France*, ed. J. G. A. Pocock (Indianapolis: Hackett Publishing Company, 1987), 68.

64. Crèvecoeur, *Letters from an American Farmer*, 56.

65. Jed Rubenfeld, *Freedom and Time: A Theory of Constitutional Self-Government* (New Haven, CT: Yale University Press, 2001), 158. I explore the iterative logic of these expanding constituent claims in *Constituent Moments*.

66. Because the people must first imagine themselves to be a people before acting as such, the imagination is an enabling—but contestable—heteronomic support. *The Federalist* offers an exemplary (and perhaps surprising) navigation of this paradox of democratic legitimacy. For recent theoretical elaborations of this paradox, see Bonnie Honig, "Between Deliberation and Decision: Political Paradox in Democratic Theory," *American Political Science Review* 101, no. 1 (2006): 1–17; Alan Keenan, *Democracy in Question: Democratic Openness in a Time of Political Closure* (Stanford, CA: Stanford University Press, 2003); and Sofia Nässtrom, "The Legitimacy of the People," *Political Theory* 35, no. 5 (2007): 624–58.

67. Danielle Allen, "Imperfect People," in *Talking to Strangers: Anxieties of Citizenship since Brown v. Board of Education* (Chicago: University of Chicago Press, 2004), 69–84, 69.

68. See, for example, Bonnie Honig, "Declarations of Independence: Arendt and Derrida on the Problem of Founding a Republic," *American Political Science Review* 85, no. 1 (1991): 97–113.

69. Hume, *Treatise*, 566.

70. Daniel T. Rodgers evaluates this debate, and its limitations, in "Republicanism: The Career of a Concept," *The Journal of American History* 79, no. 1 (1992): 11–38.

71. Accounts of the sacred origin of the founding are generally embedded in broader tropes of American exceptionalism. See Sacvan Bercovitch, *American Jeremiad* (Madison: University of Wisconsin, 1978), and Ernest Lee Tuveson, *Redeemer Nation: The Idea of America's Millennial Role* (Chicago: University of Chicago Press, 1968).

72. Thomas West explores some of the main lines of difference in "Leo Strauss and the American Founding," *Review of Politics* 53, no. 1 (1991): 157–72.

73. Diamond, "Democracy and the Federalist," 53. The "assembly of demi-gods" is Jefferson's characterization.

74. Pangle, *Spirit of Modern Republicanism*, 8.

75. Gary Rosen, *American Compact: James Madison and the Problem of Founding* (Lawrence: University Press of Kansas, 1999), 464; also see his "James Madison and the Problem of Founding," *The Review of Politics* 58, no. 3 (1996): 561–95.

76. Diamond, "Democracy and the Federalist," 67.

77. Ralph Lerner, *Thinking Revolutionary: Principle and Practice in the New Republic* (Ithaca, NY: Cornell University Press, 1987), 30.

78. Diamond, "Democracy and the Federalist," 68.

79. Rosen, "James Madison," 581.

80. Jeremy Elkins, "Constitutional Enactment," *Political Theory* 33, no. 2 (2005): 280–97, 289.

81. Hume, *Treatise*, 566.

82. Frank I. Michelman, "How Can the People Ever Make the Laws? A Critique of Deliberative Democracy," in *Deliberative Democracy: Essays on Reason and Politics*, ed. James Bohman and William Rehg (Cambridge, MA: MIT Press, 1997), 145–72; Jürgen Habermas, "Constitutional Democracy: A Paradoxical Union of Contradictory Principles?" *Political Theory* 29, no. 6 (2001): 766–81, 775.

THREE

Governing Interest

Political writers have established it as a maxim that, in contriving any system of government and fixing the several checks and balances of the Constitution, every man ought to be supposed a knave, and to have no other end, in all his actions, than private interest. By this interest we must govern him, and by means of it, make him . . . cooperative to public good.

—David Hume, "Of the Independency of Parliament"[1]

There is no quarrel between government and liberty; the former is the shield and protector of the latter. The war is between government and licentiousness, faction, turbulence, and other violations of the rules of society.

—*Virginian Independent Chronicle*, March 12, 1788[2]

Four days after the Philadelphia Convention's delegates had assembled a quorum on May 25, 1787, Edmund Randolph "opened the main business" by proposing an entirely new system of federal government, one the Virginia delegates had drafted before the convention working largely from the notes of James Madison.[3] Randolph preceded his presentation of the Virginia Plan with a "long and elaborate speech" describing the crisis that brought the delegates to Philadelphia that summer and that threatened the "fulfillment of the prophecies of the American downfall." Randolph's account was multifaceted and overlapped on several points with the preparatory notes Madison had made earlier that spring detailing the "Vices of the Political System of the United States."[4]

Both men focused on the "imbecility" of the federal government created by the Articles of Confederation, but also criticized the popular politics that had taken hold in the states following the Revolution. "Our chief danger," Randolph warned the delegates, "arises from the democratic parts of our Constitutions."[5] There were defects not only in the decentral-

75

ized political institutions and powerful state legislatures created under the Articles but in the factious and licentious dispositions of "the people themselves." According to Randolph, the "prospect of anarchy" that loomed over America derived "from the laxity of government everywhere."[6] In his famous speech before the Philadelphia Convention Randolph argued that the Crisis Period of the 1780s was best understood as a crisis in governance, broadly understood. While "the year 1776 is celebrated for a revolution in favor of *Liberty*," one anonymous Federalist would write later that year, "the year 1787, it is expected, will be celebrated with equal joy, for a revolution in favor of *Government*."[7] For Randolph's contemporaries no term captured the broad crisis of governance in the 1780s better than "democracy" itself.[8]

Randolph and Madison were not the only convention delegates who feared "the prevailing rage of excessive democracy—this fashionable contempt of government."[9] Robert Morris of Pennsylvania argued that the convention must work to "restrain the democratic spirit."[10] Elbridge Gerry of Massachusetts declared "the evils we experience flow from the excess of democracy."[11] All sides agree, Publius would write, that "something is necessary to be done to rescue us from impending anarchy."[12] Summarizing these views, the historian Woody Holton argues that the prevailing sentiment of the convention delegates was that "the American Revolution had gone too far," and their "greatest hope was that the federal convention would find a way to put the democratic genie back in the bottle."[13] It was, in short, "the excesses of democracy that lay behind the elite's sense of crisis in the 1780s."[14]

But what did these founding figures and soon-to-be Federalists mean when they invoked democratic "excess"? Did they refer to the persistence of mobbing in the postrevolutionary years and the troubling appearance of popular insurrections against established republican government like Shays' Rebellion? Or was it the unchecked legislative power of many of the states, and their profuse and erratic legislation? Did they have in mind particular policies like Rhode Island's prodebtor paper money laws? Or perhaps they meant the licentiousness and jealousy of the people themselves and the disappearance of what Washington called "the spirit of subordination"?[15] Perhaps it was all of these elements combined?

Gordon Wood has argued that the Federalist worry about the excesses of democracy most importantly described their "deep disgust with the localist and interest-ridden politics" that characterized postrevolutionary America.[16] Reversing his famous claim in the conclusion of the *Creation of the American Republic* that the Federalist new science of politics marked "the end of classical politics," Wood more recently has argued that the Federalists instead "stood for a classical world" and that the "Constitution looked backward as much as it looked forward."[17] Conversely, the Anti-Federalists, despite their usual depiction as "men of little faith," "conservative," "backward looking," civic republican critics of political modernity,[18] are now presented by Wood as the true harbingers of modern politics: it was the Anti-Federalists "who really saw best and furthest," in that they prefigured the interest group pluralism that would come to define the politics of modern America.[19]

This reversal in Wood's historical assessment revolves around a changed evaluation of the concept of interest, a concept that has long preoccupied scholarly investigations into the political theory of *The Federalist*. Some of these investigations have treated interest as the key to Publius's understanding of moral psychology and human motivation.[20] Others have emphasized interest's central role in Publius's theory of political obligation, placing it at the center of his purportedly "economic theory of political attachment."[21] For many political theorists, both admiring and critical, Publius's embrace of interest as the foundation of politics is the hallmark of *The Federalist*'s political modernity and of Publius's *bona fides* as a political realist.[22]

This chapter also places interest at its conceptual center, but it tells a different story. With the crisis of the 1780s as the relevant background, I suggest we approach Publius's reliance on interest through the rubric of governance, understood not only in terms of the formal institutions of government (for example, *Federalist* No. 51's mechanistic understanding of checks and balances), or in terms of the behavior of elected representatives and government officials (*Federalist* No. 10's theory of filtration and invocation of a "chosen body of citizens, whose wisdom may best discern the true interest of their country") (*F*, 62), but also in terms of the governance of the conduct of the people themselves. This chapter, like the previous one, shifts the usual focus from the imagined conduct of the governors to that of the governed, to how Publius envisioned the organization of this conduct by the institutional mechanisms of the constitutional state.

"Nothing is more certain," Publius wrote, "than the indispensible necessity of Government," (*F*, 8) but only a *republican* government was "reconcilable with the genius of the people of America" (*F*, 166): "all our political experiments" must be based "on the capacity of mankind for self-government" (*F*, 250). *The Federalist* argued that the proposed Constitution would provide "a Republican remedy for the diseases most incident to Republican Government" (*F*, 65), a "powerful means by which the excellencies of republican government [most notably its liberties] may be retained and its imperfections [most notably its tendency to "tempestuous waves of sedition and party-rage"] lessened or avoided" (*F*, 51). Interest, I will argue here, was an essential part of Publius's new logic of republican governance, one that aimed through institutional design to effect what Publius described as an unprecedented "amelioration of popular systems of government" (*F*, 51).

If government is best and most broadly understood as what Michel Foucault calls "the conduct of conduct,"[23] interest, as Albert O. Hirsch-

man similarly argues, is best understood as "a manner or *style* of conduct," one organized by reasoned calculation and considered instrumen-
tal action.[24] The citizen whose conduct is organized by interest is not only
a reliable, productive, and reasonable citizen, but also an "eminently
governable" citizen.[25] The same may be said, as we will see, of the interested faction. Approaching interest as a mode of governance leads to a
different understanding of the role of interest in *The Federalist*, and, following this, a different understanding of the oft-proclaimed modernity of
The Federalist's new science of politics. This emphasis situates *The Federalist* within what Foucault described as a "new economy of government
reason" that emerged in the eighteenth century, one that conceived of the
interested "freedom of the governed as a technical means of securing the
ends of government."[26] "Governmental reason in its modern form," Foucault writes, "is a reason that functions in terms of interest."[27] While
scholars have attributed a number of dramatic innovations to *The Federalist*—marking a paradigm shift from civic humanism to liberalism, for
example, or marking the emergence of a modern "scientific" approach to
the study of politics—few have approached the text as an exemplary
theoretical articulation of emerging logics of governmentality.[28] This is
one of the central tasks of this chapter.

Certain theoretical and historiographical preoccupations have obscured the governmental operation of interest in Publius's argument. The
familiar opposition between virtue and interest, for example, which has
often preoccupied proponents of the liberal and civic republican interpretations of *The Federalist*, has obscured the governmental dimensions of
interest, because the opposition mistakenly conceives of interest as *prior*
to politics rather than itself the *outcome* of political organization. In *The
Federalist*, interest is not opposed to the formative politics associated with
earlier forms of civic republicanism—forms that, in Herbert Storing's
words, treated the "whole organization of the polity as having an educative function"[29]—but is itself profoundly formative. In *The Federalist*,
interest works as both a premise of human behavior and a program of
reform, as both a descriptive and a normative category.[30]

Interest is at once what Hamilton called "the principle of human nature on which all political speculation, to be just, must be founded," and
an instituted mode of conduct that establishes a "broad and even foundation" for republican governance.[31] While classical republicanism typically depicted interest as "dangerously disruptive and corrosive of the foundations of society," Publius, following Hume, understood interest as a
cornerstone of modern governance. Publius agreed with Hume that men
must be governed by interest, "and by means of it, [made] . . . cooperative
to public good."[32] "Rather than being limited, [interests] are multiplied
and diversified" in Publius's argument and through "a spontaneous
combinatory scheme . . . they converge" around a long-term national
interest.[33]

The project of governance defended by Publius sought to institutionally interpellate citizens into a more efficiently regulated and stable economy of power and freedom—a *novus ordo seclorum*—that was not subject to the "perpetual vibrations," "rapid succession of revolutions," and "tempestuous waves of sedition and party rage" that "disfigure the annals of [past] republics," throwing them into recurrent Polybian cycles of decline and regeneration (*F*, 50–51). It was Publius's hope that such "endless cycles of history could be finally broken."[34] Interest promised a more governable republicanism, one not subject to the debilitating "vicissitudes and uncertainties" of earlier republics, and their lamentable tendency to be overwhelmed by "perpetual vibration," popular "paroxism," "fluctuation," and "convulsions" (*F*, 234, 50, 104, 426, 28). Under the logic of this new governmental reason, the order of republican governance would not spring from uncertain collective deliberations over competing public goods—deliberations that have introduced "the instability, injustice, and confusion . . . into the public councils," and that Publius describes as "the mortal diseases under which popular governments have every where perished" (*F*, 57)—but rather from the mechanical combination of competing interests establishing a stable and productive order of governance " behind the backs" of its interested agents. As clearly argued in *Federalist* No. 10, while Publius hoped that national representatives could transcend narrow parochial interests to govern in the interest of the country as a whole, he held out no such faith for the people themselves. Publius offered a political economy that forecast the probabilistic and indirect emergence of "an enlarged and permanent interest" over time (*F*, 283). The ends of republican government were not the product of collective will and design, then, but, mimicking the economic logic of the invisible hand, emerged from an economy of indirect, aggregative, and invisible mechanisms. It was governance by aggregative tendency.

Rather than holding interest responsible for the *crisis* of governance in the 1780s—and therefore treating interest as a *problem* for republican government to overcome—interest is envisioned by Publius as an important part of the *solution* to that crisis. In *The Federalist*, Publius converted interest from an obstacle into a tool of republican governance. In doing so, he established a political economy of freedom and power that contrasted sharply with the prevailing assumptions of much Revolutionary American political discourse about republican governance and its relation to popular liberties (a contrast frequently exploited by his Anti-Federalist critics). Explaining these assumptions, Bernard Bailyn writes that "the public world" of the Revolution was "divided into distinct, contrasting and innately antagonistic spheres: the sphere of power and the sphere of liberty. The one was brutal, ceaselessly active, and heedless; the other was delicate, passive, and sensitive. The one must be resisted, the other defended, and the two must never be confused."[35]

Through the concept of interest Publius united these formerly antagonistic spheres into a different logic of republican governance, one that
would govern through the (interested) freedom of citizens rather than in
direct opposition to this freedom, where power would be self-limiting or
self-correcting rather than dependent wholly on the external checks of a
vigilant and mobilized citizenry. For Publius, the postrevolutionary reliance on jealousy and vigilance, with its presumed opposition between
liberty and power, had greatly contributed to the crisis of governance in
the 1780s. This chapter examines Publius's departure from the understanding of republican governance exemplified by the radical Whig political discourse of the American Revolution, and the central role that interest plays in Publius's alternative.

I.

The American Revolution, which had engendered a remarkable outpouring of public-spirited action and political virtue, also fueled the rapid
expansion of commerce in the former colonies. "No event in the eighteenth century accelerated capitalistic development of America more than
did the Revolutionary War."[36] To many political writers in the 1770s and
1780s the Revolution's outpouring of virtuous action in defense of popular liberties was all too quickly replaced by narrowly self-seeking and
interested behavior by the newly independent citizenry. Jefferson, for
example, was repulsed by the spectacle of Americans abandoning all else
but "the sole faculty of making money."[37] Understood through the classical republican narratives that shaped American understandings of the
Revolution, this worrisome development seemed to herald the corruption of the citizenry and threaten the subversion of the new republican
states. "The failure of the people to display the public spirit on which all
republics were assumed to rest," Lance Banning writes, "produced a crisis of the Revolution."[38] "Self-immersion" or what Tocqueville would
later theorize in terms of a narrowing "individualism" was considered
fatally dangerous in a republic, and to many observers the proliferation
of self-interested behavior seemed to signal a premature decline of America's republican experiment.[39]

In part, this concern was rooted in the traditional civic republican
opposition of virtue to interest, a conceptual opposition that has also
often framed the historiographical debates between proponents of the
republican and liberal paradigms. Montesquieu influentially captured
this opposition in *The Spirit of the Laws* when he wrote that republics
require the inculcation of virtue. "One can define this virtue as love of the
laws and the homeland. This love, requiring continuous preference of the
public interest over one's own, produces all the individual virtues."[40] For
many historians of the period, this contrast serves as an important criteria

for distinguishing between a classical and a modern republicanism, or between republicanism and liberalism. In the *Machiavellian Moment*, for example, J. G. A. Pocock writes,

> The decline of virtue had as its logical corollary the rise of interest. . . . Interest was both a limiting and an expanding force. As Federalist thought took shape, and people were less and less seen as possessing virtue in the classical sense, it is not surprising to find, in Madison's writings and those of others—the tenth issue of *The Federalist* is the *locus classicus*—an increasing recognition of the importance, and the legitimacy, in human affairs of the faction pursuing a collective but particular interest, which in older Country and republican theory had figured as one of the most deadly means to the corruption of virtue by passion.[41]

The contrast between virtue and interest, and the concomitant equation of interest with corrupting passion, signals for Pocock and many others the Federalist departure from "the classical theory of the individual as a civic and active being" and toward an individual "conscious chiefly of his interest" and who takes "part in government in order to press for its realization."[42] How this interested conduct was to be managed and regulated was an important topic of political discussion in the period. In the 1780s there was a growing division, Wood writes, between those "who clung to moral reform and the regeneration of men's hearts as the remedy for viciousness and those who looked to mechanical devices and institutional contrivances as the only lasting solution for America's ills."[43] The moralists tended to emphasize virtues and the qualities of individual character whereas the institutional thinkers tended to emphasize the indirect management and regulation *of* interests rather than their direct overcoming.

This classical republican contrast of (bad) self-interested behavior with (good) altruistic virtuous behavior obscures the historical understanding of the postrevolutionary American approach to virtue and interest. For one thing, as James Kloppenburg has shown, virtue carried diverse and competing connotations in the period: republican martial virtues, Christian morality, bourgeois civility, and so forth.[44] While there was widespread concern in the period with declining public virtue, the political discourses of the 1770s and 1780s, like those of the decade leading up to the Revolution, very rarely demanded altruistic selflessness or the wholesale sacrifice of private interest to the public good. Instead, a central and frequently reiterated claim of the radical Whig discourses of the Revolution was that public vigilance or "jealousy" was the only way to maintain the liberty of the republic, check the power of government, and *also* protect the private interests of its citizens. Interested behavior was, in other words, acceptable so long as it was limited to its proper sphere outside of politics. While virtuous self-sacrifice was not the key to postrevolutionary American understandings of republican governance, it was widely believed that political and civil liberties could only be secured through public vigilance and the jealousy of power. "There is a degree of watchfulness," as Samuel Adams wrote to Elbridge Gerry, "upon which the liberties of mankind much depend."[45] "Jealousy and suspicion of all bodies set above the people was," Wood summarizes, "a cardinal principle of radical Whiggism."[46] The contrast of interest with "jealousy" reveals aspects of Publius's arguments that are obscured by the more familiar contrast of interest with virtue.

In *The Federalist* Publius described these widespread American assumptions as the "spirit" or "maxims" of "republican jealousy" (*F*, 183, 245). These assumptions were paradigmatically articulated in *Cato's Letters*, which Clinton Rossiter accurately described as "the most popular, quotable, esteemed source of political ideas in the colonial period."[47] Writing under the pseudonym Cato, John Trenchard and Thomas Gordon railed against the corruption of the English court and Robert Walpole's Ministry in the early 1720s, and warned of the devastating effect of this corruption on popular liberties, public spirit, and the principles of the Ancient Constitution. Cato appealed time and again to virtue, but not to a "philosophical virtue," which he understood as an unrealistic altruism or selflessness. Instead, Cato asked readers "only that they follow virtue as their interest"[48] — that is, recognize that political participation and vigilant civic mindedness were necessary securities of their private interests. "To say that private men have nothing to do with government," Cato wrote, "is to say that private men have nothing to do with their own happiness and misery."[49] Because the private goods of men are preserved by the collective, "it is the duty of every individual to be concerned for the whole."[50] This concern was manifest first and foremost in vigilant attention to "all publick Measures," because power is never "possessed without some abuse."[51] "Jealousy and revenge, in a whole people are," Cato remarks, "laudable and politick virtues, without which they will never thrive, never be esteemed."[52] Rome itself owed "the long preservation of its liberties," Cato continued, "to this spirit of jealousy and revenge."[53] Jefferson would later gave this maxim a classic and concise formulation in the Kentucky Resolution: "confidence is everywhere the parent of despotism — free government is founded in jealousy and not in confidence; it is jealousy and not confidence which prescribes limited Constitutions, to bind down those whom we are obliged to trust with power."[54]

The "spirit" or "maxims" of "republican jealousy" are one of the basic assumptions underwriting many Anti-Federalist criticisms of the Constitution. For Anti-Federalists, as Herbert Storing succinctly writes, "the spirit of '76 was not to trust in rulers."[55] For prominent Anti-Federalists like Elbridge Gerry and Patrick Henry, popular jealousy and vigilance were the principal — but also very fragile — means of checking the always-encroaching power of government. Anti-Federalists feared that the Constitution removed governors from direct accountability and asked citizens to place an undue trust or "confidence" in their governors. "The Anti-Federalists saw themselves in 1787–1788 fighting the good old Whig cause," writes Gordon Wood, "in defense of the people's liberties against the engrossing power of their rulers."[56] Anti-Federalists likened the Philadelphia Convention to a corrupt aristocratic conspiracy, and the federal government proposed at Philadelphia to the tyranny of George III. The prominent Anti-Federalist Cato argued that Federalists were intent on "preventing [the people's] interference in government."[57] Cato was responding in part to the New York Federalist Caesar (Alexander Hamilton), who had argued that the people were "very ill qualified to judge for themselves what government will best suit their peculiar situations," and that the people should therefore assume "a tractable and docile disposition."[58] As a question of "political safety," Cato responded, citizens must be forever vigilant against these "vultures of power."[59]

Underwriting this opposition between a vigilant or jealous citizenry and the encroaching power of government, is a logic of governance that directly opposed power to liberty and that identified the terrain of politics as a perpetual struggle between these forever contrasting forces. Nowhere is this logic more clearly exemplified in the ratification debates than in the vociferous arguments provoked by the convention's failure to provide a bill of rights with the proposed Constitution. The absence of a bill of rights was one of the most frequent—and, for Federalists, most worrisome—Anti-Federalist criticisms of the Constitution, and the eventual inclusion of the Bill of Rights is frequently hailed as the Anti-Federalists greatest political legacy. "While the Federalists gave us the Constitution," Storing writes, "the legacy of the Anti-Federalists was the Bill of Rights."[60]

Anti-Federalists worried that the absence of a bill of rights further eroded the liberties of the people in the face of the consolidation of federal power organized under the proposed Constitution. They typically sought an enumeration of popular liberties like those that prefaced many of the state constitutions created after Independence was declared. The purpose of these sometimes quite elaborate lists was to educate the citizenry about their inalienable rights so as to make them more vigilant and watchful of their governments. "The fundamental case for a bill of rights," as Storing writes, "is that it can be a prime agency of that political and moral education of the people on which free republican government depends." I agree, but the morality that Storing emphasizes here can be easily misleading. It is not virtue that the Anti-Federalists typically demanded of the citizenry, but virtù.[61] Anti-Federalists did not hope that a bill of rights would produce simply a more moral citizenry but a more vigilant and jealous citizenry. Announcing the rights and liberties of citizens was not a call for virtuous altruism but a catalyst of the popular protection of these rights and liberties. It was envisioned as a catalyst of populist republican accountability.

Publius took a dim view of these invitations to popular vigilance and jealousy in *The Federalist*, which he feared contributed significantly to the perpetuation of the postrevolutionary crisis in governance that the Constitution sought to resolve. While Publius acknowledged that bills of rights were essential in a mixed monarchy like Britain's, he denied their usefulness in a republic whose authority was based in the consent of the people. "Bills of rights are in their origin," Publius argued in *Federalist* No. 84, "stipulations between kings and their subjects, abridgements of prerogative in favor of privilege. They have no application to Constitutions professedly founded upon the power of the people, and executed by their immediate representatives and servants" (*F*, 578). For Publius, the only bill of rights needed was the preamble's invocation of "We the People" and the institutional organization and safeguards of the Constitution itself. Indeed, he argued that the careful enumeration of rights demanded by Anti-Federalists "are not only unnecessary in the proposed Constitution but would even be dangerous" (*F*, 579).

According to Publius and other prominent Federalists like James Wilson, the danger of including such provisions was that in their very claims of protection they would imply that more power had been granted to the federal government under the Constitution than was indeed the case. Whatever was not explicitly granted to the federal government under the Constitution was presumed to be reserved to the states. Publius, in effect, argued that if a right declaring the freedom of the press was included in a bill of rights, it would dangerously imply that the federal government had the right to regulate the press. This, as many Anti-Federalists noted, was a somewhat disingenuous argument. The proposed Constitution explicitly granted a great deal of power to the energized federal government, including the power of Congress to tax citizens directly and the worrisome ambiguities of the "necessary and proper" clause. What actually animated the Federalist critique of the Anti-Federalist demand for a bill of rights was the "seldom explicitly stated fear that a bill of rights, especially undue emphasis on a bill of rights might weaken *government*."[62]

Publius's multifaceted and not entirely consistent arguments against including a bill of rights never directly confronted the Anti-Federalist's main argument about the vital educative function such an enumeration would have for a vigilant citizenry. Indeed, Publius neglects this central issue entirely when in *Federalist* No. 84 he seems to at once quietly acknowledge and displace this Anti-Federalist argument. Declarations of rights, he argues there, "must altogether depend on public opinion, and on the general spirit of the people and of the government. And here . . . must we seek the only solid basis of all our rights" (*F*, 580). However, it was precisely such a "solid basis" of opinion that many Anti-Federalists hoped the bill of rights would work to effect and sustain.

In arguing against the inclusion of a bill of rights, Publius was also trying to shape the "solid basis" of public opinion and popular imagination, albeit in a very different way. By arguing that the Constitution itself *is* a bill of rights in that it "declares and specifies the political privileges of the citizens in the structure and administration of the government" (*F*, 581), Publius hoped to overcome the antagonistic relationship between the people, their liberties, and the government, and instead integrate them without remainder within the institutional organization of the constitutional state.

Publius believed that the antagonistic logic between power and liberty of the radical Whigs—so crucial, as Bailyn shows, to the political discourses of the Revolution—no longer held true in a representative republic. He sought to replace the "ferocious populism" and vigilance of radical Whig republicanism, with an elite republicanism premised upon the "solid basis" of a citizenry primarily animated by its imagined self-interest.[63] One of the many difficulties faced by Publius in the ratification debates—alongside the well-known association of republicanism with small territories and the association of commerce with political corruption—was to overcome the popular assumptions woven into the oppositional logic of republican governance associated with the discourses of the Revolution itself. Publius understood the radical Whig remedy to the encroachments of power—jealousy and vigilance cultivated by the people themselves—as a contributing factor to the postrevolutionary crisis of governance; he therefore sought to base the liberty of the republic on more secure and reliable foundations than the volatile political passions of vigilance or jealousy.

"Jealousy," Publius writes in *Federalist* No. 1, "is the usual concomitant of violent love" (*F*, 30). He warns readers against the lures of "an indiscriminate and unbounded jealousy, with which all reasoning must be vain":

> The sincere friends of liberty who give themselves up to the extravagancies of this passion are not always aware of the injury they do their own cause. As there is a degree of depravity in mankind which requires a certain degree of circumspection and distrust, so there are other qualities in human nature which justify a certain portion of esteem and confidence. Republican government presupposes the existence of these qualities in a higher degree than any other form. Were the pictures which have been drawn by the political jealousy of some among us faithful likenesses of the human character, the inference would be that there is not sufficient virtue among men for self-government. (*F*, 378)

While jealousy had been useful in the context of the Revolution, Publius argued, it was now working to undermine America's fragile experiment in republican government. He worried that "an overscrupulous jealousy of danger to the rights of the people" was serving as "bait to popularity at the expense of the public good" (*F*, 5). Postrevolutionary Americans had forgotten that "the vigor of government is also essential to the security of liberty" (*F*, 5). As I argued in the preceding chapter, the freedoms of a jealous citizenry were too prone to excess; they relied on volatile passions rather than understanding and based political judgments in unfounded assumptions rather than analysis.

Publius's critique of the "spirit" and "maxims" of "republican jealousy," alongside his embrace of a more durable republicanism based on interests, resonates closely with arguments from Hume's *Essays*, and, as Douglas Adair and Gary Wills have persuasively shown, were very likely influenced by these arguments. Hume, too, worries that the popular vigilance and public virtue celebrated in radical Whig political discourse was itself a source of republican instability. "The virtue and good intentions of CATO and BRUTUS are highly laudable," Hume writes, "but to what purpose did their zeal serve? To nothing, but to hasten the fatal period of ROMAN government, and render its convulsions and dying agonies more violent and painful."[64] More than any other set of theoretical texts, Hume's *Essays* modeled the new logic of governance based on interest that Publius would apply to his explanation of American constitutionalism.

In the *Essays* Hume argued that his contemporaries had been so captivated by the virtue of ancient republican examples that they had failed to see how modern institutional organization might resolve the cyclical volatility characteristic of past republics, and establish government on reliable institutional mechanisms rather than on the always changing "humors and tempers of men."[65] As Publius would later do, Hume completely rejected the supposed conflict that radical Whigs had established between civic strength and commerce or luxury. Hume greatly influenced what Ralph Lerner has characterized as the "commercial republicanism" of Publius and other Federalists.[66] Consider Hume's characterization of the governance of conduct in the following passage from "Of Commerce":

> Could we convert a city into a kind of fortified camp, and infuse into each breast so martial a genius, and such a passion for the public good, as to make every one willing to undergo the greatest hardship for the sake of the public; these affections might now, as in ancient times, prove alone a sufficient spur to industry and support the community. . . . But as these principles are too disinterested and too difficult to support, it is requisite to govern men by other passions, *and animate them* with a spirit of avarice and industry, art and luxury. . . . [In this case,] the harmony of the whole is still supported; and the natural bent

of the mind being more complied with, individuals, as well as the public, find their account in the observance of those maxims.[67]

The shift from the image of a "fortified camp" imposing virtue on a recalcitrant humanity to the orchestrated animation of passions compliant with "the natural bent of the mind" is a powerful example of what Foucault characterized as the logic of modern governmentality, where "government doesn't dictate so much as orchestrate conduct," and where power is not envisioned in opposition to freedom, but instead "requires the activity and freedom of the governed."[68] The interested passions of "avarice and industry, art and luxury," are, moreover, not to be simply presumed, but must be *animated* to support and establish a "harmony of the whole." According to Publius, as we will see, the governmental strategy of "supplying by opposite and rival interests, the defect of better motives," could "be traced through the whole system of human affairs, private as well as public" (*F*, 349).

For Hume and Publius, then, the self-seeking and interested behavior of a commercial society, far from being an impediment to republican government, would found it on more reliable and reasonable conduct. It would base governance in a "system of natural liberties." "Laws, order, police, discipline," Hume writes, "these can never be carried to any degree of perfection, before human reason has refined itself by exercise, and by an application to more vulgar arts, at least of commerce and manufacture." Similarly, Publius argued that the "commercial character of America," and its "unequalled spirit of enterprise," would have a refining and calming effect on popular manners and conduct. Tocqueville would celebrate the success of this strategy of governance several decades later by describing Americans as a "host of law-abiding, sober, moderate, careful and self-controlled citizens."[69]

II.

In his 1978 and 1979 lectures at the *Collège de France*, Foucault argued that the emergence of a "new governmental reason" in the eighteenth century is premised first and foremost on interest. It is a "government of interests, a government which works through and with interests, both those of individuals and increasingly those attributed to the population itself."[70] While recent studies of governmentality have looked for dynamics of governmentality apart from or below the state—an approach captured, for example, by the very title of Nikolas Rose's and Peter Miller's "Political Power Beyond the State: Problematics of Government"[71]—Publius's arguments, along with Hume's, show that these arguments were also central to late eighteenth-century debates about the organization of the constitutional state itself and the political conduct of its citizens. This would seem to accord with Foucault's own views. Governmentality, Foucault argues, "is at once internal and external to the state." "In framing a government," Publius writes, "the great difficulty lies in this: You must first enable the government to control the governed; and in the next place, oblige it to control itself." Publius's navigation of this "great difficulty" in framing government rejected the "polemic understanding of politics directed against the state apparatus" characteristic of the radical Whigs, and the jealous and vigilant conduct of citizens implied by that more populist republicanism.[72] In its place, Publius argued for an integrated economy of freedom and power premised on the interested conduct of citizens not only in their economic transactions within civil society, but also in their explicitly political or civic behavior as well. Supporting this broad claim requires a closer look at the role of interest in Publius's argument, as well as in the broader political discourses of the period.

Any study of interest in *The Federalist* should begin—although not end—with *Federalist* No. 10's account of factions. In attempting to provide "a Republican remedy for the diseases most incident to Republican Government," Publius elaborated there the alternative governmental logic described above. The alternative logic is in fact already captured in the famous contrast that frames the argument of *Federalist* No. 10. "There are . . . two methods of curing the mischiefs of faction," Publius writes, "the one, by removing its causes; the other by controlling its effects" (*F*, 58). In opting for the latter method, Publius establishes a strategy of governance that not only rejects tyrannical attempts to destroy the liberty essential to factions, but that also abandons the classical republican attempt to give every citizen "the same opinions, the same passions, the same interests" (*F*, 58). However, this in itself does not point to Publius's abandonment of "formative politics." As we will see, interest, too, is envisioned as an effect of formative politics and the organized political imagination.

The centrality of interest to the argument of *Federalist* No. 10, for both its admirers and its critics, was first emphasized in the work of Charles Beard, who set the stage for subsequent investigations into Publius's reevaluation of the role of interest in republican politics. In his *Economic Interpretation of the Constitution of the United States* (1913), Beard not only claimed to expose the narrow economic interests motivating participants in the Philadelphia Convention, and thereby debunk the heroic authority of the Founding, but to do so by following the "political science" laid out by the founders themselves. In *Federalist* No. 10, an essay that Beard canonized as, in Douglass Adair's words, "the essay most often quoted to explain the philosophy of the Fathers and thus the 'ultimate meaning' of the United States Constitution itself,"[73] Beard discovered what he called "a masterly statement of the theory of economic determinism in politics."[74] "Politics and Constitutional law," Beard proclaimed on the basis of this theory, are "inevitably a reflex of . . . contending [class] interests."[75]

Beard based this now thoroughly discredited claim on a lengthy—and self-servingly selective—quotation from *Federalist* No. 10. While Beard emphasized Publius's claim that "those who hold and those who are without property have ever formed distinct interests in society," and that "the various and unequal distribution of property" has been "the most common and durable source of factions," he omitted entirely from his discussion the preceding sentences regarding the *multiple* sources of faction. These sentences surveying many other causes of faction undermine Beard's attempt to reduce No. 10's account of interest to a narrow economic determinism (and to sharply separate "interest," for example, from "imagination"). I quote the relevant omitted passage in full:

> The latent causes of faction are thus sown in the nature of man; and we see them every where brought into different degrees of activity, according to the different circumstances of civil society. A zeal for different opinions concerning religion, concerning Government and many other points, as well of speculation as of practice; an attachment to different leaders ambitiously contending for pre-eminence and power; or to persons of other descriptions whose fortunes have been interesting to the human passions, have in turn divided mankind into parties, inflamed them with mutual animosity, and rendered them much more disposed to vex and oppress each other, than to co-operate for their common good. So strong is this propensity of mankind to fall into mutual animosities, that where no substantial occasion presents itself, the most frivolous and fanciful distinctions have been sufficient to kindle their unfriendly passions, and excite their most violent conflicts. (*F*, 59)

Like Hume, Publius makes it clear in this passage that while the *latent* sources of faction are "sown into the nature of man," how these become actualized or animated is contextually dependent on "the different circumstances of civil society." Interest is presented in *Federalist* No. 10 as *one* source—and for Publius, again as for Hume, a far preferable and governable source—of faction. It is, moreover, a source of faction that does not naturally precede politics, but is "brought into . . . activity" by pre-existing social and political relations. It is a product of social or political organization.

Many of Beard's critics have shown that a richer and more complicated theory of faction was at work in *The Federalist*, one more attuned to the complexities of human motivation and moral psychology than Beard's reductive and determinist account of material interest. The lists of factors influencing human action in *The Federalist*—"such as honor, oaths, reputation, conscience, the love of country, and family affections and attachments"—are worlds away from both the quasi-Marxist class analysis of Beard and the reductive economism of utility-maximizing methodologies in the social sciences.

Publius notes that "the supposition of universal venality in human nature is little less an error in political reasoning than the supposition of universal rectitude," and he councils that one should "see human nature as it is" without "flattering its virtues or exaggerating its vices" (*F*, 514). In this, too, Publius closely followed Hume, who, in his essay "Of Parties in General," makes clear that "factions are not mere interest groups. They can galvanize behavior that is simultaneously selfless and unspeakably vicious toward others."[76] Just as Hume divided the sources of factions into different types ("personal," and "real") and subtypes (real factions divided into those "from *interest*, from *principal*, and from *affection*"), so did Publius, as the above quote indicates, dwell on the multiple causes of faction.[77]

These important corrections to Beard's economistic and reductive view of interest aside, most explorations of the role of interest in *The Federalist's* political theory still miss the formative or programmatic dimension of Publius's account. Like Beard, many of the revisionists understand interest as first and foremost a (realist) theory of human motivation; they treat it as a moral psychology, a crucial aspect of Publius's supposed philosophy of human nature, rather than a problem of governance and a style of conduct. James P. Scanlon, for example, describes *The Federalist* as "one of the most comprehensive treatments of political motivation in existence," and parses out passions, virtue, and interest as different and competing motivations.[78] Similarly, Morton White in his careful reconstruction of the implied philosophical arguments of *The Federalist* distinguishes reason, passion, and interest as conceptually distinct—but practically blurred—psychological motives. "There *is* a psychological theory of human nature to be found in *The Federalist*," he writes, "even though it is never systematically expounded by the authors."[79]

These accounts persuasively reveal the fine texture of Publius's understanding of human motivation, and they agree that, again like Hume, Publius downgrades the motivating power of reason in politics: "a nation of philosophers is as little to be expected as the philosophical race of kings wished for by Plato." But in weaving interest into the nature of man, they neglect Publius's understanding of it as a product and tool of governance. In treating interest as a part of a philosophy of human nature, these approaches neglect how interest can be elicited, activated, or animated by government and directed in its service. Foucault's focus on governmentality brings this dimension much more clearly into view.

Just as Hume believed that "of all factions," those based on interest "are the most reasonable, and the most excusable," so did Publius argue that factions of interest could convert factions from the principal source of republican instability, to the key of durable republican governance.[80] David Epstein has insightfully explored the different kinds of faction spawned by opinions, passions, and interests. As the "springs" of action, these "latent" propensities, Epstein writes, give birth to factions of differ-ent character.[81]

But what was it about *interested* factions that Publius found so salu-tary? A full answer to this question has to turn not only to interest as a component of human motivation, a particular *end* of human action, but also as a "style of conduct," a *means* of action. Publius envisioned interest as a tool of government ("the conduct of conduct") in both senses. As a reliable motivation, interest could more securely attach the people to a government that protected those interests. As a more reasonable style of conduct, interest made for what Tocqueville called "law-abiding, sober, moderate, careful and self-controlled citizens." In both instances the most illuminating contrast is not between interest and virtue, but between interest and passion (and in particular, I would argue, the political pas-sion of jealousy).

In his classic study of the passions and the interests, Albert Hirschman writes that in the eighteenth century interest is "wedged between two traditional theories of human motivation: passion and reason. . . . Interest was seen to partake, in effect, of the better nature of each, as the passion of self-love upgraded and contained by reason, and as reason given di-rection and force by that passion. The resulting hybrid form of human action was considered exempt from both the destructiveness of passion and the ineffectuality of reason."[82] While appeals to reason and virtue aimed to repress the dangerous passions, a goal that most postrevolu-tionary Americans agreed was naïve and unrealistic, interest "harnessed" (Hirschman) or "canalized" (Foucault) the passions. But for Hirschman it is not the ends of interest that are most important in understanding the increasingly prominent role in played in eighteenth-century Anglophone political thought, but its manner. Hirschman's central thesis is that inter-est emerged as a privileged term of first political, and then economic, thought not in opposition to selfless virtue, but in opposition to volatile and ungovernable passions. The focus of much of the literature Hirsch-man covers in his study contrasts "the favorable effects that follow when men are guided by their interests with the calamitous state of affairs that prevails when men give free rein to their passions."[83]

Publius clearly fits this broader view. When Publius writes that "the regulation of various and competing interests forms the principal task of modern Legislation," he is referring explicitly to "the most common and durable source of faction," which is the diverse interests that "grow up of necessity in civilized nations": those who have and do not have property, creditors and debtors, "a landed interest, a manufacturing interest, a mer-cantile interest, a monied interest, and many lesser interests" (*F*, 59). Pub-lius thereby contrasts more modern, civilized, and acceptable factions of interest with premodern, barbaric, and volatile factions of passion. These latter factions, as Publius makes clear in *Federalist* No. 10, are far more likely to "vex and oppress each other." While Publius is clear that "the spirit and party of faction" is involved in the "necessary and ordinary operations of Government," this necessity, he seems to hope, will be limited to the more reliable and governable factions of interests.

"Why has government been instituted at all?" Publius famously asked in *The Federalist*. "Because the passions of men will not conform to the dictates of reason and justice, without constraint . . . [:] passions ought to be controlled and regulated by the government" (*F*, 96). This constraint, control, and regulation is necessary because impulsive passions in politics are dangerous, changing, unpredictable. Publius rails, for example, against the "impulses of rage, resentment, jealousy, avarice, and of other irregular and violent propensities" (*F*, 32). He emphasizes throughout the series the dangerous "impulse of sudden and violent passions." However, Publius also admits the futility of governing the passions through simple repression: citizens cannot be reliably governed by reason or virtue alone. Interest is a crucial way that passions may be "controlled and regulated," if not simply opposed or repressed.

It is true that Publius frequently couples passion and interest in his argument (I count sixteen times), or seems to suggest their interchangeability. In *Federalist* No. 10, for example, Publius defines faction as a number of citizens "united and actuated by some common impulse of passion, or of interest." But here and elsewhere this very coupling makes it clear that Publius distinguishes conceptually between passions and interests. He also makes a distinction between interests and "immediate interests" or "momentary interests," equating these latter categories more closely with the passions. There are several components of interested conduct—both individual and collective—that lead Publius to rely on it as a solution to the crisis of governance, and to thereby assert a new and more perpetual logic of republican governance than that characterized by the radical Whig discourses of the Revolution. Three important components of governable interest are duration, communicability, and suitability to mechanical economies of governance and representation. In each instance the operative contrast is interest and passion rather than interest and virtue.

Interests have constancy and duration and are reliable. Like Hume, Publius contrasts the institutional regularities and rule-bound procedures of modern republics with the unreliable dependency on personal character, whim, and passion in ancient republics. The writings of both are filled with what Publius calls the "horror and disgust" of the vicissitudes of classical republics and their unreliable dependence on the whims of personal power. Political science, as both make clear, cannot be based on whimsical acts of extraordinary individuals, but only on calculable and rule-governed behavior that works in terms of aggregate, probabilistic regularities. Interest is the behavioral correlate of these concerns with institutional regularities. Passions, by contrast, are defined in part by their fluctuating and convulsive nature. Publius thus insists on the danger of a politics subject to "every sudden breeze of passion," (*F*, 482) and worries about the "transient impulse which the people may receive from the arts of men, who flatter their prejudices to betray their interests" (*F*, 482). This contrast between momentary and unreliable passion and durational and calculable interest is broadly consistent throughout *The Federalist*. Publius makes the intrinsic relationship between duration and interest explicit in *Federalist* No. 71: "It is a general principle of human nature, that a man will be interested in whatever he possesses, in proportion to the firmness or precariousness of the tenure, by which he holds it; will be less attached to what he holds by a momentary and uncertain title, than to what he holds by a durable or certain title" (*F*, 481).

This emphasis on the duration and reliability of interests when compared to the passions (or even what Publius sometimes qualifies as "immediate" or "momentary" interests) reveals the governmental dimensions of interest in *The Federalist*, while also avoiding theoretical preoccupations with the distinction between "real" or "objective" interests and "apparent" interests, preferences, or inclinations. This distinction may trouble philosophers of social science, but they have little bearing on Publius's new science of politics. Publius does distinguish interest from inclinations in *The Federalist*, and even refers to "supposed interests" at one point in his argument (*Federalist* No. 38). "When occasions present themselves in which the interests of the people are at variance with their inclinations," he writes, for example, "it is the duty of the persons whom they have appointed to be the guardians of those interests to withstand the temporary delusion, in order to give them time and opportunity for more cool and sedate reflection" (*F*, 483). The significance of this contrast between interest and inclination, however, is not to place greater epistemological weight on the former and reject the falsity of the latter. It is instead to emphasize the more reliable governance of a long-term interest rather than momentary and delusive inclination. Publius would agree with Hume that "though men be much governed by interest; yet even interest itself, and all human affairs, are entirely governed by opinion." Interest is a problem of governance not a problem of truth. Its duration is more important for Publius than its supposed objectivity.

Interests can be shared but are not contagious. Interest is a property of both individuals (self-interest) and of groups (i.e., interested factions, the interest of the nation). While interest may, therefore, be shared and communicated, Publius argues that this typically proceeds by way of calculation of mutual advantage rather than contagion (as is the case with passions). One of the great advantages of the "extended republic," for example, was its ability to prevent such contagious passions from becoming a "general conflagration" (*F*, 64). "People spread over an extensive region, cannot like the crouded inhabitants of a small district, be subject to the infection of violent passions" (*F*, 425). There is a marked concern throughout *The Federalist* with the infectious spread of shared passions, not only within the small territory of ancient republics, but also in the popular assemblies that typically governed them. "In all very numerous assemblies, of whatever characters composed, passion never fails to wrest the scepter from reason," Publius writes in *Federalist* No. 55, "Had every Athenian citizen been a Socrates; every Athenian assembly would still have been a mob" (*F*, 374). Popular "paroxysms" of this kind "do not fall within any ordinary rules of calculation" (*F*, 104). Publius fears the contagion of popular passions that act in spite of interest, or that override interest. The communication of interests, by contrast, does not require a physical proximity, and is based in more considered reflections of mutual advantage.

Interests enable mechanical economies of governance and representation. Publius's reliance on mechanical and machine metaphors is well known. The description of the Constitution as a "machine that would go of itself," while of later origination, clearly derives from Publius's own mechanistic account of American constitutionalism. *Federalist* No. 10 and No. 51, rightly singled out as exemplary of the innovations of Publius's new science of politics, are also the essays that rely most explicitly on a mechanical economy of freedom and power to describe the operations of republican governance. In *Federalist* No. 10 the proliferation of competing and countervailing "parties and interests" in an extended republic establishes a constitutional equilibrium that indirectly controls the heretofore dangerous "effects" of factions rather than directly "removing the causes." Similarly, in *Federalist* No. 51, Publius argues that the "interior structure of government" must be organized in such a way that "its several constituent parts may, by their mutual relations, be the means of keeping each other in their proper places" (*F*, 347). "Ambition must be made to counteract ambition," Publius writes, "The interest of the man must be connected with the constitutional rights of the place." In both *Federalist* No. 10 and No. 51, stability is secured through institutional organization that indirectly governs through the free conduct of the governed (in the first case of political factions, in the second case of interested politicians), rather than in direct opposition to that conduct. In both instances, Publius relies on and develops the common eighteenth-century principle of countervailing passions.

"The idea of engineering social progress by cleverly setting up one passion to fight another," Hirschman writes, "became a fairly common intellectual pastime in the course of the eighteenth century."[84] However, while the principle of countervailing passions can be traced back to classical republican arguments about "mixed government," including the populist republicanism advocated by Machiavelli in the *Discourses*, by the end of the eighteenth century this broader discourse was replaced by a more refined and mechanistic argument that replaced countervailing passions with a political economy of interests. Publius exemplifies this teaching perfectly when he writes that the "policy of supplying by opposite and rival interests, the defect of better motives, might be traced through the whole system of human affairs, private as well as public," (*F*, 349) as does Helvetius when the latter writes "as the physical world is ruled by the laws of movement so is the moral universe ruled by the laws of interest."[85]

Through these three interdependent dimensions of interest, Publius aimed to govern the conduct of the citizenry and establish "predictability and constancy" in the political life of the republic. In contrast to the volatile *opposition* between "power" and "liberty" that defined an earlier republican paradigm (and that mandated the vigilance, virtù, and jealousy of citizens as the necessary conditions of liberty), this alternative logic of republican governance envisions power working *through* liberty construed as interest. Rather than being understood as an external limit— power as a definite limit on popular liberty—power is instead envisioned as the immanent regulation of the conduct it governs. The republican governmentality of *The Federalist* enacts an insinuation of governmental power, in that it works through the free interested actions of citizens. This new logic of republican governance shaped not only the "interior structure" of the government and the envisioned conduct of the governors (the argument of 51), but also the way that Publius envisioned the "exterior provisions" of political representation and the political conduct of the people themselves. "To surmise the acting of multitudes, contrary to their own interests—is to take all assurance out of humane affairs."[86]

Scholars on the left and the right have frequently noted that Publius sought to establish the political conditions for economic expansion, if not empire. Publius looked forward to a time when America would be able to exploit her vast natural resources, develop her "national wealth," and take her rightful place as a powerful nation among nations. Publius embraced the "industrious habits of the people of the present day, absorbed in the pursuits of gain, and devoted to the improvements of agriculture and commerce" (*F*, 47). However, if I am correct that Publius's overriding concern was the problem of governance, then these familiar considerations should be viewed as preeminently political goals rather than solely economic ones. Interest was not simply useful for tapping the economic productivity of a commercial republic and its "wide field of Western territory" (*F*, 38), but was essential for governing the citizens of that republic and ensuring its stability across time. The "possibility of a mutual gain emerged from the expected working of interest *in politics*," as Hirschman writes in a similar vein, "quite some time before it became a matter of doctrine in economics."[87]

In her concluding chapter to *On Revolution*, Hannah Arendt argues that the "treasure" of the American Revolution—its commitment to public happiness and the experience of "beginning anew"—had been tragically "lost" because the Founders of the Constitution failed to provide the spaces or institutions required for the continual reenactment of this "spirit" among the people themselves. "The machinery of government," Arendt writes, "could not save the people from lethargy and inattention to public business, since the Constitution itself provided public space only for the representative of the people, and not for the people themselves."[88] For Arendt, this failure was the result of a tragic oversight or misunderstanding. The Founders took the spirit of public attentiveness "for granted, because it was a spirit which had been formed and nourished throughout the colonial period."[89] They mistakenly empowered the people only in their "private capacity" as interested individuals and voters not in the "public capacity" as citizens. If the above analysis is correct, nothing could be further from the truth. The republic of interests that Arendt bemoans was not a sad but unintended consequence, but a product of design.

Closer to the mark, its seems to me, is Norman Jacobson, who in a remarkable article in the *American Political Science Review*, wrote that the Federalists "erected institutions designed to train generations of citizens to prefer certain goods and conduct over all others."[90] While classical republicans were educated first and foremost to "feel and affirm themselves as citizens," the Federalists envisioned a republic less dependent on public identification and popular vigilance in the face of power. For Jacobson, this signaled America's "second founding": the birth of the economic republic, the displacement of equality with equality of opportunity, and the eclipse of "the political." However, this turn to interest should not be understood as a departure from a pure realm of "the political," so much as a distinctive refinement of modern practices of governance.

NOTES

1. David Hume, "Of the Independency of Parliament," in *Political Essays*, ed. Knud Haakonssen (Cambridge: Cambridge University Press, 1994), 24–27, 24.

2. Herbert J. Storing, *What the Anti-Federalists Were For* (Chicago: University of Chicago Press, 1981), 71.

3. *RFC Vol. 1*, 18.

4. James Madison, "Vices of the Political System of the United States," in *The Papers of James Madison, Vol. IX*, ed. William T. Hutchinson et al. (Chicago: University of Chicago Press, 1977), 348–57.

5. *RFC Vol. 1*, 26.

6. *RFC Vol. 1*, 19.

7. *DHRC Vol. XIII*, 192.

8. Robert B. Shoemaker, "'Democracy' and 'Republic' as Understood in Late Eighteenth-Century America," *American Speech* 41, no. 2 (1966): 83–95.

9. *DHRC Vol. XIII*, 141.

10. Quoted in Woody Holton, *Unruly Americans and the Origins of the Constitution* (New York: Hill and Wang, 2007), 227.

11. James Madison, *Notes on the Debates in the Federal Convention of 1787, Vol. I.* (Buffalo, NY: Prometheus Books, 1987), 39.

12. Jacob E. Cooke, ed. *The Federalist* (Middletown, CT: Wesleyan University Press, 1961), 90. All subsequent citations to *The Federalist* will be to this edition, titled *F* with paginations in parentheses in the text.

13. Holton, *Unruly Americans*, 5.

14. Gordon Wood, "Interests and Disinterestedness in the Making of the Constitution," in *Beyond Confederation: Origins of the Constitution and American National Identity*, ed. Richard Beeman, Stephen Botein, and Edward C. Carter II (Chapel Hill: University of North Carolina Press, 1987), 69–112, 72.

15. George Washington, *Writings*, ed. John Rhodehamel (New York: Library of America, 1997), 526.

16. Wood, "Interests and Disinterestedness in the Making of the Constitution," 76.

17. Gordon Wood, *The Creation of the American Republic, 1776–1787* (Chapel Hill: University of North Carolina Press, 1969), 606–15; Wood, "Interests and Disinterestedness in the Making of the Constitution," 76, 92. My emphasis.

18. Cecelia Kenyon, "Men of Little Faith: The Anti-Federalists on the Nature of Representative Government," *The William and Mary Quarterly* 12, no. 1 (1955): 3–43; Storing, *What the Anti-Federalists Were For*, 7–14.

19. Wood, "Interests and Disinterestedness in the Making of the Constitution," 70–71.

20. See, for example, James Scanlon, "*The Federalist* and Human Nature," *Review of Politics* 21, no. 4 (1959): 659.

21. Samuel Beer, *To Make a Nation: The Rediscovery of American Federalism* (Cambridge, MA: Harvard University Press, 1993).

22. Martin Diamond, "Democracy and *The Federalist*: A Reconsideration of the Framers' Intent," in *As Far as Republican Principles Will Admit: Essays by Martin Diamond*, ed. William A. Schambra (Washington, DC: AEI Press, 1992), 17–36; Richard Hofstadter, "The Founding Fathers: An Age of Realism," in *The American Political Tradition* (New York: Vintage, 1989 [1948]), 3–22.

23. Michel Foucault, "The Subject and Power," in *Essential Works of Foucault, 1954–1984, Vol. III: Power*, ed. James D. Faubion (New York: New Press, 1994), 326–48. "Government concerns the shaping of human conduct and acts on the governed as a locus of action and freedom. It therefore entails the possibility that the governed are to some extent capable of acting and thinking otherwise. . . . *Liberal* modes of government are distinguished by trying to work through the freedom or capacities of the governed. Liberal ways of governing thus often conceive the freedom of the governed as a technical means of securing the ends of government," in Mitchell Dean, *Governmentality: Power and Rule in Modern Society* (Beverly Hills, CA: Sage Publishers, 1999), 15.

24. Albert O. Hirschman, "The Concept of Interest: From Euphemism to Tautology," in *Rival Views of Market Society and Other Recent Essays* (New York: Viking, 1986), 35–47, 35. In addition to the work of Hirschman and Foucault, I have learned a great deal from two recent studies examining the political organization and governance of interest within liberal politics. See Stephen G. Engelmann, *Imagining Interest in Political Thought: Origins of Economic Rationality* (Durham, NC: Duke University Press, 2003); Dean Mathiowitz, *Appeals to Interest: Language, Contestation, and the Shaping of Political Agency* (State College: Pennsylvania State University Press, 2011).

25. Michel Foucault, *The Birth of Biopolitics: Lectures at the Collège de France, 1978–1979*, ed. Michel Senellart (New York: Palgrave Macmillan, 2008), 270.

26. Dean, *Governmentality*, 15; Foucault, *The Birth of Biopolitics*, 27–50, 267–90.

27. Foucault, *Birth of Biopolitics*, 44.

28. Catherine Holland is an important exception. In her essay "Becoming Unnatural: The Federalist's Techniques of Government" she argues that the proliferation of factional differences in *Federalist* No. 10 serves to "transform political differences from dangers to resources for the national state," and, in doing so, "disciplines citizen-subjects even as it enables and empowers their actions." However, Holland's insightful account of "aggregate universalism" does not engage the central historical importance of "interest" to this alternative logic of governance, instead focusing on a some-

what vague theorization of deployed "difference." See Holland, *The Body Politic: Foundings, Citizenship, and Difference in the American Political Imagination* (New York: Routledge, 2001), 57–92, 80, 58.

29. Storing, *What the Anti-Federalists Were For*, 31.

30. See Stephen Holmes, "The Secret History of Self-Interest," in *Passions & Constraint: On the Theory of Liberal Democracy* (Chicago: University of Chicago Press, 1995), 42–68.

31. Alexander Hamilton, "Phocion," in *Works of Alexander Hamilton, Vol. II* (New York: Charles Francis & Co., 1851), 298.

32. Hume, "Of the Independency of Parliament," 612.

33. Graham Burchell, "Peculiar Interests: Civil Society and Governing 'The System of Natural Liberty,'" in *The Foucault Effect: Studies in Governmentality* (Chicago: University of Chicago Press, 1991), 119–50, 132.

34. Wood, *Creation of the American Republic*, 614.

35. Bernard Bailyn, *Ideological Origins of the American Revolution* (Cambridge, MA: Harvard University Press, 1967), 57–58.

36. Wood, "Interests and Disinterestedness in the Making of the Constitution," 78.

37. Thomas Jefferson, *Notes on the State of Virginia*, ed. William Peden (Chapel Hill: University of North Carolina Press, 1982), 161.

38. Lance Banning, "Some Second Thoughts on Virtue and the Course of Revolutionary Thinking," in *Conceptual Change and the Constitution*, ed. Terence Ball and J. G. A. Pocock (Lawrence: University Press of Kansas, 1988), 194–212, 196.

39. Banning, "Some Second Thoughts," 199.

40. Montesquieu, *The Spirit of the Laws*, ed. Anne Cohler, Basia Miller, and Harold Stone (Cambridge: Cambridge University Press, 1989), 36.

41. J. G. A. Pocock, *The Machiavellian Moment: Florentine Political Thought and the Atlantic Republican Tradition* (Princeton, NJ: Princeton University Press, 1975), 521–22.

42. Pocock, *The Machiavellian Moment*, 523.

43. Wood, *Creation of the American Republic*, 428.

44. James T. Kloppenburg, "The Virtues of Liberalism: Christianity, Republicanism, and Ethics in Early American Political Discourse," *Journal of American History* 74, no. 1 (1987): 9–33.

45. Samuel Adams, *Writings of Samuel Adams, Vol. IV*, ed. Harry Alonzo Cushing (Fairford, UK: Echo Library, 2006), 302.

46. Wood, *Creation of the American Republic*, 520.

47. Clinton Rossiter, *Seedtime of the Republic* (New York: Harcourt, 1953).

48. John Trenchard and Thomas Gordon, *Cato's Letters: Essays on Liberty, Civil and Religious, and Other Important Subjects*, ed. Ronald Hamowy (Indianapolis, IN: Liberty Fund, 1995), 282.

49. Trenchard and Gordon, *Cato's Letters*, 284.

50. Trenchard and Gordon, *Cato's Letters*, 271.

51. Caroline Robbins, *The Eighteenth-Century Commonwealthman* (Indianapolis, IN: Liberty Fund, 1959), 115.

52. Trenchard and Gordon, *Cato's Letters*, 41.

53. Trenchard and Gordon, *Cato's Letters*, 42.

54. Thomas Jefferson, "Draft of the Kentucky Resolutions," in Jean M. Yarbrough, ed., *The Essential Jefferson* (Indianapolis, IN: Hackett, 2006), 48–54, 53.

55. Storing, *What the Anti-Federalists Were For*, 51.

56. Wood, *Creation of the American Republic*, 521.

57. "Cato VII," *DHRC Vol. XV*, 242.

58. "Caesar II," *DHRC Vol. XIII*, 397.

59. "Cato I," *DHRC Vol. XIII*, 257.

60. Storing, *What the Anti-Federalists Were For*, 65.

61. See Bonnie Honig, *Political Theory and the Displacement of Politics* (Ithaca, NY: Cornell University Press, 1993), 1–117.

62. Storing, *What the Anti-Federalists Were For*, 69.

63. John McCormick, "Machiavellian Democracy: Controlling Elites with Ferocious Populism," *American Political Science Review* 95, no. 2 (2001): 297–313.

64. David Hume, "That Politics May Be Reduced to a Science," in *Political Essays*, 4–15, 14.

65. Hume, "That politics may be reduced to a science," 5.

66. Ralph Lerner, "Commerce and Character," in *The Thinking Revolutionary: Principle and Practice in the New Republic* (Ithaca, NY: Cornell University Press, 1987), 192–222.

67. David Hume, "Of Commerce," in *Political Essays*, 93–104, 100. My emphasis.

68. Burchell, "Peculiar Interests," 119.

69. Alexis de Tocqueville, *Democracy in America* (New York: Penguin, 2003), 612.

70. Burchell, "Peculiar Interests," 127.

71. Niklolas Rose and Peter Miller, "Political Power Beyond the State: Problematics of Government," *The British Journal of Sociology* 43, no. 2 (1992): 173–205.

72. Jürgen Habermas, *Structural Transformation of the Public Sphere: An Inquiry Into a Category of Bourgeois Society*, trans. Thomas Burger (Cambridge, MA: MIT Press, 1991), 26.

73. Douglass Adair, "The Tenth Federalist Revisited," in *Fame and the Founding Fathers: Essays by Douglass Adair*, ed. Trevor Colbourn (New York: W. W. Norton, 1974), 75–92, 76.

74. Charles Beard, *An Economic Interpretation of the Constitution of the United States* (New York: Free Press, 1913), 15.

75. Beard, *An Economic Interpretation*, 16.

76. David Hume, "Of Parties in General," in *Political Essays*, 33–39, 39.

77. Hume, "Of Parties in General," 36.

78. Scanlon, "Federalist and Human Nature," 661.

79. Morton White, *Philosophy, The Federalist, and the Constitution* (New York: Oxford University Press, 1989), 102.

80. Hume, "Of Parties in General," 33–40.

81. David Epstein, *The Political Theory of* The Federalist (Chicago: University of Chicago Press, 1984), 59–110.

82. Albert O. Hirschman, *The Passions and the Interests: Political Arguments for Capitalism before Its Triumph* (Princeton, NJ: Princeton University Press, 1977), 44.

83. Hirschman, *The Passions and the Interests*, 32.

84. Hirschman, *The Passions and the Interests*, 26.

85. Hirschman, *The Passions and the Interests*, 43.

86. Hirschman, *The Passions and the Interests*, 49.

87. Hirschman, *The Passions and the Interests*, 50. According to Hirschman "the main impact of *The Wealth of Nations* was to establish a powerful *economic* justification for the untrammeled pursuit of individual self-interest, whereas in the earlier literature . . . the stress was on the *political* effects of the pursuit" (100).

88. Hannah Arendt, *On Revolution* (New York: Penguin, 1990 [1963]), 238.

89. Arendt, *On Revolution*, 239.

90. Norman Jacobson, "Political Science and Political Education," *American Political Science Review* 57, no. 3 (1963): 561–69, 561.

FOUR

Publius and Politeia

> Any constitution [*politeia*] which is truly so-called . . . must devote itself
> to the end of encouraging goodness. Otherwise, a political association
> sinks into a mere alliance . . . and law becomes a mere covenant or a
> guarantor of men's rights against another instead of a rule of life that
> will make the members of the polis good and just.
>
> —Aristotle, *Politics*[1]

Recent investigations into the influence of Leo Strauss and his students
on contemporary American conservatism have typically focused on the
impact Strauss's thought has had on neoconservative foreign policy. Shadia Drury, Anne Norton, and Nicholas Xenos have each attempted to
show that core ideas driving the unilateralism of the Bush administration
resonated with the thinking of Strauss and his followers: their rejection of
low-sighted political realism, their disdain for international institutions
like the UN, their embrace of a fundamentalist moralism as the basis for
an aggressively unilateralist foreign policy, and their reliance on duplic-
ity in persuading the American public for war.[2] The discovery of a now
infamous letter that Strauss wrote to Karl Löwith in 1933, declaring his
fidelity to "principles of the right," that is to "fascist, authoritarian and
imperial principles," instead of "crawling to the cross of liberalism" and
to "the ludicrous . . . appeal to *droits imprescriptibles de l'homme*" has
sensationalized these discussions, and provoked a blogosphere cottage
industry of accusation and recrimination that continues unabated even
with neoconservatives out of power in Washington's foreign policy establishment.[3]

Strauss's admirers have come to his defense, most notably in several
book-length rehabilitations written by such prominent Straussian scholars as Thomas Pangle, Steven Smith, and Michael Zuckert and Catherine
Zuckert.[4] The twofold task of these studies is to first, and quite persua-

sively, disassociate Strauss's scholarly work from the political positions adopted by the likes of William Kristol, Abram Shulsky, and Paul Wolfowitz. Second, and less persuasively, these books struggle to downplay Strauss's radical antimodernism, his proximity to the thinking of Nietzsche, Heidegger, and Schmitt, and argue for what William Galston has recently called Strauss's "qualified embrace of liberal constitutional democracy."[5]

This chapter takes up this last claim about modern liberal constitutionalism but asks a slightly different set of questions. While recent controversies around Strauss's purported influence on American politics have understandably focused on American foreign policy, there has been relatively little work examining the quite remarkable influence of Strauss's political thought on understandings of American constitutionalism and the political thought of the American Founding, and most importantly on *The Federalist* (at least little work that is not written by Straussians).[6] There has been a good deal of discussion of the Straussian influence on regime change without a corresponding discussion of what is meant precisely by Strauss's understanding of regime—a concept central to any account of Straussian constitutionalism—and how that understanding has been brought to bear on political theory's understanding of Publius and other Founders.

In a 1988 review essay in the *New York Review of Books*—provocatively titled "The Fundamentalists and the Constitution"—Gordon Wood wrote that in the explosion of scholarship on the United States Constitution occasioned by the 1987 bicentennial, Straussians more than any other single group were attempting to "set the agenda for public debate over the Constitution." "They have sought to define the terms," Wood wrote, "to organize the conferences, and to dominate the discussions." The remarkable number of "Straussian" books and anthologies published on the American Founding during the bicentennial and in subsequent years seems to support Wood's conclusion.[7] Most recently, Straussian scholarship on American constitutionalism and the Founding has again helped to shape and give intellectual heft to public discourse as "constitutional conservatism" has become the rallying cry of a resurgent right wing in American politics, as Glenn Beck and Tea Party activists made the interpretation of American constitutional history the central framing narrative of their political orientation, and as prominent signatories of the Mount Vernon Statement, an influential statement of unifying conservative principles, declare the fundamental truth of these principles by paraphrasing Strauss's opening lines from *Natural Right and History*.[8]

What goes missing in much of this popular appropriation of broadly Straussian approaches to the political theory of the Founders are the divisions that have often bitterly separated students of Strauss on these questions: "the Crisis of the Strauss Divided." The bicentennial itself and the newfound access of Straussian scholars to the money and power of the

Reagan administration and conservative think tanks corresponded with a quite dramatic and politically advantageous shift in the meaning of American constitutionalism for many of them, from an earlier generation of Straussians—most influentially Martin Diamond and Herbert Storing—who closely followed Strauss in his critical wariness of America's modern liberal constitutionalism, to a group of scholars—influenced most importantly by Harry Jaffa—who celebrate, bizarrely for readers outside the fold, American constitutionalism as itself a product of the political wisdom of ancient political philosophy.[9] These more ideological figures are usually referred to as West Coast Straussians, and they include, aside from Jaffa himself, Thomas West, Charles Kesler, and a number of lesser-known activist-scholars affiliated with the Claremont Institute and other conservative think tanks. In their work—once piously focused on the writings of Lincoln and the Founders, but now preoccupied with the apostasy of American Progressivism and the personified evil of Woodrow Wilson—we see what Mark Lilla has described as "the slow adaptation of Straussian doctrine to comport with neoconservative Republicanism."[10]

Instead of the somewhat misleading geographic categorization, I will refer to this more politically prominent group as "American exceptionalist Straussians," because for these scholars the American republic is not what Joseph Cropsey once called "the arena in which modernity is working itself out," nor what Martin Diamond declared "the paradigm of modernity," but instead the glorious exception to Strauss's grand narrative of decline, wherein classical natural right is abandoned for the low-sighted and hedonistic political philosophy of modern liberalism, which slides inexorably through the three waves of modernity into historicism, relativism, and nihilism.[11] American exceptionalist Straussians place new philosophical garb on a very old American story: that America is outside of the depredations of history and tradition, now figured as the history of Western metaphysics itself. This politically convenient convergence of metanarratives provides a quasiphilosophical updating of the old exceptionalist myth. In the place of "Nature's Nation" we now have Aristotelian America: once the primary example of a wholly modern constitutionalism, America and Americans are now flattered as citizens of Aristotle's best regime.

This chapter examines and explains the considerable influence of Straussian readings of *The Federalist* by proceeding in two parts. In the first, I offer an outline of what I take to be the core element of Strauss's constitutional thinking—and an important basis for his qualified rejection of the sufficiency of liberal constitutionalism—focused around his reappropriation of the Aristotelian concept of the *politeia* (translated as "regime" by Strauss and his students). The 1932 encounter between Strauss and Carl Schmitt provides the relevant background for understanding the constitutional stakes of Strauss's theory of the *politeia* most forcefully and influentially articulated in *Natural Right and History*. I will focus on what I see as the theoretically revealing relationship between Strauss's concept of *politeia*, and Carl Schmitt's influential theory of constituent power examined above in chapter 1. More thoroughgoing investigation into the relationship between these two concepts than I can provide here will reveal, I suspect, important lines of proximity and distance in the political theories of these two great critics of modern liberal constitutionalism. The relationship between these concepts illuminates their mutual attention to the paradoxes and blind spots—in short, the illiberalism—that haunts modern liberal constitutionalism. Like Schmitt, Strauss aimed to show that liberal pluralism, openness, and tolerance masked its own disavowed forms of fundamentalism and dogmatism. "Liberal relativism," he writes, "has roots in the natural right tradition of tolerance or in the notion that everyone has a natural right to the pursuit of happiness as he understands happiness, but in itself it is a seminary of intolerance."[12] While Strauss and Schmitt converge on this point, Strauss's conception of *politeia* points in very different directions from Schmitt's existential decisionism. This examination will elaborate on some of the larger theoretical stakes underwriting the Straussian approach to the modernity of Publius's argument.

In the second section, I will turn directly to how Strauss's concept of *politeia* was brought to bear on the experience of the American Founding, and particularly on interpretations of *The Federalist*, in the work of some of his most prominent students. I will focus my discussion on the work of two Straussian scholars whose research has arguably been most influential on interpretations of *The Federalist*—Martin Diamond and Herbert Storing. I do so not only because I believe their work brings the stakes of a Straussian approach to American constitutionalism most clearly into focus, but also because I admire this work and think it offers an important and critical examination of the thought of founding thinkers like Publius, without engaging in the inventive hagiography of some of the more recent scholarship.

I.

"Wisdom," Strauss once wrote, "requires unhesitating loyalty to a decent constitution, and even to the cause of constitutionalism."[13] Strauss's defenders cite this passage as evidence of his commitment, albeit somewhat qualified, to the cause of modern liberal constitutionalism in general and to American constitutionalism in particular. They cite it as evidence of his embrace of political moderation. There are, needless to say, numerous passages in Strauss's work that challenge the adequacy of this view, particularly those passages where Strauss seemingly embraces nonconsensual forms of political rule based in the "counsels of the wise."[14] Rather than focusing on Strauss's invocations of what David Estland has recently described as an "epistocracy of the educated," however, in what follows I will take a very broad view of Strauss's understanding of constitutionalism, focusing on his reconstruction of ancient constitutionalism as a premodern alternative to the formal constitutionalism or proceduralism characteristic of the liberal *Rechtsstaat*, one that serves to illuminate, as did Schmitt, the controversial fundamental commitments that go hidden or disavowed by liberal constitutionalism's self-proclaimed neutrality in the face of competing ends.[15]

Strauss's recovery of ancient constitutionalism and its theoretically productive opposition to the assumptions underwriting liberalism can, by his own account, be traced to his important dialogue with the work of Carl Schmitt, and in particular with Strauss's deservedly famous 1932 review of *The Concept of the Political*.[16] Heinrich Maier has written a rigorous account of the background theoretical issues that framed this debate—in particular what Strauss called the "theologico-political predicament"—and I will not reconstruct the entirety of Strauss's argument here.[17] What I will do is outline how Strauss's framing of Schmitt's book shows it to remain within the horizons of the modern liberal constitutionalism it aims to transcend, in effect being guilty of a constitutional formalism, while opening up a theoretical space for Strauss's own subsequent return to ancient constitutionalism articulated most influentially in *Natural Right and History*, a book that, in Lilla's words, "prepared generations of conservative intellectuals in America to see nihilism lurking in the interstices of modern life, threatening to turn America into Weimar."[18]

Strauss's argument against Schmitt's *Concept of the Political* is that Schmitt's "critique of liberalism occurs in the horizon of liberalism," and that Schmitt's "unliberal tendency is nonetheless restrained by the still unvanquished systematics of liberal thought."[19] The purpose of Strauss's review is to provide a more encompassing view of these "systematics" than Schmitt provides, and thereby to gain a true "horizon beyond liberalism," a more radical critique of liberal constitutionalism's founding assumptions than those offered by Schmitt himself.[20] In order to attain this more encompassing view, Strauss provides what to some readers has seemed like an odd or idiosyncratic approach to Schmitt's famous book— one that hinges on an analysis of "culture" in its opposition to "nature." It is revealing that Strauss's approach did not appear odd or idiosyncratic to Schmitt himself, who wrote to a colleague shortly after the appearance of the review that Strauss "saw right through me and x-rayed me as nobody else had."[21] In order to grasp the core of Strauss's own critique of liberal constitutionalism then, it is important to engage what he means when he writes in his review of *The Concept of the Political* that the "final awareness of liberalism is the philosophy of culture."[22]

Strauss argues that by affirming a political ontology—the irreducibility of the polemical opposition between friend and enemy—Schmitt denies the foundational order of a teleological nature and natural right just as clearly as the liberalism he critiques. Schmitt's work becomes symptomatic of what Strauss will later characterize as the Nietzschean third wave of modernity.[23] It is modernity's affirmation of human self-sufficiency and autonomy taken to its fullest nihilistic extreme. In this early review Strauss reframes Schmitt's famous critique of liberalism's evasion of the political as first and foremost a critique of culture. Liberalism divides the genus that is specific to the political—"culture" or the "totality of human thought and action"—into various independent domains—the moral, the aesthetic, the economic, and so forth. So, according to Strauss, Schmitt's understanding of the political implies a fundamental critique of "at least the prevailing concept of culture," which is a critique first and foremost of the assumption that these spheres are relatively autonomous, or of the depoliticizing liberal strategy of removing these spheres to the private realm beyond the space of public controversy.

Here Strauss draws out more fully what is implied by Schmitt's affirmation in *The Concept of the Political* of a "political homogeneity" that overrides and takes existential precedence over these subordinate spheres of human activity. According to Strauss, Schmitt understands that the "prevailing concept of culture" affirms or entails the vision of a state in which social conflict is impartially regulated through the medium of man-made law. But here is where Strauss believes Schmitt stops short of drawing out the full consequences of his critique of the "prevailing concept of culture"; Strauss aims to more radically expose the fundamental presuppositions of this view.

In Strauss's review "culture" stands in for a project of human autonomy and self-sufficiency that he comes to identify with modernity as such. For Strauss, the abandonment of nature for culture already contains the seeds of nihilism within it, and marks modernity's fateful departure from ancient political philosophy and classical natural right. Liberalism's inaugurating gesture is to break from natural right theories based in a transcendent objective standard or law, a hierarchy of ends that human activity aims to teleologically fulfill, and posits value and meaning as, instead, wholly human creations—creations of "culture." Liberalism is equated with the abandonment of man by God and nature, which no longer give guidance on how to live. "If Martin Heidegger indicted modernity for its *Seinsvergessenheit* ("forgetfulness of Being")," as Richard H. King has recently written, "then Strauss can be said to indict it for an analogous *Naturvergessenheit* ("forgetfulness of Nature")."[24]

Schmitt's *Concept of the Political*, on Strauss's account, reveals this truth but remains trapped within its terms. Like the liberalism he critiques, Schmitt forgets that culture always presupposes that something is cultivated: "culture is always the culture of nature."[25] For Schmitt, nature is still the "sovereign creation of the spirit," which fundamentally rein-scribes him within the horizon that he had hoped to escape. In affirming the irreducibility of the political, Schmitt's decisionism ends up duplicat-ing the very "value neutrality" that he criticizes, which prevents him from asking the fundamental questions of right that motivate politics on Strauss's account. The *seriousness* of the question of what *is* right is what legitimates the political, and defines its space of contention. If Schmitt seems to affirm the irreducibility of the political over the moral, Strauss wants to show that "the position of the political must be tracked back to the position of the moral."[26] The political for Schmitt focuses on the irre-ducibility of the threat or the existential fight, not on what is being fought *for*. In this focus, Schmitt, like the liberalism he assails, presumes a posi-tion of neutrality among combatants. This is a neutrality of a different sort than that associated with liberalism's "age of neutralizations and depoliticizations" — one that doesn't seek to avoid decision but to "affirm an eagerness of decisions regardless of content."[27] "He who affirms the political as such," Strauss insightfully writes, "respects all who want to fight; he is just as tolerant as the liberals, but with the opposite intention: whereas the liberal tolerates all honest convictions so long as they merely acknowledge the legal order as sacrosanct, he who affirms the political as such respects and tolerates all serious convictions, all decisions oriented to the real possibility of war."[28] Schmitt merely affirms a liberalism with "the opposite polarity." However, in doing so Schmitt clears the ground for a reassertion of "a new order of human things" that takes its orienta-tion from a teleological nature rather than the autonomous self-assertion associated with culture, and this is, of course, the path that Strauss him-self takes in his subsequent work.

For Strauss, "liberalism stands or falls by the distinction between state and society, or by the recognition of a private sphere, protected by the law, with the understanding above all that religion belongs to the private sphere."[29] Through a contrasting recovery of the profoundly formative constitutions of the ancient world, the form of constitutionalism that Strauss develops to reveal the hidden dogmatism underwriting liberal-ism's proclaimed procedural fairness and toleration rejects the neutrality of the liberal art of separation. Strauss's theologico-political critique of modern liberal constitutionalism, his critique of the idea that a social and private sphere can be wholly set off from the ends of the state, while suggested in his critique of Schmitt, is more fully and influentially devel-oped through his encounter with the ancient Greek idea of the *politeia* in *Natural Right and History*. At the risk of simplification, where Schmitt's critique of liberalism in the *Concept of the Political* focused on liberal con-stitutionalism's inability to account and provide conceptual resources for the encounter with the extralegal decision that is the constitution's very condition of possibility and impossibility (see the discussion of constitu-ent power in chapter 1), Strauss more directly elaborates on the meaning of "political homogeneity" argued for in Schmitt's book, on the moral ordering of the polity, or on modern liberalism's seeming refusal of a formative politics—its claim to establish a "regimeless regime." Here it is important to note that Strauss's understanding of liberalism's depoliticizing strategy does not only involve the privatization of conflicting goods, as emphasized by so many of liberalism's critics on both the left and right, but also the faith in technological and procedural advances to neutrally adjudicate between conflicting goods. This will become an important aspect of the most influential Straussian interpretations of *The Federalist*, as we will see below.

The recovery of ancient constitutionalism only suggested at the end of Strauss's review of Schmitt is most developed in the chapter on "Classical Natural Right" from *Natural Right and History*. Strauss does not urge there (or elsewhere) a wholesale recovery of ancient constitutionalism as though that could "supply us with recipes for today's use";[30] his "deepest intent," as one scholar puts it, "was not to revive classical natural right as a positive doctrine of public law."[31] But Strauss's reconstruction of the ancient Greek idea of the *politeia* did allow a more deeply critical perspective to be achieved on modern liberal constitutionalism and its purported shortcomings than that provided even by radical critics like Schmitt. Strauss writes that while *politeia* is often translated as "constitution," moderns typically mean by that a merely "legal phenomenon, something like the fundamental law of the land, and not something like the constitution of the body or soul."[32] The *politeia* refers therefore to more than the form of government in its narrowly legal sense, but rather to the entire way of life of a community, its habits, customs, and moral beliefs—the assemblage of practical orientations I have grouped in this study under the category of political imagination.

Following this primary distinction, some Straussians distinguish between the "parchment regime" and the "living regime" embodied in experience and practical behavior, and they often celebrate Tocqueville's *Democracy in America*, a book that has comparatively little to say about American constitutional jurisprudence, as the classic study of the American *politeia* or regime.[33] Crucial to this conception of *politeia* is the role of formative political education. "The single most important source of the preservation of any regime," Strauss writes, "is the education of its citizens with a view to the ends of the regime."[34] Here and elsewhere Strauss is following Aristotle, as indicated in the passage from the *Politics* with which I began: "any constitution [*politeia*] which is truly so-called . . . must devote itself to the end of encouraging goodness."[35] This formative dimension—the interrelationship of statecraft and soulcraft—is a widely recognized component of Straussian political thought. There are, however, other aspects of Strauss's reconstruction of the *politeia* that are less frequently noted, and that promise to open up new insights into what is distinctive about the Straussian approach to the American Founders in particular.

I agree with Robert Howse that Strauss's discussion in "Classical Natural Right" offers an elaboration of his critique of Schmitt in the "Notes on the Concept of the Political." Howse emphasizes what he broadly considers Strauss's "hidden exchange" with Schmitt's decisionism in that chapter, but I want to focus more narrowly on how Strauss's elaboration of the Aristotelian concept of *politeia* can be read as a response to Schmitt's theory of constituent power (*die verfassunggebenden Gewalt*), which is related to his decisionism but also has a more specific function in his constitutional theory.[36] As we saw above in chapter 1, in his book *Constitutional Theory*, Schmitt defines constituent power as "the political will whose power or authority is capable of adopting the concrete global decision on the mode and form of political existence." Schmitt likens constituent power to an unstructured *"Urgrund,"* or "formless formative capacity."[37] It is an "absolute beginning" that springs out of "normative nothingness and from concrete disorder." Where Schmitt conceives of constituent power as an unconstrained act of formative will—thereby still operating within the "systematic of liberal thought" as elaborated in "Notes"—Strauss conceives of *politeia* as teleologically motivated by a particular and true vision of what is highest and good: culture on the one hand, nature on the other. Just as Schmitt argued that constituent power was essential to the understanding of any constitutional order, but that the liberal *Rechtsstaat* disavowed, Strauss argued that to discover the constitution's full meaning as *politeia* one had to be clear about its overarching moral goals, its way of life, the characters and forms of life that the constitution tends to bring about, and those it prevents from emerging.

In passages that resonate with those on constituent power in Schmitt's *Constitutional Theory*, Strauss calls the *politeia* "the supreme political phenomenon, the core of a society's self definition." "The *politeia* is more fundamental than any laws; it is the source of all laws. . . . The *politeia* is . . . the factual distribution of power within the community [rather] than what constitutional law stipulates in regard to political power."[38] Schmitt's constituent power and Strauss's *politeia* are differently inflected attempts at the theoretical recovery of "the political" threatened for both by modern liberalism's overriding tendency "to neutralization and depoliticization," by liberalism's attempt to overcome the intransigent conflicts over competing ends that structure political life through appeal to better technological means: democratic procedures, parliamentary forms, electoral mechanisms, and so forth. From the perspective of modern liberalism, as Strauss once quipped, "what you need is not so much formation of character and moral appeal as the right kind of institutions, institutions with teeth in them."[39] Liberal constitutionalism's emphasis on the instrumentalities of political technology and institutional design—not on this or that institution, but on the adjudicatory power of institutionalism *as such*—is, as we will see now, an important factor of early Straussian scholarship on the defining aspects of the American Founding and the regime it established, especially as read through the lens of *The Federalist*.

II.

Strauss wrote very little on the American Founding, and his most famous remarks—the opening lines of *Natural Right and History*—are not very encouraging. There he suggests that modern Americans have replaced their original commitment to the self-evident truths of the rights to "life, liberty, and the pursuit of happiness" with the historicist belief that "all men are endowed by the evolutionary process or by mysterious fate with many kinds of urges or aspirations."[40] According to Strauss, early Americans openly followed the teachings of Locke, but surreptitiously followed the teaching of Hobbes, and built their regime on the "low but solid ground" of the modern right of self-preservation, abandoning the ancient preoccupation with the good life for the modern preservation of mere life. "It is not an exaggeration," as Steven Smith writes, "to say that Strauss's judgment on Locke *is* his judgment on America."[41] And while Strauss seems to affirm the Declaration's Lockean commitment to modern natural right in this opening passage, the overall argument of his influential book was that the seeds of historicism, relativism, and nihilism were already lurking within these originary commitments—that America's founding documents affirmed the principles of their own eventual undoing.

For Strauss, the low ends of the American regime were the deep and hidden cause of the dangerous crisis of confidence afflicting postwar liberalism, a crisis that left America—like Weimar—"uncertain of its purpose" and exposed to threats from the extreme left and the extreme right, unable to affirm an unqualified commitment to the truth of its core principles.[42] Strauss was not alone in arguing against relativists and unprincipled liberals during the 1950s. Although Strauss critiqued the resurgence of natural law orthodoxy and dogmatism in postwar legal theory—popularized by Walter Lippmann's *The Public Philosophy* (1955)—his work can be read as part of a wave of postwar "thinking that questioned the adequacy of positive law and legal realism (in America) in the face of the totalitarian menace."[43] However, in contrast to much of this literature Strauss innovatively carried this critique beyond the purview of jurisprudence to the preoccupations of American social science, and to the preoccupations of political science in particular.

While American social scientists increasingly proclaimed their value neutrality and sought to explain the dynamics of American political life by appeal to such extrapolitical variables as economy, psychology, or sociology, Strauss urged his students to study the defining political commitments of the American regime as a precondition to fully understanding its political behavior.[44] "The distinctive human types nurtured in each regime manifest the ethos of the regime," as Martin Diamond would later write, "Each political regime is . . . in the business of handicrafting distinctive human characters. Indeed, each political order is literally constituted by the kind of human character it aims at and tends to form."[45] At a time when the behavioral revolution was well underway in American political science departments and prominent social scientists were declaring the death of political philosophy, Strauss affirmed the autonomy of the political realm and audaciously claimed that political philosophy should be understood as the variable of variables; the serious study of political life should preoccupy itself first and foremost with the normative commitments underwriting a polity's political institutions and animating the lives of its citizens.

Positivist political science was (and is) unable to engage with the substantive principles that comprise its own hidden conditions of possibility, because the political "facts" they empirically studied—behaviors, opinions, institutions—were not natural facts in the world but facts formed by prior theoretical commitments to a particular vision of justice, legitimacy, authority, and so on—formed, that is, by the stated ends of political life. Because all political communities must be understood as a regime, as a comprehensive organization of collective life oriented toward a particular vision of the common good, supposedly value-neutral political science unknowingly echoed the tenants of modern liberalism in claiming it could avoid relying upon or presuming such fundamental commitments. It was an important goal of Strauss's critical engagements with postwar American social science to make those disavowed fundamental commitments legible—a project taken up and elaborated by those of his students who turned their attention to sustained study of the American Founding.

That this study would focus on the political thought of the American Founding is sui generis, because it was in the thought of the Founders that the fundamental orientations of the regime were most clearly articulated. According to Diamond, "the political thought of the Founders remains the finest American thought on political matters."[46] In Storing's words, it "sets the horizon," because the Founders "laid down our most basic rules . . . and established the primary terms of our moral and civic discourse" (an interesting contrast with Arendt's focus on the centrality of the *act* of Founding, discussed in the introduction).[47] According to Strauss and his students, by investigating the political thought of the Founders we come to comprehensively understand the *arche* of the American regime. This is a foundational presupposition of Straussian scholarship on the American regime—not the consequence of empirical investigations, but the foundational framework in which these investigations occur. That this broadly originalist perspective seems relatively uncontroversial today only attests to the widespread dissemination—and political utility—of what was originally taken to be a very idiosyncratic approach to the study of American political life. As examined above, it invests a select group of texts with a remarkable authority and explanatory power, which leads Sheldon Wolin to describe this kind of scholarship in terms of a "misplaced Biblicism."[48]

In one important sense, however, Wolin's biblical metaphor is misleading. While most recent Straussian scholarship on the American Founding is permeated with sanctimonious affirmations of the truth, wisdom, and unsurpassed excellence of America's founding principles, this was not true of all of the most prominent first generation Straussian scholars of the American regime. This first generation examined the thought—or, as they usually put it, the intentions—of the Founders to identify their "constitutive opinions," to reconstruct the fundamental commitments of the American regime articulated at its Founding so as to better understand and *evaluate* these commitments, not to uncritically affirm them. Straussian scholarship on early American political thought has undoubtedly contributed to the conservative jurisprudence of original intent in ways that have not yet been fully appreciated and understood. Indeed, it was Gary McDowell, a Straussian in Reagan's Justice Department, who authored Attorney General Edwin Meese's influential speeches in the 1980s calling for a return to "a jurisprudence of original intention."[49] However, for the first generation of Straussian scholars the return to original intent was not the end of the investigation, or the final ground of interpretive authority, as it has become for conservative jurists.

Strauss taught that it is better *not* to understand America as Americans have understood themselves, a view hardly shared by Robert Bork and Clarence Thomas. Following Strauss, early Straussian scholarship on the American Founding did not return to original intent as a way of suturing a horizon of normative evaluation, so much as a way of illuminating fundamental orientations to political life excluded by that horizon. In attempting to open up a space of critical reflection and evaluation on the fundamental commitments of American constitutionalism — albeit criticism that was "decent" and "respectful"—early Straussian scholarship on the American regime was as critical of prevailing discourses of pluralism, consensus liberalism, and the proclaimed "end of ideology," as were critics on the left like those associated with Berkeley School political theory.[50] The goal of their return to original intention was in line with Strauss's effort in his critique of Schmitt to reconstruct a "horizon beyond liberalism," and thereby to achieve what Diamond called an "educated ascent" from the fundamental commitments of the American Founding.[51] "If there is no standard higher than the ideal of our society," Strauss once wrote, "we are utterly unable to take a critical distance from that ideal."[52]

In the remainder of this chapter, I will survey how two of the most prominent Straussian students of the American Founding, and *The Feder-*

alist in particular, undertook this study: Martin Diamond and Herbert Storing. The main lines of their interpretations of early American political thought converge, as does the particular defining ends of the regime on which they focus. Much recent Straussian scholarship on the American Founding is preoccupied with the meaning of the Declaration's Lockean affirmation of rights, and with painting a more inspirational portrait of these rights than the Hobbesian account provided by Strauss himself. This is true of Thomas Pangle's emphasis on the importance of natural law doctrine, Michael Zuckert's emphasis on implied duties and obligations of rights, as well as Harry Jaffa's bolder claim (also taken up by many of his students) that the American invocation of right is not modern at all but, instead, a glorious restatement of teleological classical natural right.[53]

In sharp contrast to these current preoccupations with rights, Diamond and Storing emphasized, as I have done in much of this book, the popular locus of authority in the American regime, and the innovative institutional mechanisms devised by the framers to respond to resulting dilemmas of democratic governance. Against an earlier generation of Progressive historians who emphasized the antidemocratic elements of the United States Constitution, the base economic motivations of the Founders, and the merely manipulative or rhetorical dimensions of early American political thought, Diamond and Storing take popular government to be a fundamental principle—but also fundamental problem—of the American regime, rational reflection to be the principle commitment of the Founders, and their political thought as the guide to this reflection. While all Straussian scholarship on American political thought rejects the historicist premises of ideology analysis, rather than pursue metaethical investigations into the philosophical foundations of natural right, Diamond and Storing approach the American "new science of politics" as primarily a problem of political technology, of institutional innovations in popular governance.

Martin Diamond was probably the most influential of Strauss's students to study early American constitutionalism. Senator Daniel Patrick Moynihan once claimed that "Martin Diamond almost singlehandedly established the relevance of the thought and doings of the Founding Fathers for his generation," and Michael Zuckert has recently written that "probably none of Strauss's students has had such a widespread influence as Diamond did."[54] That Diamond's interpretation of the American Founding was initially considered authoritative for Straussians themselves is indicated by his authorship of the chapter on *The Federalist* in the famous Strauss/Cropsey anthology on the *History of Political Philosophy*.[55] The main outlines of Diamond's interpretation are succinctly articulated in that chapter on *The Federalist*, because, for Diamond, the *Federalist* provided "the consistent, comprehensive, and true account of the Constitution and of the regime it was calculated to engender."[56]

The key to Diamond's interpretation of the *Federalist*, and therefore American constitutionalism, is a famous line from the conclusion of *Federalist* No. 10 that has already been cited above: "In the extent and proper structure of the Union," Publius writes, "we behold a Republican remedy for the diseases most incident to Republican government."[57] This search for a "Republican remedy for the diseases most incident to Republican government" is what Publius called "the great desideratum of government": "to preserve the spirit and the form of popular government," while also securing the public good and private rights against the dangers of faction and the tyranny of the majority. Diamond argued that the fundamental characteristics of the American regime are fixed in its commitment to "republican" government, coupled with the Constitution's remedy to the diseases that spring from that commitment (the "tempestuous waves of sedition and party rage," which had kept all past republics "continually agitated," and "in a state of perpetual vibration," between the extremes of tyranny and anarchy"). This remedy, Diamond emphasized, was focused not on shaping the *ends* of political life but on improving the mechanism and *means* ("the extent and proper structure of the Union"). While Diamond acknowledged that *The Federalist* "does not discuss systematically . . . the question of ends and purposes of government," he follows Strauss in arguing that the end of the American regime was ultimately a restatement of the modern liberal preservation of rights negatively defined.[58]

For Diamond, as for Strauss, the innovations of the Founders did not occur in the terrain of normative political philosophy, but in governmental technique. It was the Constitution's institutional organization—the extended republic, federated system of political representation and authority, separation of powers, and checks and balances between the different branches of government—that measures the Founders' advances in the new science of politics. American constitutionalism therefore exemplified—indeed was paradigmatic of—the liberal faith in the ability of technological means to overcome and reconcile the conflicts that structure and define political life, most importantly those conflicts animated by competing conceptions of the good life. Like Strauss before him, and Storing after, Diamond did not store much faith in such technological solutions to intractable political dilemmas.

Diamond elaborated this argument most influentially in a 1959 article from the *American Political Science Review* entitled "Democracy and *The Federalist*: A Reconsideration of the Framers' Intent." The "inconveniences" and "sickness" of popular government are there presented as a familiar conflict between the commitment to formal democratic procedures and the corruption of particular democratic outcomes. Diamond engaged this conflict in terms of the dilemmas posed for democratic government by majority tyranny, and focused in particular on Madison's confrontation with this problem in *Federalist* No. 10. Diamond, rightly I think (as argued in the previous chapter), takes this essay to be emblematic of a general shift in strategy in dealing with popular government's intrinsic forms of degeneration and corruption. There Madison proposes two "methods" for dealing with the "disease" of faction in popular government, "the one by removing its causes; the other by controlling its effects." To do the former is to either destroy the citizens' liberty that is the source of popular government, or to impose a particular end on the citizenry, to "give every citizen the same opinions, the same passions, and the same interests" (*F*, 58). This would be a premodern rather than modern "remedy." The American Constitution, as explained and justified by *The Federalist*, pursues the modern strategy of "controlling effects" rather than "removing causes"; it is an exemplary instance of the art of indirect governance.

This alternative strategy of governance is a source of both admiration and critique for Diamond. It is a source of admiration because it takes "man" as he "is" rather than how he "ought" to be. It recognizes man as a dangerous animal and derives from this recognition a clear-sighted analysis of the dangers of "popular inclination" and more direct expressions of popular will. However, it is a source of critique because institutional safeguards in themselves, neutral as to questions of end, are ultimately insufficient to the diseases they are meant to remedy. In developing this critique, Diamond invokes the very conceptions of *politeia* that Strauss elaborates in *Natural Right and History*. While ancient forms of constitutional government had "ranked highly as objects of government, the nurturing of a particular religion, education, military courage, civic spiritedness, moderation, individual excellence," he writes, "on all of these *The Federalist* is either silent, or has in mind only pallid versions of the original, or even seems to speak with contempt."[59]

The United States Constitution does not make it the business of government to "cultivate virtue or improve souls," and but instead regulates the behavior of the citizenry through "shrewd institutional arrangement." "Not to instruct or transcend these passions and interests, but rather to channel and use them," Diamond writes, becomes the hallmark of American constitutionalism.[60] It does not dictate particular results, but organizes institutions in such a way to make beneficial results probable in "aptitude and tendency." As explained by Publius, the mechanisms of electoral representation, for example, don't only focus narrowly on criteria as to who will be qualified to run for office, but rather extend the sphere of electoral districts so that "men who possess the most attractive merit, and the most diffusive and established characters" will tend probabilistically to be elected (*F*, 63). Similarly, the legislative procedure is organized in such a way that the legislation ultimately turned into law will not reflect the popular whims of the moment, but the more refined and enlarged views of an objective or unattached public interest. And the federal division of authority alongside the intricately balanced organization of the separate branches of government will not only enable the government to control the people, but incline it to "check itself" through a policy of "supplying by opposite and rival interests, the defect of better motives" (*F*, 349).

Because American constitutionalism removes "character formation from its previously prominent place on the agenda of politics," it exemplifies for Diamond a broader, modern, liberal strategy of depoliticization. "Madison was following the general tendency of modern political thought," he writes, to "solve the problems of politics by reducing the scope of politics."[61] This strategy, Diamond argued, established a remarkably successful system in maintaining social stability and security (Diamond even claims that Madison offered what he called a "beforehand response to Karl Marx," a serious compliment coming from a former Trotskyist), but he also catalogues the hidden costs—or what he calls the "collateral consequences"—of this attempt to formulate technological solutions to intransigent political problems. He thereby poses a delicate rhetorical problem for his own work (later echoed in the work of Storing): how to defend the American Founding and the United States Constitution from Progressive critics who approached it as an expression of class interests and as fundamentally antidemocratic, while also developing a more thoroughgoing critique than the Progressives of the fundamentals upon which the Constitution rests? Diamond navigates this tension by affirming a dramatic distinction between the virtues and the rationality required of the Founders, and the selfish pursuit of interests and self-gratification required or elicited by the constitutional system they instituted. "There is a profound distinction," he writes, "between the qualities necessary for the founders and those necessary for the men who come after."[62] In establishing a constitutional regime on the "low but solid ground" of self-preservation and self-interest, the Founders wisely provided security and stability to their republican experiment, but they did not recognize that over time their technological solutions could only be palliative, and in fact could ultimately work to magnify or enhance the very dangers they were guarding against.

> In order to defuse the dangerous factional force of opinion, passion, and class interest, Madison's policy deliberately risks magnifying and multiplying in American life the selfish, the interested, the narrow, the vulgar, and the crassly economic. That is the substratum on which the American political system was intended to rest and where it rests still.[63]

For Diamond, the "educated ascent" enabled by careful study of the American Founding and the exemplarity of *The Federalist* reveals that the dangers of popular government were too narrowly conceived by Publius and other Founders, and therefore their technical remedies merely mitigated without resolving these dangers. They presumed a virtue in the citizenry, for example, that their institutional mechanisms did not require and elicit, leading Diamond to ask, "Does not the intensity and kind of our modern problems seem to require of us a greater degree of reflection and public spiritedness than the founders thought sufficient for the men who came after them?"[64] His answers to this question are somewhat gestural, but the central implication is that contemporary Americans require not only a better appreciation of the ends of the regime and the technologies of governance that the regime relies upon, but also a simultaneous awareness of their basic limitations.

Herbert Storing's research into early American political thought took up and developed these questions. If Diamond is best known for his pioneering studies of *The Federalist*'s explanation of the principles of American constitutionalism, Storing is best known for his research into the political thought of their Anti-Federalist opponents. Storing edited a seven- volume collection of Anti-Federalist writing, *The Complete Anti-Federalist*, that was the authoritative scholarly edition of Anti-Federalist writing until the publication of the University of Wisconsin's exhaustive and still-appearing *Documentary History of the Ratification of the United States Constitution*.[65] Storing's book-length introductory essay to *The Complete Anti-Federalist*, published separately as *What the Anti-Federalists Were For*, remains the best available theoretical treatment of Anti-Federalist thought. Rejecting the familiar argument that Anti-Federalists were simply "men of little faith" or "partisans without principle,"[66] Storing attempts to reconstruct in that book what is "fundamental" to their thinking—to "discover a set of principles that is a good deal clearer and more coherent, and also more relevant to an understanding of the American founding and the America polity than is usually been supposed."[67]

In their fundamental commitments, Storing sees much more continuity than discontinuity between Federalists and Anti-Federalists. If they were divided in their polemics over constitutional ratification "they were, at a deeper level," Storing writes, "united with one another. Their disagreements were not based on different premises about the nature of man or the ends of political life. They were not the deep cleavages of contending regimes."[68] For Storing, Federalists and Anti-Federalists were united in their commitment to a basic set of liberal principles: that "the purpose of government is the regulation and thereby the protection of individual rights, and that the best instrument for this purpose is some form of limited, republican government."[69] However, the Anti-Federalists were inconsistent in their attachment to these principles, and Storing argues that they lost the debate over the Constitution in large part because "they had the weaker argument." He identifies "a dilemma or a tension" in Anti-Federalist thought that adds up to a "critical weakness."[70]

This weakness can be summed up in terms of what Storing considers their inconsistent attachment to competing ends. "Anti-Federalists were committed to the union and the states," Storing writes, "to both the great American republic and the small self-governing community; to commerce and to civic virtue; to both the private gain and the public good."[71] However, like Diamond, whose reading of the Federalists he follows in its main outlines (while emphasizing more than Diamond the Federalist faith in the ability of efficient public administration to secure the reasoned and self-interested attachments of the citizenry), Storing does not believe that these tensions or contradictions were resolved by the Constitution's innovations in political technology, but merely mitigated or attenuated by them. In this, he argues the Anti-Federalists, even with their "weaker argument," have nonetheless something important to teach contemporary Americans.

The tensions Storing identifies in Anti-Federalist thought are not only "critical weaknesses," but also indicate "the strength of their thought and even its glory": they illuminate tensions underwriting the fundamental commitments of the American regime itself.[72] I don't have time to detail Storing's elaborate (and in many ways convincing) argument here, but I will emphasize those aspects of the argument that bring it most clearly in line with Diamond's own and that suggests the "horizon beyond liberalism" approach to constitutionalism invoked by Strauss. For Storing, the Anti-Federalists, whatever their inconsistencies, saw clearly that the Federalist focus on improving the technical instruments of political life was ultimately insufficient to sustaining the political life of the republic.

Anti-Federalists tended to see the crisis of the 1780s as a result of the corruption of the citizenry, the loss of revolutionary virtues, and the proliferation of "vicious manners." Federalists, on the other hand, attributed the crisis—and its primary symptom of Shays' Rebellion—to the "the excesses of democracy" and to the weak and decentralized forms of government instituted in the wake of the Revolution.[73] Following from these very different diagnoses of the crisis of the 1780s, Anti-Federalists did not share the Federalist faith in the ability of institutional reorganization to adequately confront or "remedy" the "diseases" inherent to popular government. While Storing claims that Anti-Federalist thought was riddled with tensions and contradictions, he also argues that they better grasped the inescapability of formative politics, and the central importance of being attentive to this dimension when framing a constitution. They were less consistent liberals than the Federalists, Storing argued, but their inconsistency actually revealed a weakness in the fundamentals of modern liberalism itself. A premodern conception of the *politeia* inhabited—albeit quite unconsciously—the Anti-Federalist reliance on well-established arguments about the viability of small republics, arguments that offered the largest rhetorical obstacle to the Federalist vision of a viable extended republic enabled by the technological innovations of a new science of politics.

The most important—and from Storing's perspective, convincing—of the Anti-Federalist's objections to the new Constitution was its disavowal of formative politics and their reliance on the classical republican idea that "only a small republic can form the kind of citizens who will maintain republican government.[74] Anti-Federalists viewed the "whole organization of the polity as having an educative function," Storing writes, and they "emphasized repeatedly that the character of a people is affected by government and laws, but that this relation had been dangerously ignored in the framing of the proposed constitution."[75] "Government operates on the spirit of the people," as the Anti-Federalist Melancton Smith put the point, as much "as the spirit of the people operates upon it." For Anti-Federalists this meant that the government could not be neutral as to ends, it could not be a mere "regulator of conduct," but had to be a "molder of character" and actively work to frame government and law in such a way that, again quoting Melancton Smith, it "will tend to cherish and cultivate a love of liberty among our citizens."[76]

Storing's elaboration of this Anti-Federalist critique opens a space for critical judgment. In a closing argument that echoes Diamond's own, Storing worries about the ultimate consequences of *The Federalist's* disavowal of formative politics and its heavy reliance on the political technologies made possible by the new science of politics. Storing argues, in effect, that serious attention to the inconsistent liberalism of the Anti-Federalists educates readers to the weaknesses lurking in the more consistent liberalism of the Federalists.

Like Diamond, Storing ends by examining the "collateral consequences" and "unforeseen dangers" lurking in the Founder's technological solutions to the dangers inherent to popular self-government. "The liberal regime, the regime dedicated to liberty and thus the regime that self-consciously turns away from the comprehensive public moral formation of classical theory," as Michael Zuckert writes, "nonetheless does engage in moral formation of its own in its own way."[77] However, this moral formation lacks the morally inspiring excellence required to prevent the corruption of citizens, which in turn contributes to the dangers Strauss invoked in the opening pages of *Natural Right and History*.

The Federalist presumes the responsibility if not the virtue of its citizens, while not eliciting these qualities from the political institutions established under the Constitution. These qualities, Storing writes, "cannot be prudently taken for granted." "The Federalist solution," he concludes, "not only failed to provide for the moral qualities that are necessary to the maintenance of republican government; it tended to undermine them."[78] "Will not the constitutional regime," Storing asks, "with its emphasis on private, self-seeking, commercial activities release and foster a certain type of human being who will be likely to destroy that very regime?"[79]

This is a question asked of American constitutionalism by critics on the left as well as the right, but Storing's response comes firmly from the social conservative right, as he interprets the Anti-Federalist insistence on virtue in a narrowly moral and, indeed, Christian frame rather than emphasizing the equally pronounced, and more clearly political and democratic, Anti-Federalist insistence on virtue as virtù: that is, as the public spiritedness, vigilance, and jealousy of power emphasized in the last chapter.[80] However, Storing shares a critique of liberalism familiar from the left. It was the left, after all, that has traditionally turned to the Anti-Federalists for political inspiration. "The Anti-Federalists saw," Storing writes, "the insufficiency of a community of mere interest. They saw that the American regime had to be a moral community if it was to be anything, and they saw that the seat of that community must be in the hearts of the people."[81] The critique here is not just of the Founders' shortsightedness, but of the potentially fatal immorality of the political community their Constitution engendered. It is a good exemplification of the unresolved tensions, exclusions, and contradictions that underwrite any regime on Strauss's account. Strauss dismissed the idea that "it is possible to create a society free of contradictions," even, or perhaps especially, one purportedly neutral as to ends, and premised on open, fair, and formal procedures of conflict adjudication.

Diamond and Storing offer, in the words of Thomas West, an extremely "disheartening view of American politics," one hardly capable of mobilizing a public to a "renewed appreciation of our fundamental institutions and a rededication to their perpetuation."[82] West, along with many other contemporary American exceptionalist Straussians, is dissatisfied with Diamond's and Storing's (and Strauss's) qualified appreciation for the Constitution's "moderation" and "decency." They have sought to invest it, instead, with an unquestionable authority worth fighting and dying for. Where Diamond's and Storing's work aimed to bring the difficulties and costs of the American commitment to modern liberal constitutionalism into a more clear view so as to achieve an "educated ascent," to return to founding principles so as to stimulate the ongoing political navigation of the tensions inherent within them, this more recent work takes up the return to founding principles to discover their truth, so as to better provide American constitutionalism with the unquestioned and unquestionable courage of its convictions.

In closing, let me note that this shift in Straussian interpretations of the American Founding correlates with a much broader historical shift in conservative political discourse in the United States on the meaning of American constitutionalism. Isaac Kramnick and R. Laurence Moore have described this shift as "a staggering historical flip flop" in socially conservative political attitudes towards American constitutionalism.[83] For most of American history, religious and social conservatives decried the modern liberalism of American constitutionalism—particularly its separation of church and state—and mobilized historical efforts, mostly failed, to change it. Now they deny this liberalism altogether—what they formerly lamented as its "godless foundation"—and embrace "constitutional conservatism" as a way of rooting out liberalism from American political institutions and cultural life. This is very much the agenda of the "thin poetry" and "fanatical obscurantism" of today's American exceptionalist Straussians, a fact brought clearly into view by examining the scholarship of an earlier generation of scholars of *The Federalist*.[84]

NOTES

1. Aristotle, *The Politics* (Cambridge: Cambridge University Press, 1988), 119.
2. Shadia B. Drury, *Leo Strauss and the American Right* (Basingstoke, UK: Macmillan, 1997); Anne Norton, *Leo Strauss and the Politics of American Empire* (New Haven, CT: Yale University Press, 2004); Nicholas Xenos, *Cloaked in Virtue: Unveiling Leo Strauss and the Rhetoric of American Foreign Policy* (New York: Routledge, 2008).
3. Leo Strauss, "Letter to Karl Löwith," *Constellations* 16, no. 1 (2009): 82–83.
4. Thomas L. Pangle, *Leo Strauss: An Introduction to His Thought and Intellectual Legacy* (Baltimore, MD: Johns Hopkins University Press, 2006); Steven B. Smith, *Reading Leo Strauss: Politics, Philosophy, Judaism* (Chicago: University of Chicago Press, 2006); Catherine H. Zuckert and Michael P. Zuckert, *The Truth About Leo Strauss: Political Philosophy and American Democracy* (Chicago: University of Chicago Press, 2006).
5. William A. Galston, "Leo Strauss's Qualified Embrace of Liberal Democracy," in *The Cambridge Companion to Leo Strauss*, ed. Steven B. Smith (Cambridge: Cambridge University Press, 2009), 193–214.
6. See the essays collected in Kenneth L. Deutsch and John A. Murley, eds., *Leo Strauss, the Straussians and the American Regime* (Lanham, MD: Rowman & Littlefield, 1999).
7. Gordon S. Wood, "The Fundamentalists and the Constitution," *New York Review of Books*, February 18, 1988, 33.
8. "The self-evident truths of 1776 have been supplanted by the notion that no such truths exist." http://www.themountvernonstatement.com/.
9. Catherine and Michael Zuckert provide a helpful survey of these debates in their chapter "The Emergence of the Straussian Study of America," in Zuckert and Zuckert, *The Truth About Leo Strauss*, 217–27.
10. Mark Lilla, "The Closing of the Straussian Mind," *New York Review of Books*, November 4, 2004, 55–59.
11. Joseph Cropsey, "The United States as Regime and the Sources of the American Way of Life," in *Political Philosophy and the Issues of Politics* (Chicago: University of Chicago Press, 1977), 5; Martin Diamond, "On the Study of Politics in a Liberal Education," in *As Far as Republican Principles Will Admit: Essays by Martin Diamond*, ed. William A. Schambra (Washington, DC: AEI Press, 1992), 280.
12. Leo Strauss, *Natural Right and History* (Chicago: University of Chicago Press, 1953), 6.
13. Leo Strauss, "Liberal Education and Responsibility," in *Liberalism Ancient and Modern* (New York: Basic Books, 1968), 24.
14. Stephen Holmes catalogues these passages in the chapter he devotes to Strauss in Stephen Holmes, *The Anatomy of Antiliberalism* (Cambridge, MA: Harvard University Press, 1993).
15. David M. Estlund, *Democratic Authority: A Philosophical Framework* (Princeton, NJ: Princeton University Press, 2008), 206–22; see also George Kateb, "The Questionable Influence of Arendt (and Strauss)," in *Hannah Arendt and Leo Strauss: German*

Émigrés and American Political Thought after World War II, ed., Peter Graf Kielmansegg, Horst Mewes, and Elisabeth Glaser-Schmidt (New York: Cambridge University Press, 1995), 29–44.

16. Strauss makes this claim in his remarkable preface to the English translation of Spinoza's *Critique of Religion*, published in Leo Strauss, "Preface to Spinoza's Critique of Religion," in *Liberalism Ancient and Modern* (New York: Basic Books, 1968), 224–59. All references to Strauss's "Notes on the Concept of the Political" are taken from the translation included in Carl Schmitt, *The Concept of the Political*, ed. George Schwab (Chicago: University of Chicago Press, 2007), 83–107.

17. Heinrich Meier, *Carl Schmitt and Leo Strauss: The Hidden Dialogue* (Chicago: University of Chicago Press, 1995).

18. Lilla, "The Closing of the Straussian Mind," 56.

19. Strauss, "Notes on the Concept of the Political," 85.

20. Strauss, "Notes on the Concept of the Political," 107.

21. Cited in Meier, *Carl Schmitt and Leo Strauss*, xvii.

22. Strauss, "Notes on the Concept of the Political," 86.

23. Leo Strauss, "The Three Waves of Modernity," in *An Introduction to Political Philosophy: Ten Essays*, ed. Hilail Gildin (Detroit, MI: Wayne State University Press, 1989), 81–98.

24. Richard H. King, "Rights and Slavery, Race and Racism: Leo Strauss, and the American Dilemma," *Modern Intellectual History* 5, no. 1 (2008): 61.

25. Strauss, "Notes on the Concept of the Political," 104.

26. Strauss, "Notes on the Concept of the Political," 105.

27. Strauss, "Notes on the Concept of the Political," 105; see Carl Schmitt, "The Age of Neutralizations and Depoliticizations," *Telos* 96 (Summer 1993), 130–42.

28. Strauss, "Notes on the Concept of the Political," 105.

29. Strauss, "Preface to Spinoza's Critique of Religion," 230.

30. Leo Strauss, *The City and Man* (Chicago: University of Chicago Press, 1978), 11.

31. Robert Howse, "From Legitimacy to Dictatorship—and Back Again: Leo Strauss's Critique of the Anti-Liberalism of Carl Schmitt," in *Law as Politics: Carl Schmitt's Critique of Liberalism*, ed. David Dyzenhaus (Durham, NC: Duke University Press, 1998), 83.

32. Strauss, *Natural Right and History*, 136.

33. See Cropsey, "The United States as Regime and the Sources of the American Way of Life."

34. Strauss, *Natural Right and History*, 140.

35. Aristotle, *The Politics*, 119.

36. Howse, "From Legitimacy to Dictatorship." For a broader account of the role Schmitt's theory of constituent power in his theory of constitutionalism, see Renato Cristi, "Carl Schmitt on Sovereignty and Constituent Power," in *Law as Politics: Carl Schmitt's Critique of Liberalism*, ed. David Dyzenhaus (Durham, NC: Duke University Press, 1998), 179–95.

37. Carl Schmitt, *Constitutional Theory*, trans. Jeffrey Seitzer (Durham, NC: Duke University Press, 2008), 125.

38. Strauss, *Natural Right and History*, 105.

39. Leo Strauss, *What Is Political Philosophy? And Other Studies* (Chicago: University of Chicago Press, 1988), 43.

40. Strauss, *Natural Right and History*, 1.

41. Smith, *Reading Leo Strauss*, 169.

42. Strauss, *The City and Man*, 3.

43. King, "Rights and Slavery, Race and Racism," 60.

44. See Edward Purcell, *The Crisis of Democratic Theory: Scientific Naturalism and the Problem of Value* (Lexington: University of Kentucky Press, 1973).

45. Martin, Diamond, "Ethics and Politics: The American Way," in *As Far as Republic Principles Will Admit: Essays by Martin Diamond*, ed. William A. Schambra (Washington, DC: AEI Press, 1992), 340.

46. Martin Diamond, "Democracy and the Federalist: A Reconsideration of the Framers' Intent," in *As Far as Republic Principles Will Admit: Essays by Martin Diamond*, ed. William A. Schambra (Washington, DC: AEI Press, 1992), 18.

47. Herbert J. Storing, *What the Anti-Federalists Were For* (Chicago: University of Chicago Press, 1981), 13. See also Thomas L. Pangle, *The Spirit of Modern Republicanism: The Moral Vision of the American Founders and the Philosophy of Locke* (Chicago: University of Chicago Press, 1988).

48. Sheldon S. Wolin, *The Presence of the Past: Essays on the State and the Constitution* (Baltimore, MD: The Johns Hopkins University Press, 1989), 3.

49. See John Brigham, "Original Intent and Other Cult Classics," *The Good Society* 11, no. 2 (2002): 13–17.

50. A full excavation of these connections has not yet been done. A good place to begin, however, would be a comparison of Diamond's *American Political Science Review* essay, "Democracy and the Federalist: A Reconsideration of the Framers' Intent" discussed below, and Norman Jacobson's remarkably similar arguments in a 1963 essay from the same journal, "Political Science and Political Education," *American Political Science Review* 57, no. 3 (1963): 561–69. Benjamin Barber outlines some of these themes in Barber, "The Politics of Political Science: 'Value-free' Theory and the Wolin-Strauss Dust-Up of 1963" *American Political Science Review* 100, no. 4 (2006), 539–545.

51. Diamond, "On the Study of Politics in a Liberal Education," 278.

52. Strauss, *Natural Right and History*, 3.

53. Michael P. Zuckert, *Launching Liberalism: On Lockean Political Philosophy* (Lawrence: University Press of Kansas, 2002); Pangle, *The Spirit of Modern Republicanism*; Harry Jaffa, *A New Birth of Freedom: Abraham Lincoln and the Coming of the Civil War* (Lanham, MD: Rowman & Littlefield, 2000).

54. Michael P. Zuckert, "Refinding the Founding: Martin Diamond, Leo Strauss, and the American Regime," in *Leo Strauss, the Straussians, and the American Regime*, ed. Kenneth L. Deutsch and John A. Murley (Lanham, MD: Rowman & Littlefield, 1999), 235.

55. Martin Diamond, "The Federalist," in *History of Political Philosophy*, ed. Leo Strauss and Joseph Cropsey (Chicago: University of Chicago Press, 1987), 631–51.

56. Diamond, "The Federalist," 632.

57. All references to *The Federalist* are from Jacob E. Cooke's definitive edition, Jacob E. Cooke, ed., *The Federalist* (Middletown, CT: Wesleyan University Press, 1961), 65.

58. Diamond, "The Federalist," 632.

59. Diamond, "Ethics and Politics," 345.

60. Diamond, "Ethics and Politics," 355.

61. Diamond, "Ethics and Politics," 353.

62. Diamond, "Democracy and the Federalist," 35.

63. Diamond, "Ethics and Politics," 355.

64. Diamond, "Democracy and the Federalist," 36.

65. Herbert J. Storing, ed., *The Complete Anti-Federalist*, 7 vols. (Chicago: University of Chicago Press, 1981); Merill Jensen et al., eds., *The Documentary Story of the Ratification of the Constitution and the Bill of Rights, 1787–1791*, 23 vols. (Madison: Wisconsin Historical Society Press, 1976–2009).

66. See Cecelia Kenyon, "Men of Little Faith: The Anti-Federalists on the Nature of Representative Government," *The William and Mary Quarterly* 12, no. 1 (1955): 3–43.

67. Storing, *What the Anti-Federalists Were For*, 6.

68. Storing, *What the Anti-Federalists Were For*, 6.

69. Storing, *What the Anti-Federalists Were For*, 5.

70. Storing, *What the Anti-Federalists Were For*, 71.

71. Storing, *What the Anti-Federalists Were For*, 6.

72. Storing, *What the Anti-Federalists Were For*, 6.

73. See, most notably, Gordon S. Wood, *The Creation of the American Republic, 1776–1787* (Chapel Hill: University of North Carolina Press, 1969).

74. Storing, *What the Anti-Federalists Were For*, 16.

75. Storing, *What the Anti-Federalists Were For*, 21.

76. Storing, *What the Anti-Federalists Were For*, 19.

77. Zuckert, "Refinding the Founding," 248.

78. Storing, *What the Anti-Federalists Were For*, 73.

79. Storing, *What the Anti-Federalists Were For*, 73.

80. For an influential discussion of the complex meanings of early American invocations of political virtue, see James T. Kloppenburg, "The Virtues of Liberalism: Christianity, Republicanism, and Ethics in Early American Political Discourse," *Journal of American History* 74, no. 1 (1987): 9–33.

81. Storing, *What the Anti-Federalists Were For*, 76.

82. Thomas G. West, "Leo Strauss and the American Founding," *Review of Politics* 53, no. 1 (1991): 157–72.

83. Isaac Kramnick and R. Laurence Moore, *The Godless Constitution: A Moral Defense of the Secular State* (New York: W. W. Norton, 2005), 148.

84. Thomas L. Pangle, "Patriotism American Style," *National Review* (November 29, 1985), 30–34.

FIVE

From "We the People" to "We the Electorate"

A Republic was inevitably the American form, and its Natural danger
Pop. Tumults and Convulsions . . . . The People, the Origin of Power,
cannot act personally, & can only exercise their power by representation.
                    —James Madison to Edward Pendleton, October 8, 1787[1]

It is clear that the principle of representation was neither unknown to
the ancients, nor wholly overlooked in their political constitutions. The
true distinction between these and the American Governments lies *in
the total exclusion of the people in their collective capacity* from any share in
the *latter*.
                                        —*Federalist* No. 63[2]

This passage from *The Federalist* has often been invoked by democratic
critics of the United States Constitution as evidence of Framers' mistrust
of popular politics in general, and of its more unruly collective manifestations in particular. As we have seen in previous chapters, *The Federalist* is
filled with foreboding about the dangers attending the people's collective
appearance on the postrevolutionary political scene. However, as Bernard Manin argues in his influential study of the principles of representative government, this passage is about more than Publius's fear of democratic excess and majority tyranny; it also points to an important transformation in the modern understanding of political representation itself
wherein political equality comes to signify "the equal right to consent to
power" rather than "an equal chance to hold office." For reasons I will
explore below, I would modify Manin's emphasis on office holding with
the broader view of participating *in* power, but I agree that a "new conception of citizenship" is envisioned by Publius's distinction between
ancient and American constitutions. "Citizens," Manin summarily writes,

"were now viewed primarily as the source of political legitimacy, rather than as persons who might desire to hold office [participate in power] themselves."[3]

The shift Manin identifies has far-reaching consequences for how the people are imagined and how their agency is institutionally interpellated, a question already raised in chapter 1's discussion of ratifying conventions and constituent power. This final chapter explores different modes of this imagining and interpellation, and suggests some of the far-reaching consequences, by turning to how the debates between Federalists and Anti-Federalists contested the meaning of political representation and the legitimacy of popular politics. A different set of theoretical issues surrounding the people as a projection of political imagination emerges from this examination—from the question of *who* the sovereign people are, to the question of *how* the sovereign people is enacted. Recounting the constitutional conversion of the expansively egalitarian and internally conflicted rhetoric of "we the people" to the individualized and routinized agency of "we the electorate" challenges the simple equation—common in both our political science and in our political life—of democratic authority with suffrage. This is a valuable historical reminder to conclude the book, considering the notorious inability of democratic electorates to significantly redress dramatic inequalities of wealth and power. There is a large and growing scholarly literature, for example, investigating the failure of formal electoral mechanisms to hold political and economic elites accountable in the United States.[4] This final chapter will argue that a reading of *The Federalist* suggests this to be less an unintended failure of the political institutions founded and ratified in 1787–1788 than an anticipated outcome.

The discussion proceeds in three parts. In the first, I outline the central theoretical issue dividing Federalists and Anti-Federalists over how the people should engage in the political life of the new republic: their competing concepts of representation. In the second section, I turn from these competing concepts of representation to the different institutional technologies they devised to achieve those ideals. In this section, I am particularly concerned to examine, more than I have up to this point, how "the great mechanical power" of representation is organized through the size of the polity and of electoral districts as a means of providing what Publius called a "republican remedy" to one of the "diseases most incident to republican government," namely faction (*F*, 84). However, as I will show in the third section, faction is only *one* of the diseases Publius believes popular republican politics have historically engendered; the other disease he describes more broadly as "insurrection." These are interrelated but conceptually distinct phenomena of republican politics that have sometimes been conflated in the scholarship on *The Federalist*. It was not particular forms of election that were devised to address this second challenge to republican governance, so much as it was elections as such.

Elections were not only envisioned by Publius as important "exterior provisions" whereby the people could check government power, but also as powerful tools *of* governance, means through which the government indirectly secured the rule of a worthy elite—a "natural aristocracy"—and controlled and channeled the political agency of the people themselves. Like the interested conduct of citizens explored in chapter 3, envisioned in this way, elections exemplify a shift in republican strategies of popular governance, wherein government power did not directly inhibit or interfere with the liberty of citizens, but was instead sublimated into the citizenry's indirectly regulated free conduct, in this case the narrowing of different forms of citizen-initiated political participation and popular enactment into voting. Publius understood how elections enable and constrain, empower and govern, political constituencies, and their central importance in securing "the amelioration of popular systems of civil government" (*F*, 51).

This chapter's focus on the duality of elections—at once the "principal mechanisms by which citizens attempt to control the state," and the tools of governance that limit popular politics and increase the power of the state—aims to recover some of the key political preoccupations of the period, not only with the frequency of elections, terms of office, spheres of jurisdiction, or qualifications for formal enfranchisement—all familiar criteria for evaluating democratic suffrage—but also with the different mechanisms and non-electoral practices through which the people's will was enacted and institutionally embodied in postrevolutionary contexts.[5] Where Manin focuses his study primarily on the contrast between election and lot as formal mechanisms of popular government, I will emphasize the complex postrevolutionary assemblage of formal and informal institutions of popular will formation and elite accountability.

Postrevolutionary Americans, as the historian Christian G. Fritz has recently demonstrated, "vigorously debated whether the people could express their sovereign will . . . only by using government-sanctioned procedures."[6] When Publius invoked the American Government's "*total exclusion of the people in their collective capacity*," he not only contrasted the Constitution's "schema of representation" with the assemblies and tribunals of ancient Rome, but also with a plenitude of postrevolutionary forms of collective participation in political power. By establishing a uniform economy of popular representation, *The Federalist*'s Constitution aimed to absorb the people's constituent power into formal procedures of electoral institutions. The Preamble's "We the People" therefore anticipates and authorizes the people's subsequent disappearance, or its severely mitigated appearance in article 1, section 2, requiring that "the House of Representatives shall be composed of Members chosen every second Year by the People of the several States." Publius and other Federalists "hoped that after ratification the collective sovereign would express itself only by electing representatives."[7] In doing so, they established the state itself as "the fixed center of political life," and reimagined politics as what Wolin calls "organizational activity aimed at a single, dominating objective, control of state apparatus."[8] This concluding chapter reconstructs the political background—and suggests the democratic costs—of that vision. In it, the arc of the book's argument—which begins with the ratifying invocation of the people's constituent capacities and then catalogues *The Federalist*'s various formative strategies to govern those capacities and discipline the political imagination—will come to a close.

I.

"Of all the conceptions of political theory underlying the momentous developments of the American revolutionary era," Gordon Wood writes, "none was more important than that of representation."[9] Representation is often invoked in the period as the key "improvement" of the modern "science of politics"—in Publius's words, a "powerful means by which the excellencies of republican government may be maintained and its imperfections lessened or avoided" (*F*, 51). Publius revealingly called representation the "great mechanical power" in government, and he defined republicanism itself—in contrast with democracy—as the form of "government in which the scheme of representation takes place." It was through modern advances and refinements of this "scheme," Publius argued, that a "republican remedy" could be found "for the diseases most incident to republican government" (*F*, 65), especially those related but conceptually distinct diseases of "faction" and "insurrection."

Political representation was most closely aligned by Publius and his contemporaries with legislative assemblies, and Publius sometimes narrowly refers to the legislative branch simply as "the representative body." He worries about the tendency of the legislature to extend the "sphere of its activity," and draw "all power into its impetuous vortex," (*F*, 333) because legislative power is most closely associated with popular authority (he also refers to it as the "popular branch"). "The representatives of the people, in a popular assembly," Publius writes, "seem sometimes to fancy that they are the people themselves" (*F*, 483). To counter this dangerous delusion, the argument of the *Federalist* is to present the entirety of the Constitution as a functioning representation of popular authority, a collective authorship indicated, of course, by the Preamble's opening invocation of "We the People."

The people's voice, Publius argues across eighty-five essays, is represented not only through the "popular branch" but also through the network of constitutional mechanisms that establish the operations—and check the power—of the legislative branch. The argument is most clearly stated in *Federalist* No. 78, where Publius equates the Constitution itself with "the people's intention" and authorizing will, and on this basis argues that no legislation "contrary to the constitution can be valid." "To deny this," he continues, "would be to affirm that the deputy is greater than his principal; that the servant is above his master; that the representatives of the people are superior to the people themselves" (*F*, 524). In No. 78 Publius makes "the Constitution," "fundamental law," and "the people themselves" equivalent terms, and audaciously presents the people's will as not only represented by the Constitution, but as strictly equivalent to it, that is, as wholly absorbed within its constituted legal form and the political channels established by it. What conception of political representation can possibly validate such a remarkable claim?

In examining this question, it is important to note how sharply this conception contrasted with the dominant view espoused by American revolutionaries. Underlying the colonial catechism "no taxation without representation" was a "mimetic" theory of political representation that evaluated representation primarily by how closely the representatives' actions corresponded to the "actual"—that is, the stated and explicit— demands and preferences of their constituents. The colonists' frequently reiterated argument regarding Parliament's tax policies in the 1760s was that representatives must be directly accountable to actual people from particular locations rather than to the abstractions of fixed social orders or the representative's own understanding of the common good. Parliament, conversely, defended itself by appealing to what George Grenville's secretary, Thomas Whately, described as a theory of "virtual representation," according to which Parliament represented not specific districts and actual constituent demands, but a deliberative body through which all "the Commons of Great Britain are represented."

The revolutionary debate around "actual" and "virtual" representation can be understood as a historic exemplification of "the mandate-independence controversy," which Hanna Pitkin describes as the "central classic controversy in the literature on political representation." "Should (must) a representative do what his constituents want, and be bound by mandates or instructions from them," the question goes, "or should (must) he be free to act as seems best to him in pursuit of their welfare?"[10] The mandate view, taken to its fullest extent, reduces the representative to a mere tool of the represented, acting only on the basis of their explicit instructions. This position reduces the representative to a passive instrument of their interests or preferences. In the terms of contemporary democratic theory, the descriptive literalism of the mandate view makes it broadly compatible with "aggregative" conceptions of democracy, which "take expressed preferences as the privileged or primary material for democratic decision making," rather than decisions based in moral justification and reasoned deliberation.[11]

The independence view, by contrast, emphasizes the normative importance of independent deliberation and judgment on the part of the representative. It is not the explicitly articulated preferences of the repre-

sented that are essential but the broader, more objective, and "unattached" interests of the constituency taken as a whole. Representation is
not evaluated here on the basis of how accurately it corresponds with the
stated interests or preferences of the represented (whether articulated
through votes or opinion polls), but with a deliberative capacity to judge
independently of them. If the mandate view risks reducing the representative to a passive instrument, the independence view seems to undermine democratic accountability and inflate the wisdom, expertise, or
superior rationality of the representative.

While the main outlines of revolutionary debates over representation
are captured in the familiar terms of the "the mandate-independence
controversy," these terms do not correspond as clearly to the central issues dividing Federalists and Anti-Federalists as is often supposed.
While the ratification debates have sometimes been portrayed as reitera-
tions of revolutionary arguments over representation—with the Anti-
Federalists cast as beleaguered colonists invoking the requirements of
actual representation, and Federalists offering a modified republican articulation of virtual representation—important features of their competing views are obscured by this familiar comparison. Some Anti-Federalists did insist on the right of constituents to "instruct" their representatives, and all of them feared that the scheme of representation established
by the Constitution severely weakened popular accountability.

However, the most provocative Anti-Federalist argument was not that
the people should be able to instruct representatives and hold them more
directly accountable to their constituents' preferences and demands, but
that the people—in the sense of the common or the many—should actually be able to participate in government and hold office. The Anti-Federalist claim was not that representatives should mirror the stated preference
of their electors, but that they should "resemble" them and "possess their
sentiments and feelings, and be governed by their interests." Brutus offers the clearest articulation of this Anti-Federalist position:

> The very term, representative implies that the person or body chosen
> for this purpose, should resemble those who appoint them—a repre-
> sentation of the people of America, if it be a true one must be like the
> people. It ought to be so constituted that a person who is a stranger to
> the country, might be able to form a just idea of their character, by
> knowing that of their representatives. They are the sign—the people
> are the thing signified. [12]

Brutus's point here is not to reduce the representative to a passive tool
of instruction—what Eric Slauter has recently described as mere "object"—but to insist that the common people—the "great body of the yeoman of the country," for example, "the mechanics of every branch"—
actually hold and participate in power. [13] Manin recognizes this point:
"The charge the Anti-Federalists repeatedly leveled was not that under

the proposed Constitution representatives would fail to act as instructed, but that they would not be *like* those that elected them."[14] Another Anti-Federalists, the Federal Farmer, argued that "fair representation . . . ought to be so regulated, that every order of men in the community . . . can have a share in it."[15] The fear of Anti-Federalists like Brutus and the Federal Farmer was that under the Constitution "the great body of planters and farmers cannot expect any of their order . . . being chosen . . . only the gentry, the rich, the well born will be elected." The "natural aristocracy of the country," "the well born," "the highest orders of life," Brutus claims, "will be ignorant of the sentiments of the middling class of citizens, strangers to their ability, wants, and difficulties, and void of sympathy and fellow feeling."[16] The Anti-Federalist account of representation rests on an epistemic claim that the independent judgment of the representative should accord with that of the representatives without the need of explicit instruction. "The great art, therefore, in forming a good constitution," Brutus writes, is "to frame it as that those to whom the power is committed shall be subject to the same feeling and aim at the same objects as the people who transfer to them their authority."[17]

While this may appear to be a radicalization of the revolutionary argument about "actual" representation, and even resemble some contemporary arguments calling for the presence of women and ethnic minorities in elected assemblies—going beyond constituent interests to constituent identities—it was not a rare or idiosyncratic argument in late eighteenth-century America, particularly after the Revolution.[18] John Adams himself, hardly a radical democrat, wrote in 1776 that a popular legislative assembly should "be in miniature, an exact portrait of the people at large. It should think, feel, reason, and act like them."[19] In 1788, however, Publius dismissed this view as an "impracticable" and dangerous fantasy. "The idea of an actual representation of all classes of the people by persons of each class," he writes, "is altogether visionary" (*F*, 219). While acknowledging the central importance that representatives "be acquainted with the general genius, habits and modes of thinking of the people at large and with the resources of the country" (*F*, 222), Publius argued that all this required was the effective and timely communication of relevant information, not resemblance of character, shared sentiments, or class identity. The necessary knowledge to effectively represent a constituency can be better obtained by a "skillful individual in his closet," Publius writes, "with all the local codes before him," than a farmer who can better sympathize with his neighbors' sentiments and feelings (*F*, 380). Publius claims, further, that "this is all that can be reasonably meant by a knowledge of the interests and feelings of the people. In any other sense the proposition has either no meaning, or an absurd one" (*F*, 222). As Suzette Hemberger has recognized, there is a clear difference in the *kind* of knowledge required for a "proper representation" on the Anti-Federalist and Federalist views: The former is focused on tacit dimensions acquired by shared lived experience, and the latter on the skills and expertise of a specialist. The one knowledge is situated and ethnographic; the other, formal and objective.[20]

It was not only the impracticability of the Anti-Federalist view that concerned Publius, but what he considered its dangerously narrow parochialism. From Publius's perspective, the Anti-Federalist insistence on the representative's resemblance to the represented was little more than the affirmation of "the bias of local views and prejudices" (*F*, 144). The distinction between the unreflective expression of aggregate "inclinations," "whims," and "preferences," and the more normatively robust and objective standard of what Publius alternately describes as "the common good of the society," "the public weal," "the good of the whole," "the great interests of the nation," and "the national prosperity and happiness" is reiterated throughout *The Federalist*. Publius returns at several points to "occasions" in which "the interests of the people" will be found to be "at variance with their inclinations" (*F*, 482). "The mild voice of reason, pleading the cause of an enlarged and permanent interest, is but too often drowned, before public bodies as well as individuals, by the clamors of an impatient avidity for immediate and immoderate gain" (*F*, 283). Publius characterized this enlarged, permanent, and objective standard as "the cool and deliberate sense of the community" (*F*, 425), thereby providing evidence for the now familiar claim that "deliberative democracy was the conscious creation of the delegates to the Constitutional Convention of 1787" as explained in *The Federalist*.[21] The opposition seems to suggest a representative articulation of a deliberated general will that contrasts with a popularly aggregated will of all.

Less amenable to the deliberative democratic appropriation of Publius's argument, however, is the latter's insistence that knowledge of "the cool and deliberate sense of the community" is not available to the people themselves—whose political participation, as we saw in chapter 3, and as I will elaborate upon below, is not at all envisioned in the terms of collective deliberations over topics of common concern—but only to elect representatives capable of taking such an "enlarged view" of matters. It is the proclaimed epistemic authority and superior judgment of the representative that led the Massachusetts Federalist Fisher Ames to succinctly claim that "the representation of the people is something more than the people,"[22] and that led Publius to write that "the public voice pronounced by the representatives of the people, will [under proper regulation] be more consonant to the public good, than if pronounced by the people themselves convened for that purpose" (*F*, 62).

Federalists rejected the Anti-Federalist position that political representation was only an unfortunate concession to necessity "because it is impossible for the people to act collectively." Instead, the Federalist conception of representation claimed a superior wisdom and authority for the representative based on "skills" and "capacities" not found among the people at large. This is not a moral incapacity of the people—"It is a just observation that the people commonly *intend* the PUBLIC GOOD," Publius writes—but an epistemic one: the people do not always "*reason right*" about the *means* of promoting it" (*F*, 482; emphasis in original). The representative government envisioned in Publius's argument shares the people's normative commitment to the public good—what Publius elsewhere calls "fidelity to the object of government, which is the happiness of the people"—but adds to this the more specialized administrative knowledge that comes with wielding power—that is, "a knowledge of the means by which that object can be best obtained" (*F*, 419).

In framing the debate over representation in this way, Publius converts the qualitative objections of the Anti-Federalists—no amount of learning, study, or skill will transform a wealthy merchant into a yeoman farmer—into a quantitative or technical problem—the wealthy merchant only requires the skill and information necessary to act representatively on behalf of constituents. Wolin has described this in terms of the contrast between the Anti-Federalist politics of place, and the Federalist politics of space.[23] The priority Anti-Federalists give to locality and physical proximity, as we have seen, was aimed at making the actual participation in government of sociologically distinct sectors of the population the essential point; it was about who substantively wielded power.

Publius sometimes responds to this familiar Anti-Federalist objection by mischaracterizing it as a sociologically detached problem of the office of the representative itself, as if Anti-Federalists were primarily concerned with "the want of a sufficient knowledge of local circumstances." "Inquisitive and enlightened statesmen," Publius writes for example, "are deemed everywhere best qualified to make judicious selection of the objects proper for revenue, which is a clear indication . . . of the species of knowledge of local circumstances requisite to the purposes of taxation" (*F*, 224). The Anti-Federalist concern with the ability of different classes to participate in governance is quietly displaced in *The Federalist* by Publius's emphasis that the representative be "a well informed man," "enlightened," and "respectable." A commonly invoked eighteenth-century category to describe the worthy is the "natural aristocracy," which at once distinguished it from the politically instituted hereditary aristocracy of monarchical regimes, while setting it apart from the common people. "Birth, education, talents, and wealth," said the Anti-Federalist Melancton Smith in the New York Ratifying Convention, "create distinctions among men as visible and of as much influence as titles, stars, and garters."[24]

While Publius denied the frequent Anti-Federalist claim that the participants of the Philadelphia Convention were motivated "by high aristocratic ideas and a contempt for the common people," he nonetheless admitted that the skills and knowledge required of the representative will typically be found in elite segments of the society, especially "pro-

prietors of the land," "merchants," "and members of the learned profes-
sions" (*F*, 223). However, to formally mandate criteria assuring the election of members of these classes would obviously undermine the basic
principles of popular government. A "republican remedy" instead had to
be found. The difficulty confronting the Federalist majority during the
Philadelphia Convention, as Woody Holton has very persuasively demonstrated, was how to put the "new government sufficiently beyond the
reach of popular influence to ensure that it acted responsibly, but without
making it so unresponsive to the popular will as to not only violate their
highest ideals but also jeopardize ratification."[25] The Federalists focused
their attention not narrowly on explicitly stated rules and prohibitions for
office holding, although these were considered, but on the indirect effects
of innovations in political technology, first and foremost the organization
of popular elections.

II.

Anti-Federalists and Federalists disagreed dramatically in their understanding and explanation of the crisis of the 1780s. For Anti-Federalists,
the loss of political virtues engendered by the Revolution—the "spirit of
'76"—and the corruption by luxury of the newly enfranchised citizenry
were the central problems that reformers had to address; they called for a
return to revolutionary austerity and for renewed moral and political
vigilance. For Federalists, however, the most important causes of the crisis were the weak and poorly organized political institutions established
in the wake of Independence—both the Articles of Confederation and the
individual state constitutions—an institutional analysis that naturally led
to proposals for institutional reform. The 1780s forced a separation, Gordon Wood has written, "between those who clung to moral reforms and
the regeneration of men's hearts as the remedy for viciousness and those
who looked to mechanical devices and institutional contrivances as the
only lasting solution for America's ills."[26] This divide clearly played itself
out in the debates between Anti-Federalists and Federalists. The difference was already stated explicitly by those Anti-Federalists critical of the
entire approach taken by the Philadelphia Convention, as exemplified by
an anonymous writer in the *Philadelphia Freeman's Journal*:

> It is taken for granted [by participants in the convention] . . . that
> something is accidentally wrong with our political machine, which a
> little skill and contrivance may at once put to rights by the magic of a
> few resolves upon paper; not considering that the evils and confusions
> we experience have originated in a great measure with the people
> themselves, and by them only can be eventually rectified. A long
> course of frugality, disuse of foreign luxuries, encouragement of indus-
> try, application to agriculture, attention to home manufactures, and a

spirit of union and national sobriety, can alone place us in the respectable rank of rich and flourishing nations.[27]

As we saw in the last chapter, more than any other approach to early American constitutionalism, it was the first generation students of Leo Strauss who most emphasized the Federalist reliance on political technology to resolve the political dilemmas of the 1780s.

Publius and other Federalists focused their attention on the operations of this intricate political machinery, and its foundation in the improvements that had been made in the new "science of politics." They also emphasized the expertise required to understand these modern improvements in political science and political technology. While the "principles of liberty" could be understood by many, because they were "matters of feeling," one Federalist wrote, the "principles of government" were much harder to grasp, being "objects of reflection and reason."[28] Anti-Federalists often responded to this line of argument by claiming that it was the very complexity of the political machinery devised by the Philadelphia Convention that obscured its operations from the mass of citizens, thereby shielding government from popular accountability. Many Anti-Federalists argued that the complexity of government outlined in the Constitution aimed to remove political matters from popular concern and the capabilities of ordinary citizens and instead make them matters of specialized knowledge and expertise. It exemplified the antirevolutionary sentiment that many Anti-Federalists attributed to supporters of the Constitution, namely, as clearly stated by the Old Whig: "THAT COMMON PEOPLE HAVE NO BUSINESS TO TROUBLE THEMSELVES ABOUT THE GOVERNMENT," "that they are not fit for it; that they should leave these matters to their superiors."[29]

The organization of elections under Publius's Constitution was an essential part of this political machinery and its attempt to safeguard government against "ill humors in the society" (*F*, 528). It was through the direct election of legislative representatives in the House and state legislatures, and indirect forms of election in the Senate and Presidency, that the abstract norms of political representation outlined above were orchestrated to achieve improved electoral outcomes "in aptitude and tendency." The Constitution left many of the details of election to the states, and there were distinctive regional political cultures around voting in the United States well into the nineteenth century.[30] However, one central point of contention between Federalists and Anti-Federalists was the size of electoral districts themselves, and especially article 1, section 2's limitation of representatives in the House to no more than one per thirty thousand residents. In what Woody Holton has described as the "dimensions debate" over the size of electoral districts we can see once again the shift in Federalist strategy away from an approach to popular governance through direct imposition, interference, or prohibition, and towards forms of governance that indirectly channel and regulate the free behavior of citizens through established institutional procedures. Politically demarcated territory and space itself became an important means of indirect popular governance in *The Federalist*, as did the political temporality established by the Constitution. Both were techniques for regulating and managing—if not overcoming—social conflict.

Through innovations in institutional organization, Publius hoped to found republicanism on a more stable constitutional foundation than ancient republics. Advances in institutional design and "contrivance" promised a more enduring republicanism with a markedly different political temporality, linear and progressive in tendency, rather than subject to Polybian cycles of decline and regeneration.[31] Republics were no longer fated to be "continually agitated," in "a state of perpetual vibration, between the extremes of tyranny and anarchy," Publius argued, but would instead endure through probabilistically reliable forms of institutionally channeled political behavior. Conflict would be accepted, even encouraged, in the "schema of representation" Publius defended and explained, but this conflict would engender a stable empire and "permanent monument" to the errors of past republics (F, 50–51).

The central component of Publius's celebrated "amelioration of systems of civil government," was the "republican remedy" he argued that the United States Constitution established for the "diseases most incident to republican government" (F, 65)—"diseases" he distinguished in the terms of "domestic faction and insurrection." The analysis of faction in *Federalist* No. 10, already discussed in chapter 3, was focused on "controlling [the] effects" of faction, rather than "removing its causes"—a shift in governing strategy that distinguished the modern constitutional improvements Publius defended in *The Federalist*. To control the causes of faction, Publius wrote, would be either to abolish the political liberty that defined republicanism or to "give every citizen the same opinions, the same passions, and the same interests" (F, 58). He associated this latter strategy with the "prevailing prejudices" of ancient republicanism and their adoption by Anti-Federalist critics of the Constitution; it was the approach Publius new science of political hoped to transcend.

The logic of Publius's argument has been the focus of intense scholarly controversy ever since Charles Beard focused attention on the argument in his *Economic History of the United States Constitution*.[32] Larry Kramer has recently argued that, based on the failure of many contemporaries to recognize the innovations of *Federalist* No. 10's argument about faction and filtration, scholars should not consider the analysis authoritative for their interpretations of American constitutionalism.[33] However, the key insight of *Federalist* No. 10's distinctive approach to curing the "instability, injustice, and confusion" in "public councils" that had been the "mortal diseases under which popular governments have everywhere perished"—that is, the "extent and proper structure of the Union"—was more widespread in Federalist political discourse than Kramer allows.[34] "In small societies," as Charles Pickney warned the South Carolina Ratifying Convention, "the people are easily assembled and inflamed"; "The schemes of the Rich will be favored by the extent of the Country," Gouverneur Morris declared in the Philadelphia Convention, "The people in such distant parts cannot communicate & act in concert. They will be the dupes of those who have more knowledge & intercourse."[35]

Publius developed these broader insights about space and popular governance in distinctive directions. The most familiar argument focused on how the extension of territory, proliferation of competing factions of interest, and distinctive dynamics of electoral politics could work to secure more stable forms of popular rule and more legitimate forms of political representation than was possible in the presumed necessity of small republics. The stability argument, as Madison admitted in a letter to Thomas Jefferson, was a classical instance of divide and rule: "Divide et impera, the reprobated axiom of tyranny, is under certain qualifications, the only policy, by which a republic can be administered on just principles."[36] Writing as Publius, Madison elaborated in *Federalist* No. 10:

> Extend the sphere, and you take in a greater variety of parties and interests; you make it less probable that a majority of the whole will have a common motive to invade the rights of other citizens; or if such a common motive exists, it will be more difficult for all who feel it to discover their own strength, and act in unison with each other. (*F*, 64)

The Federalist's art of popular separation and the institutional safeguards it envisions against "the danger of combining" (*F*, 425) are not merely about stability, but also engage a more assertively normative argument that the larger the territory of a society "the more duly capable it will be of self-government" (*F*, 353). However, the capacity for self-government envisioned by Publius has little do with the capacities elicited from the people themselves, and much more to do with those of their representatives. The people are not *themselves* required to focus political attention and deliberation on "the public weal," but are in fact institutionally discouraged from doing so. Their ability to "feel" common motives, "discover their own strength, and act in unison with each other" is institutionally undermined. While we have seen Publius elicit the constituent capacities of the people in chapter 1, the dominant popular imaginary offered in *The Federalist* does not envision a citizenry capable of cultivating arts of collective self-government and deliberation, except as this emerges incrementally and indirectly across time. Publius organized institutions in such a way that the people's representatives would tend to have and acquire these capacities, for "the whole power of the proposed government is to be in the hands of the representatives of the people," which Publius argues was "the only efficacious security for the rights and privileges of the people which is attainable in civil society" (*F*, 178). The alchemy of electoral representation, Publius insisted, could turn the base metals of narrow and prejudicial popular political input into the gold of wise governance and efficient administration.

The Federalist's argument about the improved capacities of self-governance in a large republic is not only about the size of political territory in general—how "extending the sphere" mitigates the dangers of democratic majorities—but also about the size of electoral districts and the likely dynamics of elections in larger districts. The key principle here is sometimes called "filtration." Through the election of representatives in larger districts, the narrow and parochial interests of locality are transcended: "men of factious tempers, of local prejudices, or of sinister designs," cannot win the votes of a majority, and "men who possess the most attractive merit and the most diffusive and established characters" will rise to popular attention and electoral victory (*F*, 62–63). The effect, Publius writes, is "to refine and enlarge the public views, by passing them through the medium of a chosen body of citizens, whose wisdom may best discern the true interest of their country, and whose patriotism and love of justice, will be least likely to sacrifice it to temporary and partial considerations" (*F*, 62).

Elections operate according to what Bernard Manin calls "the principle of distinction," and both Federalists and Anti-Federalists recognized that "election by itself carries an aristocratic effect."[37] By electing an aristocracy of talent you typically elect an aristocracy of wealth, Federalists argued, since the natural inequality of the human "faculties" resulted in corresponding inequalities of wealth and property. This effect was obviously increased in larger electoral districts, which, as Madison argued in the Philadelphia Convention, would "be manifestly favorable to the election of persons with a probable attachment to the rights of property," or as he put it elsewhere, would "extract from the mass of the society the purest and noblest characters which it contains."[38]

Madison's language of probability is important here. Publius would later emphasize that this aristocratic effect was not *mandated* by law, but instead indirectly was achieved through the operation of electoral procedures that would reliably *tend*, when multiplied over a large number of elections conducted in large expanses of time, to produce this favorable result. Political probability is an essential part of Publius's argument in defense of the Constitution.

In defending the convention's plan, Publius emphasized the guarantee of republican forms of government and the openness of free elections: "No qualification in monied or landed property is required by the proposed plan" (*F*, 432). There were lengthy discussions during the convention over such qualifications for enfranchisement and office holding— whether or not there should be property qualifications for participation in Federal elections, for example. The decision to leave these questions to the states protected participants from the expected charge they were intent on limiting the franchise. The strategy elaborated and defended by Publius was both more reliable and less open to direct contestation because it made the same result probable in "aptitude and tendency" without direct inhibitions on the people's political freedom — and without the direct opposition such inhibitions would likely engender. In Woody Holton's words, Publius and other Federalists rejected "blatant restrictions on popular power in favor of subtler ones."[39] While Publius at one point in *Federalist* No. 60 argues that "there is no method of securing to the rich the preference [of likely election], but by prescribing qualifications of property either for those who may elect, or be elected" (*F*, 408), the arc of his argument relies on the aggregate probability of precisely such electoral outcomes without direct prescription.

The sought-after effect of the insistence on large electoral districts was to achieve substantially undemocratic ends through the innovative organization of (relatively) open and democratic means. The electoral rhetoric of formal political equality was employed to entrench and sustain the practical reality of political inequality. This form of elite governance through probabilities of electoral outcome not only helped deflect the resistance that open disenfranchisement, for example, would engender, but also built flexibility into the political machinery to safely accommodate what Publius describes as the "tides" and "vicissitudes" of political life, basing its stability in long-term tendencies of political behavior.

Some Anti-Federalists grasped the more subtle forms of popular disempowerment that the proposed political machinery would institute. Indeed, even while the convention was still in session, it was rumored in newspapers that "schemes . . . have been projected which preserve the form, but effectually destroy the spirit of democracy."[40] Once the convention's plan was publicly revealed it became an Anti-Federalist commonplace that the republican *form* of the proposed Constitution distracted the public from properly understanding its aristocratic *substance*. Some Anti-Federalists argued that this combination of republican form with aristocratic substance would have the effect of making citizens feel that they were acting freely while practically disempowering them, leaving the people with a deflated sense of their own political capacity and turning them away in disgust from public life.

The Federal Farmer, who Publius described as his most "plausible" Anti-Federalist opponent (*F*, 457), was a penetrating analyst of just this dynamic. "It is deceiving the people to tell them they are electors, and can choose their legislators," he wrote, "if they cannot in the nature of things, choose men among themselves and genuinely like themselves."[41] The elite would benefit from "silent operations . . . which are not immediately perceived by the people in general." The overall machinery of government, another Anti-Federalist worried, was "calculated to induce the freemen to imagine themselves at liberty, while they are thus destined to be allured or driven round as if impounded, being at the same time told that nothing confines them, although they have not the powers of escape."[42] The likely result was what Richard Henry Lee called "elective despotism," "chains being still chains, whether made of gold or of iron."[43]

Anti-Federalists did not oppose systems of elections as such, but the particular schema established under the Constitution. They urged a variety of electoral counterproposals—larger representation in the House, for example, direct election of senators, and sovereign authority of state legislatures—all of which were built on their core representative ideal: that the common people should not just be able to consent to power, but able to participate in power by holding electoral office. Without this practical reality, the electoral schema established by the Constitution was "merely nominal—a mere burlesque,"[44] nothing but "the shadow of representation."[45] That being said, some of the more radical Anti-Federalist writers—those Saul Cornell categorizes as "plebian" Anti-Federalists—also worried that the "schema of representation" established by the Constitution would not only deflate the formal authority of the local legislatures constituted under the Articles of Confederation, but that it would also delegitimate the myriad informal expressions of popular authority that emerged in revolutionary and postrevolutionary America and defined its politics.[46]

If extended territory and large electoral districts were republican means of confronting the disease of "faction," elections as such, established as the hegemonic form of popular authorization and political participation, were the republican means of confronting the republican disease of "insurrection." By envisioning—and institutionally interpellating—the people as an individualized and sociologically homogeneous electorate, and reducing their political agency to voting, Publius made a Janus-faced intervention. He hoped to establish a *novus ordo seclorum* that transcended the cyclical history of ancient republics plagued by "tempestuous waves of sedition and party rage" (*F*, 50), and looked forward to the more severely minimalist and routinized conceptions of democratic politics that govern the inquiries and imperatives of post-Schumpeterian political science.

III.

The most obvious way Publius envisioned elections to remedy the republican disease of insurrection was by endowing the federal government with far more authority than it had under the Articles of Confederation. "Virtually all the delegates" to the Philadelphia Convention "conceived direct popular election of national leaders to be a means of increasing the authority and influence of the new national government,"[47] and Publius developed these arguments at length in *The Federalist*. Just as the federal government would be able to legislate for individuals rather than "for states or governments, in their corporate or collective capacities," thereby extending "the authority of the union to the persons of the citizens, the only proper objects of government" (*F*, 95), so would the legislative authority of the union be drawn from individual citizen-electors rather than mediated through other political bodies. James Wilson offered the paradigmatic image of this new arrangement when he described the increased power of the "federal pyramid" raised to "considerable altitude," but supported by as "broad a base as possible."[48] This dynamic was increased through subsequent developments in electoral law and practice in the United States—through the Seventeenth Amendment's direct election of senators, for example, and changes in the electoral college's function in presidential elections. However, Publius already envisioned the direct election of representatives in the House to be a powerful means of inflating the authority of the national government and endowing it with the ability to, when necessary, "command more extensive resources for the suppression of disturbances . . . than would be in the power of any single member" (*F*, 104). The force of the union backed by popular consent was the government's most direct means of suppressing insurrection, but Publius also envisioned more subtle means through which elections could mitigate the disease of insurrection—means focused on the power of elections to shape the political imagination and the political activity of citizens themselves.

As we have seen throughout this study, Publius was attentive to the various ways that institutions rely upon the anticipated motivations and conduct of the individuals working within them, and how they work to reliably *elicit* these motivations and forms of conduct. Publius's formative understanding of political institutions—how institutions operate not merely as neutral means of achieving political goals (output), but actively shape the conduct (input) of the actors working within them—is most often applied to individuals working within the government itself. The most familiar example is *Federalist* No. 51's explanation of how the different branches of government are organized to balance and check the power of the others, how "ambition must be made to counteract ambition" in the organization of these institutions, so that "the interest of the man must be connected with the constitutional rights" of the office he holds (*F*, 349). However, there are many other examples in *The Federalist* of how Publius anticipates the institutions and offices established by the Constitution to work upon and mold thoughts and behaviors. For example, in countering Anti-Federalist arguments about the aristocratic dimensions of the Senate, Publius argues that the Senate's six-year term will actually encourage the ambitious men likely to hold the office to honorable rather than avaricious conduct because the status conferred by the position will outweigh the perceived benefits of seeking temporary private advantage;

the appetite for honor will outweigh the appetite for gain (*F*, 489). Publius appeals several times to the moral psychology of the ambitious and fame-hungry men likely to hold federal office. It is through the interface of institutional design and predicted behavior of officeholders that government will not only "control the governed," but also be obliged to "control itself" (*F*, 349).

Less frequently noted, however, is what I have emphasized in this book: how heavily Publius relies on the capacity of governing institutions to shape the thoughts and channel the conduct of the governed, of the people themselves. While Publius develops famous arguments about the delicate counterbalancing of different branches of government, and of the disaggregated authority of federalism, he also insists that "dependence on the people is no doubt the primary control on the government" at all levels (*F*, 349).

The figuration of the people as "exterior provisions" and "natural guardians of the constitution" is a structural component of Publius's argument and of the constitutional equilibrium he envisions (*F*, 104). Publius relies on the anticipated response of the people to check the authority of the different branches of government at several points in the argument, to maintain balance between state and federal government, and even circumscribe the power of the executive. "Strength is always on the side of the people" in a republic, Publius declares, where much "must be left to the prudence and firmness of the people; who, as they will hold the scales in their own hands, it is hoped, will always take care to preserve the constitutional equilibrium" (*F*, 198). "If the Fœderal Government should overpass the just bounds of its authority, and make a tyrannical use of its powers," he writes, "the people whose creature it is must appeal to the standard they have formed, and take such measures to redress the injury done to the constitution, as the exigency may suggest and prudence justify" (*F*, 206). While Publius conclusively rejects Thomas Jefferson's more radical reliance on frequent "recurrence to the people" as the primary constitutional check on government power in *Federalist* No. 49 (*F*, 338–343), he nonetheless invokes such recurrence at several points in his account of constitutional equilibrium.

This argument presumes, of course, the sustained pressure of an active and vigilant citizenry—Publius invokes "the disquietude of the people," concerted "plans of resistance" (*F*, 319), even the ever-present threat of "popular revolution"—yet Publius also emphasizes the power of the institutions created by the Constitution to curb the dangerous excesses of such popular vigilance. "The circumstances of a revolution quickened the public sensibility on every point connected with the security of popular rights," Publius worried, "and in some instances raised the warmth of our zeal beyond the degree which consisted with the due temperature of the body politic" (*F*, 166). The widespread concern with postrevolutionary "insurgency" best exemplified by the 1786 debtors' rebellion in western Massachusetts is a familiar leitmotif of debates over constitutional ratification. Publius and other Federalists sometimes presented Shays' Rebellion as a symptom of a virulent political disease afflicting the body politic of postrevolutionary America. It served as a reminder to all Americans that the dangers of postrevolutionary insurrection "are not merely speculative" (*F*, 131).

However, it was not only the extralegal regulation of rebellions like Shays' that concerned Publius and other Federalists. They were also troubled by the motley assemblage of forms of popular representation that took hold in revolutionary and postrevolutionary America. This assemblage was made up of a complex array of formal institutions of government beyond state legislatures and Congress—such as popular jury trials, councils of censors, local militias, and town assemblies—and also informal mechanisms of elite accountability that had been engendered by the Revolution itself—crowds, petitioning publics, and independent self-created political associations and societies—all basing their authority on popular voice.[49]

While Gordon Wood is surely right that the revolutionary insistence on "actual" rather than "virtual" representation made elections a central component of early American political culture, it is an overstatement to claim that voting "became the sole criterion of representation" in postrevolutionary America.[50] The problem of insurrection was not, in other words, only about the occasional bouts of open resistance that punctuated the political life, but also concerned the formal and informal institutions to which the Revolution had given rise and that challenged the establishment of an orderly economy of popular representation sought by the majority of participants in the Philadelphia Convention.[51]

These improvisational and citizen-initiated assemblies—Wood describes them as "spontaneous organizations of the people"—drew (some) citizens into political life without necessarily placing them into an office.[52] While these different formal and informal institutions operated in very different ways, they all provided spaces and opportunities for relatively large segments of the white male citizenry not only to consent to power, but also to actually participate in power. Publius emphasized that *how* the people participated in politics, was also closely related to *who* participated. He invokes, for example, that "unhappy species of population abounding in some states, who during the calm of regular government are sunk below the level of men; but who in tempestuous scenes of civil violence may emerge into the human character, and give a superiority of strength to any party with which they may associate themselves" (*F*, 294). While the various forms of politics engaged in by the "people out of doors" cannot all be understood as formal "offices" in the way Manin conceptualizes it, they were nonetheless spaces where political power was enacted or popular governance enforced. They were manifestations of "the people in their collective capacity" that Publius hoped to definitively exclude from the broader constitution of the American polity. If "supporters of the federal constitution hoped its formation would establish a constitutional order after which little would be heard of the sovereign people except in an attenuated, symbolic, and theoretical sense," it was these animated, substantive, and practical incarnations of popular voice that they had in mind.[53]

That elections would be the primary means of sustaining the people's constitutional presence in this "attenuated, symbolic and theoretical sense" was already indicated in what the editors of *The Documentary History of the Ratification of the Constitution* consider the opening salvo of the ratification debates: Benjamin Rush's "Address to the People of the United States." In that essay, published in advance of the Philadelphia Convention, Rush established a central point repeated in the writing of many other prominent Federalists. "It is often said," Rush wrote, "that 'the sovereign and all other power is seated *in* the people.' This idea is unhappily expressed. It should be—'all power is derived *from* the people.' They possess it only on the days of their elections. After this, it is the property of their rulers, nor can they exercise or resume it, unless it is abused."[54] Writing as a "Citizen of America," Noah Webster echoed this point in October of the same year:

> The distinction between the powers of the *people* and their representatives in the legislature, is as absurd in *theory*, as it proves pernicious in *practice*. A distinction, which has already countenanced and supported one rebellion in America; has prevented many good measures; has produced many bad; has created animosities in many States, and embarrassments in all. It has taught the people a lesson, which if they continue to practice, will bring laws into contempt, and frequently mark our country with blood.[55]

And, finally, Washington in his famous Farewell Address in 1796, and responding to the radical democratic republican clubs that had emerged throughout the states, would write that "all combinations and associations, under whatever plausible character, with the real design to direct, control, counteract, or awe the regular deliberation and action of the constituted authorities, are destructive of this fundamental principle [the citizen's obligation to obey the government] and of fatal tendency."[56]

Publius, Rush, Webster, Washington, and many other Federalists hoped that by establishing a uniform economy of political representation based around elections, the new federal constitution would simultaneously secure the rule of worthy elites on a broad basis of popular consent, while safely channeling myriad forms of postrevolutionary political enactment into one governing mechanism. Elections would not only provide popular mechanisms of elite rule, as Manin emphasizes, but give more reliable form to the motivations and political conduct of the people themselves. Elections were not only devices for managing conflict and securing advantageous political outcomes, in other words, but of regulating and governing political input. If Publius was attentive to how institutions could shape and mold the behavior of those working in government, elections were a powerful means of channeling the political behavior of the governed as well.

The capacity of electoral politics to govern constituencies and not only hold government accountable is recognized by some political scientists. Elections, Benjamin Ginsberg writes, "transmute what might otherwise take the form of sporadic, citizen-initiated activity into a routine public function."[57] Publius was wary of forms of popular politics that "do not fall within any ordinary rules of calculation" (*F*, 104). "Where the whole power of the government is in the hand of the people," Publius writes, "there is the less pretence for the use of violent remedies, in partial or occasional distempers of state. The natural cure for an ill administration, in a popular or representative constitution, is a change of men" (*F*, 132). Here we have an early articulation of a minimalist conception of democracy and democratic theory.

Publius's apprehension of the instabilities attending large popular assemblies is well known. "In all very numerous assemblies," he writes, "of whatever characters composed, passion never fails to wrest the scepter from reason. Had every Athenian citizen been a Socrates; every Athenian assembly would still have been a mob" (*F*, 374). The reasoning behind this claim is that "bodies of men" are even less capable of "rectitude" and "disinterestedness" than "individuals" (*F*, 96). There is a shamelessness in large public assemblies that inherently corrupts their judgments and actions. "A spirit of faction which is apt to mingle its poison in the deliberations of all bodies of men," Publius writes, "will often hurry the persons of whom they are composed into improprieties and excesses for which they would blush in a private capacity" (*F*, 96). Voting was envisioned by Publius as a way of acting publically in just such a "private capacity."

While electoral practices differed dramatically in different regions of the country—and in the South they were still primarily an oral and public act, with citizens waiting for their names to be called by an election official and then voicing their support of a particular candidate—in all instances elections work to disaggregate the demos into individual parts and proceduralize popular voice; they are the primary means of excluding "the people in their collective capacity" from participation in governance.[58]

In converting "We the People" into "We the Electorate" Publius envisioned a representative government committed to the "public weal," but one that would not have to rely on such commitments from citizens themselves. *The Federalist*'s new science of politics contained in embryo a vision of popular politics that would become central to postwar American political science, the idea that "people can coordinate with each other without anyone's coordinating them, without a dominant common purpose, and without rules that fully prescribe their relations to each other."[59] The public weal Publius envisioned would emerge indirectly through the probable workings of the political machinery itself, rather than through the common deliberation of its citizens.

Critics of this vision—from Anti-Federalists to contemporary radical democrats—often demonstrate how clearly such institutional coordination worked in favor of elites. However, its formative impact on the citizenry it coordinates is also worth emphasizing. In the final chapter of *On Revolution*, Hannah Arendt provided an idiosyncratic but productive interpretation of Jefferson's political thought that engages with just this issue. More than any of his contemporaries, Arendt argued, Jefferson recognized the costs of narrowly privatizing political behavior in the form of elections. What Jefferson "perceived to be the mortal danger to the republic," she writes, "was that the Constitution had given all the power to citizens, without giving them the opportunity of *being* republicans and *acting* like citizens. In other words, the danger was that power had been given to citizens in their private capacity, and that there was no space [beyond "the ballot box"] established for them in their capacity of being citizens."[60]

The Federalist's authoritative interpretation of the constitutional who and how of American peoplehood plays an important role in the shift to which Arendt refers, and may still help orient contemporary theoretical engagements with the people as an object of democratic analysis. It may help us recognize the costs of the basic fact Hans Kelsen once recognized about modern democracies: "in modern democracies political rights are reduced in the essential to a simple right to vote."[61]

Six years after ratification, in 1794, Noah Webster wrote a letter to Joseph Priestley declaring that in America the word "democrat" had "come to signify a person who attempts an undue opposition or influence over government by means of private clubs, secret intrigues, or by public popular meetings which are extraneous to the Constitution"; in the first edition of his 1828 *Dictionary of the American Language* Webster simply defined a democrat as "one who favors universal suffrage."[62] The term democrat underwent a dramatic semantic shift over these years, as did the practice of democratic politics. The simple equation of democracy with suffrage remains a basic presupposition of most contemporary political discourse and most contemporary political science. However, this equation is a historical artifact marked by a long history of contention. The American "great national discussion" of 1787–1788 is one important chapter in that history.

In reconstructing some of the elements of this debate here, my hope is to unsettle some of the prevailing assumptions behind this simple equation. Manin has provocatively written that "the aristocratic nature of elections has prompted no conceptual investigation or political debate since the beginning of the nineteenth century."[63] That is surely an overstatement, but it does point to an important truth: once democratic government is constitutionally established in electoral terms, other forms of popular representation lose their legitimacy, and other forms of political conduct lose their salience and legibility. There are democratic advantages as well as costs incurred by this loss, which democratic theory might productively identify and recover. In addition to focusing on the question of *who* the people are and the dilemmas posed by the "boundary problem"—investigations that have reinvigorated democratic theory in recent years, and that were examined in chapter 1—we might also reexamine the important and timely question of *how* the agency of the people has been envisioned and enacted. *The Federalist Papers* engages with both of these questions, and demonstrates their historical entanglement during the American Founding, and its legacy for our political present.

NOTES

1. *DHRC Vol. XIII*, 46.
2. Jacob E. Cooke, ed., *The Federalist* (Middletown, CT: Wesleyan University Press, 1961), 428. Emphasis in the original. Hereafter *F*, with paginations in parentheses in the text.
3. Bernard Manin, *The Principles of Representative Government* (New York: Cambridge University Press, 1997), 92.
4. See, for example, Larry Bartels, *Unequal Democracy: The Political Economy of the New Gilded Age* (Princeton, NJ: Princeton University Press, 2008); and Lawrence R. Jacobs and Theda Skocpol, eds., *Inequality and American Democracy: What We Know and What We Need to Learn* (New York: Russell Sage Foundation, 2007).
5. Benjamin Ginsberg, *The Consequences of Consent: Elections, Citizen Control, and Popular Acquiescence* (London: Longman Higher Education, 1982), 3.
6. Christian G. Fritz, *American Sovereigns: The People and America's Constitutional Tradition Before the Civil War* (New York: Cambridge University Press, 2008), 3.
7. Woody Holton, *Unruly Americans and the Origins of the Constitution* (New York: Hill and Wang, 2007), 134.
8. Sheldon S. Wolin, "Norm and Form: The Constitutionalization of Democracy," in *Athenian Political Thought and the Reconstruction of American Democracy*, ed. J. Peter Euben, John R. Wallach, and Josiah Ober, (Ithaca, NY: Cornell University Press, 1994), 39.
9. Gordon S. Wood, *Representation in the American Revolution* (Charlottesville, VA: University of Virginia Press, 2008), 2.
10. Hanna Pitkin, *The Concept of Representation* (Berkeley, CA: University of California Press, 1972), 145.
11. Amy Gutman and Dennis Thompson, *Why Deliberative Democracy?* (Princeton, NJ: Princeton University Press, 2004), 13–21, 15.
12. *DHRC Vol. XIV*, 122.
13. Eric Slauter, *The State as a Work of Art: The Cultural Origins of the Constitution* (Chicago, IL: The University of Chicago Press, 2009), 137.
14. Manin, *Principles of Representative Government*, 110.
15. *DHRC Vol. XIV*, 26.
16. *DHRC Vol. XIV*, 123.
17. *DHRC Vol. XIV*, 297.

18. See, for example, Anne Phillips, *The Politics of Presence* (New York: Oxford University Press, 1998).

19. John Adams, "Thoughts on Government," in *Works of John Adams*, Vol IV, 195.

20. Suzette Hemberger, "A Government Based on Representations," *Studies in American Political Development* 10, no 2 (1996), 289–332; see also Sheldon Wolin, *The Presence of the Past: Essays on the State and the Constitution* (Baltimore, MD: The Johns Hopkins University Press, 1990).

21. Joseph M. Bessette, *The Mild Voice of Reason: Deliberative Democracy and American National Government* (Chicago, IL: The University of Chicago Press, 1997), 6.

22. Fisher Ames, "Speech in the Convention of Massachusetts, January 15, 1788," in *Works of Fisher Ames*, ed. W. B. Allen (Indianapolis: Liberty Fund, 1983), 543.

23. Wolin, *Presence of the Past*, 100–120.

24. Cited in Gordon Wood, *The Creation of the American Republic, 1776 – 1787* (Chapel Hill, NC: University of North Carolina Press, 1969), 488–489.

25. Woody Holton, "'Divide et Impera': 'Federalist 10' in a Wider Sphere," *William and Mary Quarterly* 62, no. 2 (2005), 175–212, 176.

26. Wood, *Creation of the American Republic*, 428.

27. *DHRC Vol. XIII*, 190.

28. *DHRC Vol. XIII*, 191.

29. *DHRC Vol. XIII*, 378; *Vol. XIV*, 248.

30. See Alexander Keyssar, *The Right to Vote: The Contested History of Democracy in the United States* (New York: Basic Books, 2000).

31. For a good discussion of this shifting conception of political time, see Michael Lienesch, *New Order of the Ages: Time, the Constitution, and the Making of Modern American Political Thought* (Princeton, NJ: Princeton University Press, 1988).

32. Charles Beard, *An Economic Interpretation of the Constitution of the United States* (New York: Free Press, 1913).

33. Larry D. Kramer, "Madison's Audience," *Harvard Law Review* 112 (1999), 611 – 679.

34. See especially Holton, "'Divide et Impera.'"

35. Farrand, *RFC Vol. I*.

36. Madison, *Papers of James Madison*, Vol. 10, 214.

37. Manin, *Principles of Representative Government*, 131.

38. The convention heatedly discussed the issue of property qualifications for suffrage on August 7, 1787. See *RFC Vol. II*, 196–212; cited in Jack Rakove, *James Madison and the Creation of the American Republic* (New York: Longman, 2002), 56.

39. Holton, *Unruly Americans*, 211.

40. *DHRC Vol. XIII*, 123.

41. *DHRC Vol. XIV*, 48.

42. Cited in Holton, *Unruly Americans*, 256.

43. *DHRC Vol. XIII*, 323.

44. *DHRC Vol. XIV*, 124.

45. *DHRC Vol. XIV*, 301.

46. Saul Cornell, *The Other Founders: Anti-Federalism and the Dissenting Tradition in America, 1787 – 1828* (Chapel Hill, NC: University Press of North Carolina, 1999).

47. Ginsberg, *The Consequences of Consent*, 19.

48. *RFC Vol. I*, 49.

49. I explore the political dynamics of these competing claims of popular authorization in *Constituent Moments: Enacting the People in Postrevolutionary America* (Durham, NC: Duke University Press, 2010).

50. Gordon Wood, "The Making of American Democracy," in *The Idea of America: The Birth of the United States* (New York: Penguin, 2012), 189–212, 215.

51. Wood, *Creation of the American Republic*, 306–343, 325.

52. Wood, *Creation of the American Republic*, 313.

53. Fritz, *American Sovereigns*, 117.

54. *DHRC Vol. XIII*, 47.

55. *DHRC Vol. II.*

56. George Washington, "Farewell Address," in *Writings*, ed. John Rodehamel (New York: Library of America, 1997), 962–978.

57. Ginsberg, *The Consequences of Consent*, 30.

58. Keyssar, *The Right to Vote*, 28.

59. Charles E. Lindblom, *The Intelligence of Democracy: Decision Making Through Mutual Adjustment* (New York: Free Press, 1965). I am grateful to Kyong-Min Son for reminding me of the centrality of this conception of "system" and "political machinery" to postwar behavioral political science in the United States.

60. Hannah Arendt, *On Revolution* (New York: Penguin, 1990 [1963]), 256.

61. Hans Kelsen, *La démocratie Sa nature Sa valeur* (Paris: Economica, 1988 [1929]), 35.

62. H. R. Warfel, ed., *The Letters of Noah Webster* (New York: Library Publishers, 1953), 208. Noah Webster, *American Dictionary of the American Language* (Philadelphia, 1828).

63. Manin, *Principles of Representative Government*, 132.

Conclusion

By the time Alexis de Tocqueville and Gustave de Beaumont arrived in the United States in 1831, America's mythology of Founding was firmly established in its public culture, and *The Federalist Papers* had already achieved canonical and authoritative status in American politics and jurisprudence.[1] Tocqueville admired Publius's account of American constitutionalism and relied extensively upon *The Federalist* when composing *Democracy in America*: perhaps more extensively than the few references to the text suggest.[2] However, his admiration aside, the overall thrust of Tocqueville's great work was to de-emphasize what is generally taken to be *The Federalist*'s preoccupation with political technology, law, and formal institutions of governance. Tocqueville also diminished the significance of the Founding itself—and the Founders—to explaining the dynamics and tendencies of America's democratic experiment. He likened the Constitution to one of those "beautiful creations of human industry that lavish glory and goods on those who invent them," but that were "sterile" without "a people long habituated to directing affairs by itself."[3] Tocqueville's emphasis on the deep, hidden, and aggregate determinations of social equality, and its formative impact on opinions, mores, practices, and beliefs—the complex assemblage of formative influence making up the political imagination—takes him beyond the Founding period of 1776–1789 to the "first founding" of Puritan New England.[4] "The form of the federal government of the United States appeared last," Tocqueville reminds his readers, "It was only a modification of the republic, a summary of the political principles spread through the entire society before it and subsisting independently of it."[5]

Far from celebrating the American Founders as a modern exemplar of the Great Lawgiver, Tocqueville wrote to disenthrall readers of such willful mythologies, which he believed belonged to heroic anachronisms of an aristocratic age rather than the aggregative tendencies of democracy. He instead drew readers' attention to the multitude of "hidden springs" that pattern democratic politics and shape the democratic citizen. Tocqueville's new science of politics is a paradigm of formative political analysis.

Publius's new science of politics is usually not read this way. On the contrary, the significance of Publius's innovations in political science is often measured by how far *The Federalist* departs from the formative ideal, and instead focuses on institutional design, federalism, the separation of powers, and electoral representation. Publius's effort to find a "Republican remedy for the diseases most incident to Republican government" is often taken to be a measure of his political modernity and to raise problems associated with modern liberal political theory more broadly, especially its inability to generate a compelling account of the "background culture" or "character" necessary to sustain and enliven liberal democratic institutions. We are often told that Publius and other Federalists, like contemporary political liberals, did not rely on the federal government's power to mold virtuous citizens through coercive schemes of civic education (although these projects were legislated vigorously in individual states). Such classical approaches were more closely associated with the Anti-Federalist opposition, and their contemporary civic republican heirs.

Publius's new science of politics thus brings into view what many consider a blind spot in political liberalism: that the liberal state must generate the support and loyalty of its subjects, but that it cannot sufficiently account for the generation of these commitments on its own terms. Political liberalism, critics often claim, lacks the resources to "inspire the loyalty of its citizen-consumers."[6] Political liberals themselves have become increasingly attentive to these issues, to investigating how "the institutions of the basic structure have deep and long-term social effects and in fundamental ways shape citizens' character and aims—the kinds of persons they are and aspire to be"[7]—but they don't usually turn to Publius for guidance on these issues, because Publius and other Federalists are said to establish the "the existence and security of the government . . . in the absence of political virtue."[8]

This familiar view of *The Federalist* has been challenged by scholars attempting to reconstruct a more robustly civic republican concern with virtue in Publius's work. Publius may have considered government to be "the greatest of all reflections on human nature," and concluded that "if men were angels, no government would be necessary," but there are indications that Publius, too, would have agreed with Samuel Adams that "neither the wisest constitution nor the wisest laws will secure liberty and happiness of a people whose manners are universally corrupt."[9] Those who emphasize Publius's classical republicanism argue that while his means were different from ancient writers, he still hoped the Constitution would engender a republican character in its citizens.

These competing interpretations of *The Federalist*'s new science of politics share a common assumption challenged by the preceding chapters: they assume that questions of formative politics are reducible to questions of civic virtue. Political imagination as I have presented it in this book is a broader category than virtue or civic education, and it brings the full extent of Publius's preoccupation with formative politics more clearly into view. It allows us to better understand and evaluate Publius's anticipatory vision of how the successful ratification of the Constitution would pattern politics in the United States and shape the practices of citizenship. In doing so, it brings Publius's analysis closer to Tocqueville's.

I have emphasized Publius's attention to the complex interdependence of formal political institutions and the political imagination they at once shape and depend upon. Publius would have agreed with Tocqueville, when the latter wrote that "what keeps large numbers of citizens subject to the same government is much less the rational determination to remain united than the instinctive and in some sense involuntary accord that results from similarity of feeling and likeness of opinion."[10] *The Federalist* helps explain the Constitution's formative role in producing this "involuntary accord."

That said, *The Federalist* invokes and enlists the political imagination in different and sometimes competing ways across its eighty-five essays. Many scholars have emphasized the contending voices, personalities, or discourses speaking through Publius, and this study also presents a text animated by occasionally discordant political visions. Perhaps the most important example of this dissonance emerges around *The Federalist's* vision of power and political capacity. The elicitation of the people's constituent capacities that I examined in chapter 1 and the reliance on their sustained vigilance that I examined in chapter 5 is embedded within a text that emphasizes, time and again, the disciplinary regulation of popular politics that I have traced in much of the rest of the book, through such mechanisms as veneration, national identification, interest formation, and our imagined relation to the authority of the Founders themselves.

Sheldon Wolin once argued "that in the American political tradition, the people has had two 'bodies,' with each one standing for a different conception of the collective identity of power, and of the terms of power. In one of these bodies the people was conceived to be politically active, while in the other it was essentially, though not entirely, passive."[11] Wolin associated the political and democratic body—the "body politic"—with the American Revolution and with the Anti-Federalists, and the economic and antidemocratic body—the "political economy"—with the Constitution and *The Federalist Papers*. I think both bodies inhabit Publius's text, and that, despite the efforts to discipline and govern the former—or to convert it into a ghost or shadow of itself—popular power reappears time and again within the text and within the political imagination the text has done so much to authorize and enact.[12] Wolin may be right that "the aim of *The Federalist* was not only to found a strong state, but to depoliticize the people," but the popular resources marshaled to achieve that goal have worked time and again against the organizing power of authorial intent.[13]

The Constitution was successfully ratified in July of 1788 and the newly elected federal government officially began to govern on March 4,

1789. A good deal of time was spent in the first Congress debating how to engender authority by cloaking the new government in the regalia of power. One historian has written that many Federalists "understood that for the new Constitution to succeed, rituals and practices would need to be developed that made the new republican government relevant and tangible to those Americans who now possessed (in theory) sovereign authority over it."[14] Publius offered contemporaries many reasons to take such considerations very seriously. Soon after ratification political disagreement quickly moved from battles over the Constitution to battles over its meaning, and political disagreement has remained there, for the most part, ever since.

Hannah Arendt once marveled at American "constitution worship" and what she called the early American ability "to look upon yesterday with the eyes of centuries to come."[15] This is a tactic urged on readers by Publius in *The Federalist*. While not wanting to be led "too far into regions of futurity," Publius asked his audience to imagine themselves looking back on their present from the perspective of posterity, to survey their deliberations from the glorious height of a future empire. We now find ourselves looking back from the very imperial perspective Publius asked his readers to imagine—latecomers often captivated by what we take to be the single and unitary act of Founding—but our challenge is different from Publius's contemporaries asked to judge from the view of the future perfect, from the view of what will have been. Perhaps our challenge is instead to disenthrall ourselves of the very political imagination that this perspective has helped shape and consider the tensions and foreclosed possibilities it makes legible to us now.

"The imagination of Americans," Tocqueville writes, "even in its greatest flights of fancy, is circumspect and cautious. Its impulses are restricted and its achievements unfinished. These habits of restraint are found in political society and to an unusual degree favor the tranquility of the people and the stability of the institutions they have adopted."[16] To tap the constituent capacities that Publius at once called upon and denied, elicited and disavowed, requires that we interrogate more closely the political "habits of restraint" he worked to enshrine, and envision anew the potential people that haunt *The Federalist* as a specter and as an unfulfilled promise.

NOTES

1. See Simon Gilhooley, "The Textuality of the Constitution and the Origins of Original Intent," PhD Dissertation, Cornell University (2013).

2. See James T. Schleifer, *The Making of Tocqueville's Democracy in America* (Indianapolis, IN: Liberty Fund, 2000).

3. Alexis de Tocqueville, *Democracy in America* (New York: Penguin, 2003), 155–56.

4. James W. Caesar, "Alexis de Tocqueville and the Two-Founding Thesis," *The Review of Politics* 73, no. 2 (Spring 2011): 219–43.

5. Tocqueville, *Democracy in America*, 56.

6. Richard Dagger, *Civic Virtues: Rights, Citizenship, and Republican Liberalism* (Oxford: Oxford University Press, 1997), 108–9. Paul Kahn has recently offered a powerful version of this critique through the framework of political theology. See his *Political Theology: Four New Chapters on the Concept of Sovereignty* (New York: Columbia University Press, 2012).

7. John Rawls, *Political Liberalism: Expanded Edition* (New York: Columbia University Press, 2005), 68. See John Tomasi, *Liberalism Beyond Justice: Citizens, Society, and the Boundaries of the Political* (Princeton, NJ: Princeton University Press, 2001).

8. Gordon Wood, *Creation of the American Republic*, (Chapel Hill: University of North Carolina Press, 1969), 429.

9. Samuel Adams Letter to James Warren, February 12, 1779. Cited in Ira Stoll, *Samuel Adams: A Life* (New York: Free Press, 2008), 25.

10. Tocqueville, *Democracy in America*,

11. Sheldon Wolin, "The People's Two Bodies," *Democracy* 1, no. 1 (1980): 11.

12. Joshua Miller, "The Ghostly Body Politic: *The Federalist Papers* and Popular Sovereignty," *Political Theory* 16, no. 1 (1988): 99–119.

13. Wolin, "The People's Two Bodies," 15.

14. Sandra Moats, *Celebrating the Republic: Presidential Ceremony and Popular Sovereignty from Washington to Monroe* (DeKalb: Northern Illinois University Press, 2010), 4.

15. Hannah Arendt, *On Revolution* (New York: Penguin, 1990 [1963]), 198.

16. Tocqueville, *Democracy in America*, 341.

References

Ackerman, Bruce. 1993. *We the People, Vol. 1: Foundations*. Cambridge, MA: Belknap Press of Harvard University Press.

Ackerman, Bruce. 1998. *We the People, Vol. 2: Transformations*. Cambridge, MA: Belknap Press of Harvard University Press.

Ackerman, Bruce, and Neal Katyal. 1995. "Our Unconventional Founding." *The University of Chicago Law Review* 62, no. 2: 475–573.

Adair, Douglass. 1974. *Fame and the Founding Fathers: Essays by Douglass Adair*, ed. Trevor Colbourn. New York: W. W. Norton.

Adams, John. 1966. "Letter to Benjamin Rush, September 30, 1805." In *Spur of Fame: Dialogues of John Adams and Benjamin Rush, 1805–1813*, ed. John A. Schutz and Douglass Adair. Indianapolis, IN: Liberty Fund, 39–44.

Adams, John. 2000. *The Political Writings of John Adams*, ed. George Carey. Washington: Regnery Publishing.

Adams, Samuel. *Writings of Samuel Adams, Vol. IV*, ed. Harry Alonzo Cushing. Fairford, UK: Echo Library, 2006.

Adams, Willi Paul. 1980. *The First American Constitutions: Republican Ideology and the Making of the State Constitutions in the Revolutionary Era*, trans. Rita Kimber and Robert Kimber. Chapel Hill: University of North Carolina Press.

Allen, Danielle. 2004. *Talking to Strangers: Anxieties of Citizenship since Brown v. Board of Education*. Chicago: University of Chicago Press.

Anderson, Benedict. 1983. *Imagined Communities*. New York: Verso.

Amar, Akhil R. 1994. "The Consent of the Governed: Constitutional Amendment Outside Article V." *Columbia Law Review* 94, no. 2: 457–508.

Arato, Andrew. 1999. "Carl Schmitt and the Revival of the Doctrine of Constituent Power in the United States." *Cardozo Law Review* 21: 1739–47.

Arato, Andrew. 2000. *Civil Society, Constitution, and Legitimacy*. New York: Rowman & Littlefield.

Arendt, Hannah. 1990 [1963]. *On Revolution*. New York: Penguin Books.

Aristotle. 1988. *The Politics*. Cambridge: Cambridge University Press.

Bailyn, Bernard. 1967. *The Ideological Origins of the American Revolution*. Cambridge, MA: Harvard University Press.

Bailyn, Bernard. 2003. *To Begin the World Anew: The Genius and Ambiguities of the American Founders*. New York: Knopf.

Balkin, Jack. 2011. *Constitutional Redemption: Political Faith in an Unjust World*. Cambridge, MA: Harvard University Press.

Banning, Lance. 1988. "Some Second Thoughts on Virtue and the Course of Revolutionary Thinking." In *Conceptual Change and the Constitution*, ed. Terence Ball and J. G. A. Pocock. Lawrence: University Press of Kansas.

Banning, Lance. 1995. *The Sacred Fire of Liberty: James Madison & the Founding of the Federal Republic*. Ithaca, NY: Cornell University Press.

Barber, Benjamin. 2006. "The Politics of Political Science: 'Value-free' Theory and the Wolin–Strauss Dust-Up of 1963." *American Political Science Review* 100, no. 4: 539–45.

Bartels, Larry. 2008. *Unequal Democracy: The Political Economy of the New Gilded Age*. Princeton, NJ: Princeton University Press.

Beard, Charles. 1913. *An Economic Interpretation of the Constitution of the United States*. New York: Free Press.

Beer, Samuel. 1993. *To Make a Nation: The Rediscovery of American Federalism*. Cambridge, MA: Harvard University Press.

Bell, Whitfield J., Jr. 1962. "The Federal Processions of 1788." *New-York Historical Society Quarterly* 46: 5–39.

Benhabib, Seyla. 1994. "Deliberative Rationality and Models of Democratic Legitimacy." *Constellations* 1, no. 1: 26–52.

Benhabib, Seyla. 2003. *The Reluctant Modernism of Hannah Arendt*. Lanham, MD: Rowman & Littlefield.

Bennett, Jane. 2002. *Thoreau's Nature: Ethics, Politics, and the Wild*. Lanham, MD: Rowman & Littlefield.

Bennington, Geoffrey. 1994. "Mosaic Fragment: If Derrida Were an Egyptian." In *Legislations: The Politics of Deconstruction*, 207–26. London: Verso.

Bercovitch, Sacvan. 1978. *American Jeremiad*. Madison: University of Wisconsin Press.

Bernal, Angelika. "Beyond Origins: Rethinking Founding in a Post-Foundational Age." Unpublished manuscript.

Bessette, Joseph M. 1997. *The Mild Voice of Reason: Deliberative Democracy and American National Government*. Chicago: University of Chicago Press.

Boorstin, Daniel J. 1953. *The Genius of American Politics*. Chicago: University of Chicago Press.

Braun, Eva. 1991. *The World of Imagination: Sum and Substance*. New York: Rowman & Littlefield.

Brigham, John. 2002. "Original Intent and Other Cult Classics." *The Good Society* 11, no. 2: 13–17.

Buck-Morss, Susan. 2002. *Dreamworld and Catastrophe: The Passing of Mass Utopia in East and West*. Boston, MA: MIT Press.

Burchell, Graham. 1991. "Peculiar Interests: Civil Society and Governing 'The System of Natural Liberty.'" In *The Foucault Effect: Studies in Governmentality*. Chicago: University of Chicago Press.

Burke, Edmund. 1987. *Reflections on the Revolution in France*, ed. J. G. A. Pocock. Indianapolis, IN: Hackett Publishing Company.

Caesar, James W. 2011. "Alexis de Tocqueville and the Two-Founding Thesis." *The Review of Politics* 73, no. 2: 219–43.

Connolly, William E. 1994. *The Ethos of Pluralization*. Minneapolis: University of Minnesota Press.

Connolly, William E. 2002. *The Augustinian Imperative: A Reflection on the Politics of Morality*. Lanham, MD: Rowman & Littlefield.

Connolly, William E. 2002. *Neuropolitics: Thinking, Culture, Speed*. Minneapolis: University of Minnesota Press.

Cooke, Jacob E., ed. 1961. *The Federalist*. Middletown, CT: Wesleyan University Press.

Coole, Diana. 2007. *Merleau-Ponty and Modern Politics After Anti-Humanism*. Lanham, MD: Rowman & Littlefield.

Cornell, Saul. 1999. *The Other Founders: Antifederalism and the Dissenting Tradition in America, 1787–1828*. Chapel Hill: University Press of North Carolina.

Cover, Robert. 1983. "Foreword: Nomos and Narrative." *Harvard Law Review* 97, no. 4: 4–68.

Crèvecoeur, Hector St. John de. 1997. *Letters from an American Farmer*, ed. Susan Manning. New York: Oxford University Press.

Cristi, Renato. 1998. "Carl Schmitt on Sovereignty and Constituent Power." In *Law as Politics: Carl Schmitt's Critique of Liberalism*, ed. David Dyzenhaus. Durham, NC: Duke University Press, 179–195.

Cropsey, Joseph. 1977. "The United States as Regime and the Sources of the American Way of Life." In *Political Philosophy and the Issues of Politics*. Chicago: University of Chicago Press, 1–15.

Dagger, Richard. 1997. *Civic Virtues: Rights, Citizenship, and Republican Liberalism*. Oxford: Oxford University Press.

Dallmayr, Fred. 2002. *G. W. F. Hegel: Modernity and Politics*. Lanham, MD: Rowman & Littlefield.

Davidson, Cathy. 1986. *Revolution and the Word: The Rise of the Novel in America*. New York: Oxford University Press.

Dean, Mitchell. 1999. *Governmentality: Power and Rule in Modern Society*. Beverly Hills: Sage Publishers.

Derrida, Jacques. 1986. "Declarations of Independence." *New Political Science* 15: 7–17.

Deutsch, Kenneth L., and John A. Murley, eds. 1999. *Leo Strauss, the Straussians and the American Regime*. Lanham, MD: Rowman & Littlefield.

Diamond, Martin. 1987. "The Federalist." In *History of Political Philosophy*, eds. Leo Strauss and Joseph Cropsey, 631–51. Chicago: University of Chicago Press.

Diamond, Martin. 1992a. *As Far as Republican Principles Will Admit: Essays by Martin Diamond*, ed. William A. Schambra, 17–36. Washington, DC: AEI Press.

Diamond, Martin. 1992b. "On the Study of Politics in a Liberal Education." In *As Far as Republican Principles Will Admit: Essays by Martin Diamond*, ed. William A. Schambra, 276–84. Washington, DC: AEI Press.

Dippel, Horst. 1996. "The Changing Idea of Popular Sovereignty in Early American Constitutionalism: Breaking Away from European Patterns." *Journal of the Early Republic* 16, no. 1: 21–45.

Drury, Shadia B. 1997. *Leo Strauss and the American Right*. Basingstoke, UK: Macmillan.

Drury, Shadia. 2008. *Aquinas and Modernity: The Lost Promise of Natural Law*. Lanham, MD: Rowman & Littlefield.

Dumm, Thomas L. 2002. *Michel Foucault and the Politics of Freedom*. Lanham, MD: Rowman & Littlefield.

Elkins, Jeremy. 2005. "Constitutional Enactment." *Political Theory* 33, no. 2: 280–97.

Ellison, Ralph. 1995. *Invisible Man*. New York: Vintage.

Elster, Jon. 2000. *Ulysses Unbound: Studies in Rationality, Precommitment, and Constraints*. Cambridge: Cambridge University Press.

Engell, James. 1981. *The Creative Imagination: Enlightenment to Romanticism*. Cambridge, MA: Harvard University Press.

Engelmann, Stephen G. 2003. *Imagining Interest in Political Thought: Origins of Economic Rationality*. Durham, NC: Duke University Press.

Epstein, David. 1984. *The Political Theory of* The Federalist. Chicago: University of Chicago Press.

Estlund, David M. 2008. *Democratic Authority: A Philosophical Framework*. Princeton, NJ: Princeton University Press.

Farrand, Max, ed. *The Records of the Federal Convention of 1787*. New Haven, CT: Yale University Press.

Ferguson, Kennan. 2007. *William James: Politics in the Pluriverse*. Lanham, MD: Rowman & Littlefield.

Ferguson, Robert A. 2004. "The Forgotten Publius." In *Reading the Early Republic*, 151–71. Cambridge, MA: Harvard University Press.

Flathman, Richard E. 2002. *Thomas Hobbes: Skepticism, Individuality, and Chastened Politics*. Lanham, MD: Rowman & Littlefield.

Fliegelman, Jay. 1993. *Declaring Independence: Jefferson, Natural Language and the Culture of Performance*. Stanford, CA: Stanford University Press.

Fleischacker, Samuel. 2003. "The impact on America: Scottish philosophy and the American founding." In *The Cambridge Companion to the Scottish Enlightenment*, ed. Alexander Broadie. New York: Cambridge University Press.

Foucault, Michel. 1994. "The Subject and Power." In *Essential Works of Foucault, 1954–1984, Vol. III: Power*, ed. James D. Faubion, 326–48. New York: New Press.

Foucault, Michel. 2008. *The Birth of Biopolitics: Lectures at the Collége de France, 1978–1979*, ed. Michel Senellart. New York: Palgrave Macmillan.

Frank, Jason. 2010. *Constituent Moments: Enacting the People in Postrevolutionary America*. Durham, NC: Duke University Press.

Franklin, Julian. 1978. *John Locke and the Theory of Sovereignty: Mixed Monarchy and the Right of Resistance in the Thought of the English Revolution*. Cambridge: Cambridge University Press.

Fritz, Christian G. 2008. *American Sovereigns: The People and America's Constitutional Tradition Before the Civil War*. New York: Cambridge University Press.

Furtwangler, Albert. 1984. *The Authority of Publius: A Reading of the Federalist Papers*. Ithaca, NY: Cornell University Press.

Galston, William A. 2009. "Leo Strauss's Qualified Embrace of Liberal Democracy." In *The Cambridge Companion to Leo Strauss*, ed. Steven B. Smith, 193–214. Cambridge: Cambridge University Press.

Geertz, Clifford. 1980. *Negara: The Theatre State in Nineteenth-Century Bali*. Princeton, NJ: Princeton University Press.

Gentile, Emilio. 2006. *Politics as Religion*, trans. George Staunton. Princeton, NJ: Princeton University Press.

Geuss, Raymond. 2010. *Politics and the Imagination*. Princeton, NJ: Princeton University Press.

Gilhooley, Simon. "The Textuality of the Constitution and the Origins of Original Intent," PhD Dissertation, Cornell University (2013).

Ginsberg, Benjamin. 1982. *The Consequences of Consent: Elections, Citizen Control, and Popular Acquiescence*. London: Longman Higher Education.

Grant De Pauw, Linda. 1966. *The Eleventh Pillar: New York State and the Federal Constitution*. Ithaca, NY: Cornell University Press.

Grossman, Jay. 2003. *Reconstituting the American Renaissance: Emerson, Whitman, and the Politics of Representation*. Durham, NC: Duke University Press.

Gutman, Amy, and Dennis Thompson. 2004. *Why Deliberative Democracy?* Princeton, NJ: Princeton University Press.

Haakonssen, Knud. 1993. "The Structure of Hume's Political Theory." In *The Cambridge Companion to Hume*, ed. David Fate Norton. New York: Cambridge University Press.

Habermas, Jürgen. 1991. *Structural Transformation of the Public Sphere: An Inquiry Into a Category of Bourgeois Society*, trans. Thomas Burger. Cambridge, MA: MIT Press.

Habermas, Jürgen. 2001. "Constitutional Democracy: A Paradoxical Union of Contradictory Principles?" *Political Theory* 29, no. 6: 766–81.

Hamilton, Alexander. 1851. *Works of Alexander Hamilton, Vol. II*. New York: Charles Francis & Co.

Hamilton, Alexander, James Madison, and John Jay. 2003. *The Federalist Papers*, ed. Clinton Rossiter. New York: Signet Classics.

Haraszti, Zoltán. 1952. *John Adams and the Prophets of Progress*. Cambridge, MA: Harvard University Press.

Harris, Marc L. 2004. "Civil Society in Post-Revolutionary America." In *Empire and Nation: The American Revolution in the Atlantic World*, ed. Eliga H. Gould and Peter S. Onuf. Baltimore, MD: Johns Hopkins University Press, 197–216.

Hemberger, Suzette. 1996. "A Government Based on Representations." *Studies in American Political Development* 10, no. 2: 289–332

Hirschman, Albert O. 1977. *The Passions and the Interests: Political Arguments for Capitalism before Its Triumph*. Princeton, NJ: Princeton University Press.

Hirschman, Albert O. 1986. "The Concept of Interest: From Euphemism to Tautology." In *Rival Views of Market Society and Other Recent Essays*. New York: Viking.

Hofstadter, Richard. 1989 [1948]. "The Founding Fathers: An Age of Realism." In *The American Political Tradition*, 3–22. New York: Vintage.

Holland, Catherine. 2001. *The Body Politic: Foundings, Citizenship, and Difference in the American Political Imagination*. New York: Routledge.

Holmes, Stephen. 1993. *The Anatomy of Antiliberalism*. Cambridge, MA: Harvard University Press.

Holmes, Stephen. 1995. *Passions and Constraint: On the Theory of Liberal Democracy*. Chicago: University of Chicago Press.

Holton, Woody. 2005. "'Divide et Impera': 'Federalist 10' in a Wider Sphere." *The William and Mary Quarterly* 62, no. 2: 175–212.

Holton, Woody. 2007. *Unruly Americans and the Origins of the Constitution*. New York: Hill and Wang.

Honig, Bonnie. 1991. "Declarations of Independence: Arendt and Derrida on the Problem of Founding a Republic." *American Political Science Review* 85, no. 1: 97–113.

Honig, Bonnie. 1993. *Political Theory and the Displacement of Politics*. Ithaca, NY: Cornell University Press.

Honig, Bonnie. 2001. *Democracy and the Foreigner*. Princeton, NJ: Princeton University Press.

Honig, Bonnie. 2006. "Between Decision and Deliberation: Political Paradox in Democratic Theory." *American Political Science Review* 101, no. 1: 1–17.

Howe, Daniel Walker. 1989. "Why the Scottish Enlightenment Was Useful to the Framers of the American Constitution." *Comparative Studies in Society and History* 31, no. 3: 572–87.

Howse, Robert. 1998. "From Legitimacy to Dictatorship—and Back Again: Leo Strauss's Critique of the Anti-Liberalism of Carl Schmitt." In *Law as Politics: Carl Schmitt's Critique of Liberalism*, ed. David Dyzenhaus, 56–91. Durham, NC: Duke University Press.

Hume, David. 1978. *A Treatise of Human Nature*, ed. L. A. Selby-Bigge. New York: Oxford University Press.

Hume, David. 1994. *Political Essays*, ed. Knud Haakonssen. Cambridge: Cambridge University Press.

Hume, David. 2006. *Essays: Moral, Political, and Literary*. New York: Casimo Classics.

Jacobs, Lawrence R. and Theda Skocpol, eds. 2007. *Inequality and American Democracy: What We Know and What We Need to Learn*. New York: Russell Sage Foundation.

Jacobson, Norman. 1963. "Political Science and Political Education." *American Political Science Review* 57, no. 3: 561–69.

Jaffa, Harry. 2000. *A New Birth of Freedom: Abraham Lincoln and the Coming of the Civil War*. Lanham, MD: Rowman & Littlefield.

Jameson, John Alexander. 1867. *The Constitutional Convention: Its History, Powers, and Modes of Proceeding*. New York: S. C. Griggs.

Jasinski, James. 1997. "Heteroglossia, Polyphony, and *The Federalist Papers*." *Rhetoric Society Quarterly* 27, no. 1: 23–46.

Jefferson, Thomas. 1958. *The Papers of Thomas Jefferson, Vol. 14*, ed. Julian Boyd. Princeton, NJ: Princeton University Press.

Jefferson, Thomas. 1982. *Notes on the State of Virginia*, ed. William Peden. Chapel Hill: University of North Carolina Press.

Jefferson, Thomas. 1984. *Thomas Jefferson: Writings*. New York: Library of America.

Jefferson, Thomas. 1999. *Political Writings*, ed. Joyce Appleby and Terence Ball. New York: Cambridge University Press.

Jefferson, Thomas. 2006. "Draft of the Kentucky Resolutions." In *The Essential Jefferson*, ed. Jean M. Yarbrough, 48–54. Indianapolis, IN: Hackett.

Jensen, Merrill, John P. Kaminski, Gaspare J. Saladino, Richard Leffler, and Charles H. Schoenleber, eds. 1976–2009. *The Documentary History of the Ratification of the Constitution*, 20 vols. Madison: Wisconsin Historical Society Press.

Kahn, Paul. 2012. *Political Theology: Four New Chapters on the Concept of Sovereignty*. New York: Columbia University Press.

Kalyvas, Andreas. 2000. "Carl Schmitt and the Three Moments of Democracy." *Cardozo Law Review* 21, nos. 5–6: 1525–66.

Kalyvas, Andreas. 2005. "Popular Sovereignty, Democracy, and the Constituent Power." *Constellations* 12, no. 2: 223–44.

Kammen, Michael. 1986. *A Machine That Would Go of Itself: The Constitution in American Culture*. New York: Alfred A. Knopf.

Kateb, George. 1995. "The Questionable Influence of Arendt (and Strauss)," in *Hannah Arendt and Leo Strauss: German Émigrés and American Political Thought after World War II*, ed. Peter Graf Kielmansegg, Horst Mewes, and Elisabeth Glaser-Schmidt, 29–44. New York: Cambridge University Press.

Kateb, George. 2002. *Emerson and Self-Reliance*. Lanham, MD: Rowman & Littlefield.

Keenan, Alan. 2003. *Democracy in Question: Democratic Openness in a Time of Political Closure*. Stanford, CA: Stanford University Press.

Kelsen, Hans. 1988. *La démocratie Sa nature Sa valeur*. Paris: Economica.

Kenyon, Cecelia. 1955 [1929]. "Men of Little Faith: The Anti-Federalists on the Nature of Representative Government." *The William and Mary Quarterly* 12, no. 1: 3–43.

Keyssar, Alexander. 2000. *The Right to Vote: The Contested History of Democracy in the United States*. New York: Basic Books.

King, Richard H. 2008. "Rights and Slavery, Race and Racism: Leo Strauss, and the American Dilemma." *Modern Intellectual History* 5, no. 1: 55–82.

Kloppenburg, James T. 1987. "The Virtues of Liberalism: Christianity, Republicanism, and Ethics in Early American Political Discourse." *Journal of American History* 74, no. 1: 9–33.

Kloppenburg, James T. 1998. *The Virtues of Liberalism*. New York: Oxford University Press.

Kramer, Larry. 1999. "Madison's Audience." *Harvard Law Review* 112: 611–79.

Kramer, Larry. 2004. *The People Themselves: Popular Constitutionalism and Judicial Review*. New York: Oxford University Press.

Kramnick, Isaac. 1988. "The 'Great National Discussion': The Discourse of Politics in 1788." *The William and Mary Quarterly* 45, no. 1: 3–32.

Kramnick, Isaac, and R. Laurence Moore. 2005. *The Godless Constitution: A Moral Defense of the Secular State*. New York: W. W. Norton.

Lepore, Jill. 2010. *The Whites of Their Eyes: The Tea Party's Revolution and the Battle over American History*. Princeton, NJ: Princeton University Press, 2010.

Lerner, Ralph. 1987. *The Thinking Revolutionary: Principle and Practice in the New Republic*. Ithaca, NY: Cornell University Press.

Lienesch, Michael. 1988. *New Order of the Ages: Time, the Constitution, and the Making of Modern American Political Thought*. Princeton, NJ: Princeton University Press.

Lilla, Mark. 2004. "The Closing of the Straussian Mind." *New York Review of Books*, November 4, 55–59.

Lincoln, Abraham. 1989. "Address to the Young Men's Lyceum of Springfield, Illinois." In *Abraham Lincoln: Speeches and Writing 1832–1858*, ed. Don E. Fehrenbacher, 28–36. New York: Library of America.

Lindblom, Charles E. 1965. *The Intelligence of Democracy: Decision Making Through Mutual Adjustment*. New York: Free Press.

Looby, Christopher. 1996. *Voicing America: Language, Literary Form, and the Origins of the United States*. Chicago: University of Chicago Press.

Loughlin, Martin and Neil Walker, eds. 2007. *The Paradox of Constitutionalism: Constituent Power and Constitutional Form*. Oxford: Oxford University Press.

Machiavelli, Niccolo. 1989. *The Prince*. In *Machiavelli: The Chief Works, Vol. 3*, trans. Albert Gilbert, 5–96. Durham, NC: Duke University Press.

Madison, James. 1977. *The Papers of James Madison, Vol. IX*, ed. William T. Hutchinson et al. Chicago: University of Chicago Press.

Madison, James. 1987. *Notes on the Debates in the Federal Convention of 1787, Vol. 1*. Buffalo, NY: Prometheus Books.

Maier, Pauline. 1972. *From Resistance to Revolution: Colonial Radicals and the Development of American Opposition to Britain, 1765–1776*. New York: W. W. Norton.

Manin, Bernard. 1997. *The Principles of Representative Government*. New York: Cambridge University Press.

Marshall, Thurgood. "The Bicentennial Speech." http://www.thurgoodmarshall.com/speeches/constitutional_speech.htm.

Martin, Terence. 1961. *The Instructed Vision: Scottish Common Sense Philosophy and the Origins of American Fiction*. Bloomington, IN: Indiana University Press.

Marx, Karl. 1973. *Surveys from Exile: Political Writings, Volume 2*, ed. David Fernbach. New York: Penguin Books.

Mason, Alpheus T. 1952. "*The Federalist*—a Split Personality." *American Historical Review* 57, no. 3: 625–43.

Mathiowitz, Dean. 2011. *Appeals to Interest: Language, Contestation, and the Shaping of Political Agency*. State College: Pennsylvania State University Press.

May, Henry F. 1976. *The Enlightenment in America*. New York: Oxford University Press.

McCormick, John. 2001. "Machiavellian Democracy: Controlling Elites with Ferocious Populism." *American Political Science Review* 95, no. 2: 297–313.

Meier, Heinrich. 1995. *Carl Schmitt and Leo Strauss: The Hidden Dialogue*. Chicago: University of Chicago Press.

Michelman, Frank. 1988. "Law's Republic." *The Yale Law Journal* 97, no. 8: 1493–1537.

Michelman, Frank. 1997. "How Can the People Ever Make the Laws? A Critique of Deliberative Democracy." In *Deliberative Democracy: Essays on Reason and Politics*, ed. James Bohman and William Rehg. Cambridge, MA: MIT Press.

Miller, Joshua. 1988. "The Ghostly Body Politic: *The Federalist Papers* and Popular Sovereignty." *Political Theory* 16, no. 1: 99–119.

Miller, Perry. 1967. *Nature's Nation*. Cambridge, MA: Harvard University Press.

Millican, Edward. 1990. *One United People: The Federalist Papers and the National Idea*. Louisville: University Press of Kentucky.

Milton, John. 2004. *Paradise Lost*, ed. Gordon Teskey. New York: W. W. Norton.

Moats, Sandra. 2010. *Celebrating the Republic: Presidential Ceremony and Popular Sovereignty from Washington to Monroe*. DeKalb: Northern Illinois University Press.

Montesquieu. 1989. *The Spirit of the Laws*, ed. Anne Cohler, Basia Miller, and Harold Stone. Cambridge: Cambridge University Press.

Morgan, Edmund S. 1989. *Inventing the People: The Rise of Popular Sovereignty in England and America*. New York: W. W. Norton.

Morganthau, Hans J. 1954. *Politics Among Nations*. New York: Knopf.

Nässtrom, Sofia. 2007. "The Legitimacy of the People." *Political Theory* 35, no. 5: 624–58.

Norton, Anne. 2004. *Leo Strauss and the Politics of American Empire*. New Haven, CT: Yale University Press.

Paine, Thomas. 2000. *Political Writings*. Cambridge: Cambridge University Press.

Palmer, R. R. 1959. *The Age of Democratic Revolution: The Challenge*. Princeton, NJ: Princeton University Press.

Panagia, Davide. 2013. *Impressions of Hume*. Lanham, MD: Rowman & Littlefield.

Pangle, Thomas L. 1985. "Patriotism American Style." *National Review*, November 29, 30–34.

Pangle, Thomas L. 1988. *The Spirit of Modern Republicanism: The Moral Vision of the American Founders and the Philosophy of Locke*. Chicago: University of Chicago Press.

Pangle, Thomas L. 2006. *Leo Strauss: An Introduction to His Thought and Intellectual Legacy*. Baltimore, MD: Johns Hopkins University Press.

Phillips, Anne. 1998. *The Politics of Presence*. New York: Oxford University Press.

Pitkin, Hanna. 1972. *The Concept of Representation*. Berkeley, CA: University of California Press.

Pocock, J. G. A. 1975. *The Machiavellian Moment: Florentine Political Thought and the Atlantic Republican Tradition*. Princeton, NJ: Princeton University Press.

Preuss, Ulrich K. 1993. "Constitutional Powermaking for the New Polity: Some Deliberations on the Relations between Constituent Power and the Constitution." *Cardozo Law Review* 14: 639–60.

Publius, James. 1989. "Jay's Treaty (April 6, 1796)." In *The Papers of James Publius, Vol. XVI*, ed. J. C. A. Stagg, Thomas A. Mason, and Jeanne K. Sisson. Charlottesville: University of Virginia Press.

Purcell, Edward. 1973. *The Crisis of Democratic Theory: Scientific Naturalism and the Problem of Value*. Lexington: University Press of Kentucky.

Rakove, Jack. 2002. *James Madison and the Creation of the American Republic*. New York: Longman.

Rawls, John. 2005. *Political Liberalism: Expanded Edition*. New York: Columbia University Press.

Remer, Gary. 2000. "Two Models of Deliberation: Oratory and Conversation in Ratifying the Constitution." *Journal of Political Philosophy* 8, no. 1: 68–90.

Rice, Grantland S. 1997. *The Transformation of Authorship in America*. Chicago: University of Chicago Press.

Ricoeur, Paul. 1984. "The Political Paradox." In *Legitimacy and the State*, ed. William E. Connolly, 250–72. New York: New York University Press.

Robbins, Caroline. 1959. *The Eighteenth-Century Commonwealthman*. Indianapolis, IN: Liberty Fund.

Rodgers, Daniel T. 1992. "Republicanism: the Career of a Concept." *The Journal of American History* 79, no. 1: 11–38.

Rosanvallon, Pierre. 2006. "Revolutionary Democracy." In *Democracy Past and Future*, ed. Samuel Moyn. New York: Columbia University Press.

Rose, Nikolas and Peter Miller. 1992. "Political Power Beyond the State: Problematics of Government." *The British Journal of Sociology* 43, no. 2: 173–205.

Rosen, Gary. 1996. "James Madison and the Problem of Founding." *Review of Politics* 58, no. 3: 561–95.

Rosen, Gary. 1999. *American Compact: James Madison and the Problem of Founding*. Lawrence: University Press of Kansas.

Rossiter, Clinton. 1953. *Seedtime of the Republic*. New York: Harcourt.

Rousseau, Jean-Jacques. 1968. *The Social Contract*, trans. M. Cranston. New York: Penguin Books.

Rubenfeld, Jed. 2001. *Freedom and Time: A Theory of Constitutional Self-Government*. New Haven, CT: Yale University Press.

Rush, Benjamin. 1947. "The Effects of the American Revolution on the Mind and Body of Man." In *Selected Writings of Benjamin Rush*, ed. Dagobert D. Runes. New York: Philosophical Library.

Saladino, Gaspare J. 1990. "Pseudonyms used in the newspaper debate over the ratification of the United State Constitution in the State of New York, September 1787–July 1788." In *New York and the Union*, ed. Stephen L. Schecter and Richard B. Bernstein. Albany: New York State Commission on the Bicentennial.

Scanlon, James P. 1959. "*The Federalist* and Human Nature." *Review of Politics* 21, no. 4.

Shklar, Judith. 1981. "*The Federalist* as Myth." *Yale Law Journal* 90, no. 4: 942–53.

Schleifer, James T. 2000. *The Making of Tocqueville's Democracy in America*. Indianapolis, IN: Liberty Fund.

Schmitt, Carl. 1965. *Verfassungslehre*. Berlin: Duncker & Humboldt.

Schmitt, Carl. 1988. *Political Theology: Four Chapters on the Concept of Sovereignty*, trans. George Schwab. Cambridge, MA: MIT Press.

Schmitt, Carl. 1992. *The Crisis of Parliamentary Democracy*, trans. Ellen Kennedy. Cambridge, MA: MIT Press.

Schmitt, Carl. 1993. "The Age of Neutralizations and Depoliticizations." *Telos* 96 (Summer): 130–42.

Schmitt, Carl. 1993. *Über die drei Arten des rechtswissenschaftlichen Denkens*. Berlin: Duncker & Humboldt.

Schmitt, Carl. 2004. *Legality and Legitimacy*, trans. and ed. Jeffrey Seitzer. Durham, NC: Duke University Press.

Schmitt, Carl. 2008. *Constitutional Theory*, ed. and trans. Jeffrey Seitzer. Durham, NC: Duke University Press.

Scheuerman, William E. 1998. "Revolutions and Constitutions: Hannah Arendt's Challenge to Carl Schmitt." In *Law as Politics: Carl Schmitt's Critique of Liberalism*, ed. David Dyzenhaus. Durham, NC: Duke University Press.

Shalev, Eran. 2003. "Ancient Masks, American Fathers: Classical Pseudonyms During the American Revolution and Early Republic." *Journal of the Early Republic* 23, no. 2: 151–72.

Shapiro, Kam. 2009. *Carl Schmitt and the Intensification of Politics*. Lanham, MD: Rowman & Littlefield.

Shapiro, Michael J. 2002. *Reading "Adam Smith": Desire, History, and Value*. Lanham, MD: Rowman & Littlefield.

Shoemaker, Robert B. 1966. "'Democracy' and 'Republic' as Understood in Late Eighteenth-Century America." *American Speech* 41, no. 2: 83–95.

Siemers, David J. 2002. *Ratifying the Republic: Anti-Federalists and Federalists in Constitutional Time*. Stanford, CA: Stanford University Press.

Simpson, Sarah H. J. 1925. "The Federalist Procession in the City of New York." *New York Historical Society Bulletin* 7: 39–57.

Skowronek, Stephen. 2006. "The Reassociation of Ideas and Purposes: Racism, Liberalism, and the American Political Tradition." *American Political Science Review* 100, no. 3: 385–401.

Slauter, Eric. 2009. *The State as a Work of Art: The Cultural Origins of the Constitution*. Chicago: University of Chicago Press.

Smith, James Morton, ed. 1995. *The Republic of Letters: The Correspondence between Jefferson and Madison, 1776–1826*. New York: W. W. Norton.

Smith, Rogers M. 2003. *Stories of Peoplehood: The Political and Morals of Political Membership*. New York: Cambridge University Press.

Smith, Steven B. 2006. *Reading Leo Strauss: Politics, Philosophy, Judaism*. Chicago: University of Chicago Press.

Smith-Rosenberg, Carroll. 1992. "Dis-Covering the Subject of the 'Great Constitutional Discussion,' 1786–1789." *The Journal of American History* 79, no. 3: 841–73.

Stoll, Iva. 2008. *Samuel Adams: A Life*. New York: Free Press.

Storing, Herbert J. 1981a. *What the Anti-Federalists Were For*. Chicago: University of Chicago Press.

Storing, Herbert J., ed. 1981b. *The Complete Anti-Federalist*, 7 vols. Chicago: University of Chicago Press.

Strauss, Leo. 1953. *Natural Right and History*. Chicago: University of Chicago Press.

Strauss, Leo. 1968a. "Liberal Education and Responsibility." In *Liberalism Ancient and Modern*, 9–25. New York: Basic Books.

Strauss, Leo. 1968b. "Preface to Spinoza's Critique of Religion." In *Liberalism Ancient and Modern*, 224–59. New York: Basic Books.

Strauss, Leo. 1978. *The City and Man*. Chicago: University of Chicago Press.

Strauss, Leo. 1988. *What is Political Philosophy? And Other Studies*. Chicago: University of Chicago Press.

Strauss, Leo. 1989. "The Three Waves of Modernity." In *An Introduction to Political Philosophy: Ten Essays*, ed. Hilail Gildin, 81–98. Detroit, MI: Wayne State University Press.

Strauss, Leo. 2007. "Notes on the Concept of the Political." In Carl Schmitt, *The Concept of the Political*, ed. George Schwab, 83–107. Chicago: University of Chicago Press.

Strauss, Leo. 2009. "Letter to Karl Löwith," *Constellations* 16 (1): 82–83.

Strong, Tracy B. 2002. *Jean-Jacques Rousseau: The Politics of the Ordinary*. Lanham, MD: Rowman & Littlefield.

Tocqueville, Alexis de. 2003. *Democracy in America*. New York: Penguin.

Tomasi, John. 2001. *Liberalism Beyond Justice: Citizens, Society, and the Boundaries of the Political*. Princeton, NJ: Princeton University Press.

Trenchard, John and Thomas Gordon. 1995. *Cato's Letters: Essays on Liberty, Civil and Religious, and Other Important Subjects*, ed. Ronald Hamowy. Indianapolis, IN: Liberty Fund.

Tuveson, Ernest Lee. 1968. *Redeemer Nation: The Idea of America's Millennial Role*. Chicago: University of Chicago Press.

Venturi, Franco. 1971. *Utopia and Reform in the Enlightenment*. Cambridge: Cambridge University Press.

Waldron, Jeremy. 1999. *Law and Disagreement*. New York: Oxford University Press.

Waldstreicher, David. 1997. *In the Midst of Perpetual Fetes: The Making of American Nationalism, 1776–1820*. Chapel Hill: University of North Carolina Press.

Warfel, H. R., ed. 1953. *The Letters of Noah Webster*. New York: Library Publishers.

Warner, Michael. 1990. *The Letters of the Republic: Publication and the Public Sphere in Eighteenth-Century America*. Cambridge, MA: Harvard University Press.

Washington, George. 1997. *Writings*, ed. John Rodehamel. New York: Library of America.

West, Thomas G. 1991. "Leo Strauss and the American Founding," *Review of Politics* 53, no. 1: 157–72.

Whelan, Frederick G. 1985. *Order and Artifice in Hume's Political Philosophy*. Princeton, NJ: Princeton University Press.

White, Morton. 1989. *Philosophy, The Federalist, and the Constitution*. New York: Oxford University Press.

White, Stephen K. 2002. *Edmund Burke: Modernity, Politics, and Aesthetics*. Lanham, MD: Rowman & Littlefield.

Wills, Gary. 1982. *Explaining America: The Federalist*. New York: Penguin Books.

Wills, Gary. 1988. "James Wilson's New Meaning for Sovereignty." In *Conceptual Change and the Constitution*, ed. Terence Ball and J. G. A. Pocock, 99–106. Lawrence: University of Kansas Press.

Wilson, James. "Oration delivered on the Fourth of July, 1788," in the appendix of Francis Hopkinson, *An Account of the Grand Federal Procession*, (Philadelphia, 1788).

Wolin, Sheldon S. 1980. "The People's Two Bodies." *Democracy* 1, no. 1: 9–24.

Wolin, Sheldon S. 1960. *Politics and Vision: Continuity and Innovation in Western Political Thought*. London: George Allen & Unwin.

Wolin, Sheldon S. 1989. *The Presence of the Past: Essays on the State and the Constitution*. Baltimore, MD: Johns Hopkins University Press.

Wolin, Sheldon S. 1994. "Norm and Form: The Constitutionalization of Democracy." In *Athenian Political Thought and the Reconstruction of American Democracy*, ed. J. Peter Euben, John R. Wallach, and Josiah Ober. Ithaca, NY: Cornell University Press.

Wood, Gordon S. 1969. *The Creation of the American Republic, 1776–1787*. Chapel Hill: University of North Carolina Press.

Wood, Gordon S. 1974. "The Democratization of Mind in the American Revolution." In *Leadership in the American Revolution, Papers Presented at the Third Symposium, May 9 and 10, 1974*, 63–89. Washington, DC.

Wood, Gordon. 1987. "Interests and Disinterestedness in the Making of the Constitution." In *Beyond Confederation: Origins of the Constitution and American National Identity*, ed. Richard Beeman, Stephen Botein, and Edward C. Carter II. Chapel Hill: University of North Carolina Press.

Wood, Gordon S. 1988. "The Fundamentalists and the Constitution," *New York Review of Books*, February 18, 33–40.

Wood, Gordon. 1993. *The Radicalism of the American Revolution*. New York: Vintage Books.

Wood, Gordon. 2003. *The American Revolution: A History*. New York: Modern Library.

Wood, Gordon. 2008. *Representation in the American Revolution*. Charlottesville: University of Virginia Press.

Wood, Gordon. 2012. *The Idea of America: The Birth of the United States*. New York: Penguin.

Xenos, Nicholas. 2008. *Cloaked in Virtue: Unveiling Leo Strauss and the Rhetoric of American Foreign Policy*. New York: Routledge.

Yack, Bernard. 2001. "Popular Sovereignty and Nationalism." *Political Theory* 29, no. 4: 517–36.

Zuckert, Catherine H., and Michael P. Zuckert. 2006. *The Truth About Leo Strauss: Political Philosophy and American Democracy*. Chicago: University of Chicago Press.

Zuckert, Michael P. 1999. "Refinding the Founding: Martin Diamond, Leo Strauss, and the American Regime." In *Leo Strauss, the Straussians and the American Regime*, ed. Kenneth L. Deutsch and John A. Murley, 235–52. Lanham, MD: Rowman & Littlefield.

Zuckert, Michael P. 2002. *Launching Liberalism: On Lockean Political Philosophy*. Lawrence: University Press of Kansas, 2002.

Index

About the Author

Jason Frank is an associate professor in the Department of Government at Cornell University.